WAR OF WORDS

WAR OF WORDS

A True Tale of Newsprint and Murder

Simon Read

UNION SQUARE PRESS
An imprint of Sterling Publishing Co., Inc.

New York / London
www.sterlingpublishing.com

FOR MY PARENTS,

WHO HAVE ALWAYS ENCOURAGED

———

STERLING and the distinctive Sterling logo are registered trademarks
of Sterling Publishing Co., Inc.

Library of Congress Cataloging-in-Publication Data
Read, Simon.
War of words : a true tale of newsprint and murder / Simon Read.
p. cm.
Includes bibliographical references and index.
ISBN 978-1-4027-5612-2 (hc- trade cloth)
1. San Francisco (Calif.)—History—19th century. 2. De Young,
Charles, 1845–1880. 3. Kalloch, I. S. (Isaac Smith), 1831–1887.
4. Newspaper editors—California—San Francisco—Biography.
5. Mayors—California—San Francisco—Biography. 6. San
Francisco chronicle. I. Title.
F869.S353D427 2009
979.4'61040922—dc22
[B]   200804868

Book design and layout by Richard Oriolo
Front matter map by Laura Hartman-Maestro

2 4 6 8 10 9 7 5 3 1

Published by Sterling Publishing Co., Inc.
387 Park Avenue South, New York, NY 10016
© 2009 by Simon Read
Distributed in Canada by Sterling Publishing
c/o Canadian Manda Group, 165 Dufferin Street
Toronto, Ontario, Canada M6K 3H6
Distributed in the United Kingdom by GMC Distribution Services
Castle Place, 166 High Street, Lewes, East Sussex, England BN7 1XU
Distributed in Australia by Capricorn Link (Australia) Pty. Ltd.
P.O. Box 704, Windsor, NSW 2756, Australia

Manufactured in the U.S.A.
All rights reserved

Sterling ISBN 978-1-4027-5612-2

For information about custom editions, special sales, premium and
corporate purchases, please contact Sterling Special Sales
Department at 800-805-5489 or specialsales@sterlingpublishing.com.

Newspapermen do not seem to be good shots. A French paper says that nearly 300 duels were fought in Paris during the last 12 months, only two of which resulted fatally. Of these belligerent gentlemen ninety-one were journalists. From this it would seem as though French dueling were a harmless pastime, scarcely dangerous enough to be exciting. California duels in the early days were much more serious affairs.

—DAILY DRAMATIC CHRONICLE (SAN FRANCISCO), WEDNESDAY, JANUARY 15, 1868

Journalism . . . a low trade and a habit worse than heroin, a strange seedy world full of misfits and drunkards and failures.

—HUNTER S. THOMPSON, GENERATION OF SWINE

CONTENTS

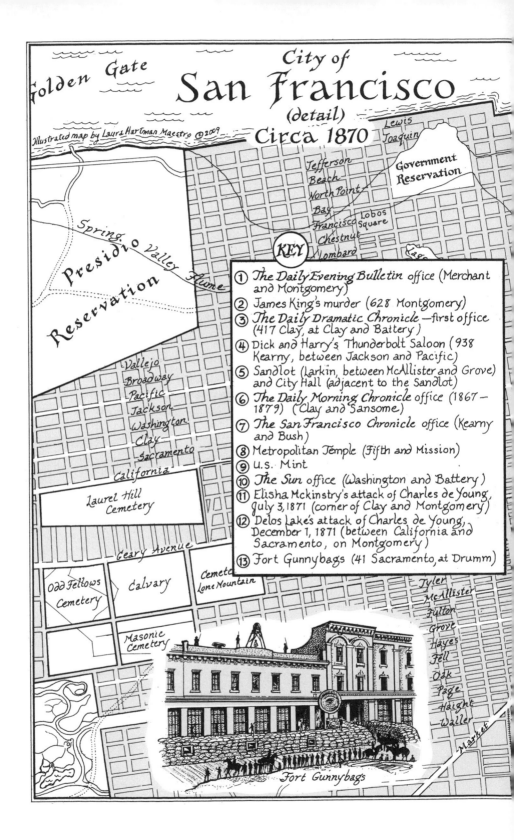

Golden Gate

City of
San Francisco
(detail)
Circa 1870

Illustrated map by Laura Hartman Maestro ©2009

Lewis
Joaquin

Jefferson
Beach
North Point
Bay
Francisco
Chestnut
Lombard

Government
Reservation

Lobos
Square

KEY

Spring Valley Flume

Presidio Valley Reservation

① The *Daily Evening Bulletin* office (Merchant and Montgomery)
② James King's murder (628 Montgomery)
③ The *Daily Dramatic Chronicle* —first office (417 Clay, at Clay and Battery)
④ Dick and Harry's Thunderbolt Saloon (938 Kearny, between Jackson and Pacific)
⑤ Sandlot (Larkin, between McAllister and Grove) and City Hall (adjacent to the Sandlot)
⑥ The *Daily Morning Chronicle* office (1867–1879) (Clay and Sansome)
⑦ The *San Francisco Chronicle* office (Kearny and Bush)
⑧ Metropolitan Temple (Fifth and Mission)
⑨ U.S. Mint
⑩ The *Sun* office (Washington and Battery)
⑪ Elisha Mckinstry's attack of Charles de Young, July 3, 1871 (corner of Clay and Montgomery)
⑫ Delos Lake's attack of Charles de Young, December 1, 1871 (between California and Sacramento, on Montgomery)
⑬ Fort Gunnybags (41 Sacramento, at Drumm)

Vallejo
Broadway
Pacific
Jackson
Washington
Clay
Sacramento
California

Laurel Hill Cemetery

Geary Avenue

Odd Fellows Cemetery

Calvary

Cemetery
Lone Mountain

Tyler
McAllister
Fulton
Grove
Hayes
Fell
Oak
Page
Haight
Waller

Masonic Cemetery

Market

Fort Gunnybags

One mile

N

San Francisco Bay

North Beach

Jefferson Beach

North Point Bay

Francisco

Chestnut

Lombard

Greenwich

Filbert

Union

Green

Vallejo

Broadway

Pacific

Jackson

Washington

Clay

Sacramento

California

Pine

Bush

Sutter

Post

Geary

O'Farrell

Ellis

Eddy

Turk

Tyler

McAllister

Fulton

Grove

Hayes

Fell

Oak

North Pt.

India Dock

Telegraph Hill

Wash. Sq.

Montgomery Avenue

St.

Merchant St.

Dupont

Kearny

Montgomery

Sansome

Battery

Front St.

Davis St.

Drumm

East St.

Stewart St.

Spear St.

Main St.

Beale St.

Fremont St.

Stockton

Powell

Mason

Taylor

Jones

Leavenworth

Hyde St.

Larkin St.

Polk St.

Van Ness St.

Union St.

Market Street

Fourth St.

Fifth St.

Sixth St.

Seventh St.

Eighth St.

Ninth St.

Tenth St.

Eleventh St.

Twelfth St.

Thirteenth St.

Fourteenth St.

Mission St.

City Hall Ave.

Park

Old Chronicle Building

Montgomery Block

Townsend St.

King St.

Berry St.

Channel St.

Hopper

Irwin

Hubbell

South

Alameda St.

El Dorado St.

Alameda St.

El Dorado St.

China Basin

Mission Rock

④ ② ① ⑩ ⑬ ⑪ ⑥ ③ ⑫ ⑦ ⑧ ⑨ ⑤

Prologue

A FALLEN KING

A PROFESSION NOT WITHOUT RISK, the job of newspaper editor attracted men of stern stuff in the testosterone-rich days of old San Francisco. Nearly fatal beatings and bloodletting by pistol and bowie knife were regularly occurring phenomena outside (and sometimes inside) the sanctity of the newsroom. Gunpowder and steel proved highly effective in expressing one's displeasure with an article—more so than a letter to the editor. An angry reader gunned down a reporter in the summer of 1852 outside Sacramento after the scribe penned an editorial criticizing the governor. One editor got the picture and posted the following notice on his office door: "Subscriptions received from 9 to 4; challenges from 11 to 12 only."

James King of William would have been wise to follow suit.

Though his name suggested royalty, King boasted no such family lineage. His beginnings were humble, his life less than majestic and his ending far short of dignified. In November 1848, the twenty-six-year-old King had ventured from the East Coast to San Francisco, then a shanty town of rickety wooden structures, sagging canvas tents and mud-strewn streets strolled by men packing Colts and Winchesters. Tall and lanky, he lacked the rugged appearance one might expect from a settler of the Western frontier. A black beard framed a naturally pursed mouth and seemed to accentuate the sharp angles of his cheekbones and nose. Forgoing boots and denim, King had a taste for black suits, narrow-cut trousers and bowties worn at crooked angles. He often draped a knee-length cape over his shoulders to combat San Francisco's ever-present chill. His choice of wardrobe, coupled with his pale complexion, gave the young man a melancholy air.

He was born under the unassuming name James King on January 28, 1822, at Georgetown in the District of Columbia. The regal-sounding moniker he went by later in life was his own creation—a way of distinguishing himself from other James Kings living in the Georgetown area. He excelled at school in literature and languages, devouring the works of English authors and acquiring a respectable command of Latin. His tongue also proved nimble when speaking French and Spanish. He left home at fifteen to find his niche, bouncing from job to job before reaching New York City and hitching a ride on a steamer in May 1848. His travels took him to Cartagena, Colombia, and over the Isthmus of Panama by mule before he reached San Francisco seven months later.

Upon his arrival, he ventured north with pick and shovel to mine the earth and streams in Placerville, then known as Old Dry Diggings and Hangtown. Three weeks of backbreaking work yielded enough gold to pay off the debt he incurred in the move. A brief stint followed in Sacramento, where he worked in the mercantile trade before going into business on his own. On December 5, 1849—after securing financing back east—King established a bank in a small, wood-framed building on Montgomery Street between Clay and Merchant.

Banking initially proved a choice profession, but economic depression in 1855, wrought by the fading gold rush and years of dubious investments to capitalize on the madness, toppled a number of banks. King's fell victim. Although friends offered him substantial sums of money to resume his business, King refused, opting instead to pursue an endeavor many considered pure madness: From the abyss of unemployment, *The Daily Evening Bulletin*— a twelve-by-fourteen-inch newspaper—was born.

Only four pages in length, the debut issue hit city streets on October 8, 1855. "Whatever may be our political bias individually, as conductor of the *Evening Bulletin* we shall act independently of either of the political parties that now divide the State," King wrote in that debut issue. "By being independent of either party, however, we by no means intend a neutrality or indifference to public affairs; but in all matters of public interest we shall advocate such measures as may seem to us best for the public good."

His tenure as newspaperman would prove short-lived.

———

SAN FRANCISCO—A CITY OF gun smoke, opium dens and brothels— might not have seemed the place for one of such timid physicality as King. "The city was overrun with the refuse and scum of the earth," noted one contemporary witness. "Robberies and murders were frequent; many of the city's officials were thieves." But such vile specimens imbued King with a sense of purpose in his newly desired role as social crusader. His weapon of choice for ridding San Francisco of corruption would not be sword or pistol, but pen: his new publishing venture.

"The apparent folly of starting a newspaper in this city where so many already exist, and at this time when so few are barely doing that, would seem to demand some explanation," wrote King, then thirty-three and a married father of six. "Necessity, not choice, have driven us to this experiment. No one can be more fully sensible than ourselves of the folly of newspaper enterprise as an investment of money. But we invest no money of our own (for we have none) and only a few hundred dollars generously advanced us by a few friends."

It was a gentle salutation that did nothing to foreshadow the fierce moral vendetta upon which King was quickly to embark. Before the week was out, King had launched his campaign with a series of stinging editorials, slamming everything from crooked banking interests to bottom-feeding politicians. In a column dated October 13, 1855, King lashed out on all that he perceived to be wrong:

A man, unworthy to serve the humblest citizen in the land, has filled the highest office in the gift of the people. Judges have sat on the bench, whose more appropriate station would have been the prison house. Men, without one particle of claim to the position, have filled the posts of Mayor and Councilmen in this city, for the sole purpose of filling their pockets with the ill-gotten gains of their nefarious schemes, their pilfering and dishonesty. City and County Treasurers, and Recorders have sought to obtain offices of trust and honor, who, had they met their desserts, would in other countries have formed part of the chain gang years ago. And all the while the *press*, THE PRESS, either silent or through base fear of personal injury, or yet more shameful, is basely bought to uphold this iniquity."

King had let his intentions be known and put the city's other papers on notice. He intended to splash stories of corruption across the *Bulletin's* four-column pages. He would highlight the rampant criminality that plagued the city and chastise papers that ignored such problems to curry political favor. He planned to name names and run all scoundrels out of town.

In doing so, he traversed dangerous ground. Two rival editors had only recently assailed one another with pistols over some perceived slight. The two combatants—one from the *Placer Times*, the other from the *Daily Alta California*—confronted one another across the Bay near Oakland.

An audience of more than two thousand people crowded the battlefield in anticipation of the spectacle. The distance was a fairly close-range twenty paces, yet neither combatant was a particularly accurate shot. "One of the editors received a bullet through his high hat, and on the fifth shot hit his antagonist in the leg," stated one contemporary account. "Honor being satisfied, the editors returned to their sanctums."

Although King initially had no "base fear of personal injury," he soon realized he might as well have been wearing a large bull's-eye on his front and back like some perverse sandwich board. Within weeks of the *Bulletin's* debut, the death threats began. "Men warned him that his life was in danger," King's son Charles recalled later, "and more than once some personal friend would rouse us up after midnight to know if he were safe, it having been reported that he had been assassinated." As a young boy, Charles would watch his father practice with a pistol in the family backyard:

> I have seen him many a time hit the mark he was aiming at repeatedly
> in succession. His idea was, if he should ever be attacked, to throw up
> his left arm as a defense while he drew his weapon with his right arm
> and fired. He never dreamed of being attacked in the streets of the
> city, where some inoffensive passer-by would be imperiled.

King placed too much faith in his fellow man.

———

KING'S PUBLISHED ATTACKS ON CRIME and corruption earned him the adulation of those in San Francisco who craved more stringent law and order. One adoring reader recalled:

> James King of William . . . was a man of indomitable energy, utterly
> destitute of fear, and with his intense hatred of injustice and wrong,
> he turned every means at his command into the work of uprooting the
> evil deeds then so prevalent in city and county management. I well
> remember meeting him two days before the curtain rose on the
> terrible tragedy that was to follow, and looking at him with a sort of
> reverent wonder, as at a man who carried his life in his hand.

King editorialized on the need for better schools, and slammed the bloated salaries of city leaders. Not even Mayor James Van Ness was spared: the paper described him as "the tool and abettor of thieves and ruffians and a malignant misanthrope." Within a month, the *Evening Bulletin*'s daily print run had grown from a few hundred copies to twenty-five hundred. Public demand soon made it the most popular paper in the city, boosting its print run to thirty-five hundred in two short months. Such success brought a backlash, as each day's mail carried with it numerous threats of death and invitations to settle scores in a manner befitting a true gentleman. Responding to one aggrieved reader who sought the pleasure of a duel, King wrote in the December 6, 1855, issue:

> Mr. Selover, it is said, carries a knife. We carry a pistol. We hope neither will be required, but if this rencontre cannot be avoided, will Mr. Selover persist in periling the lives of others? We pass every afternoon about 4:30 to 5 o'clock along Market Street from Fourth to Fifth Street. The road is wide and not so much frequented as those streets farther in town. If we are to be shot or hacked to pieces, for heaven's sake let it be done there. Others will not be injured, and in case we fall, our house is but a few hundred yards beyond and the cemetery not much farther.

ON THE AFTERNOON OF MAY 13, 1856, King set his crusading pen to paper and inked a vicious editorial, referencing a dispute between James P. Casey, county supervisor for the Presidio district and founding editor of the *Weekly Sunday Times*, and another gentleman. The cause of the quarrel, apparently, was not as important as the participants' moral fiber. King leveled his command of the written word at Casey, whom he had long disdained. The article said in no uncertain terms that Casey was a thief whose political ascension had been achieved through crooked means:

> The fact that Casey has been an inmate of Sing Sing prison in New York, is no offence against the laws of this State; nor is the fact of his having stuffed himself through the ballot-box as elected to the Board of Supervisors from a district where it is said he was not even a candidate, any justification for Mr. Bagley to shoot Casey, however richly the latter may deserve to have his neck stretched for such fraud of the people.

The article assailed the "shallowness" of Casey's character and heaped upon him other indignities.

Indeed, Casey had been tried and convicted for grand larceny in New York's Court of General Sessions on September 5, 1849, after stealing a hundred and forty dollars' worth of furniture from the apartment of his former mistress. He had purchased the bedstead, mattress and bureaus for her in happier times and believed them to be his when the relationship soured. A jury thought otherwise and sent him to Sing Sing for two years.

The Casey exposé ran in the May 14, 1856, issue of the *Bulletin*, which by then boasted a daily circulation of fifty-eight hundred readers. A man who at that time enjoyed the company of bartenders and gamblers, Casey bristled at any mention of his past. Having read the biting copy, he mustered his courage and stormed the *Bulletin*'s building on the southeast corner of Merchant and Montgomery streets. King was sitting at his desk in a small office adjacent to the newsroom when Casey, short of breath and waving a copy of the offending article, confronted him.

"What do you mean by such a statement?" he demanded.

"It is not the truth?" King replied, not making any effort to get up.

"That is not the point. I don't wish my past acts raked up," Casey said. "On that point, I am sensitive."

"Are you done?" King asked, shrugging his shoulders in casual dismissal. "There's the door—go! Never show your face here again."

"I'll say in my paper what I please," Casey said, invoking his own editorial power before turning to leave.

"You have a right to do as you please," King replied. "I'll never notice your paper."

"If necessary, I shall defend myself," said Casey. He placed his hand on his chest as though taking some oath.

"Leave my office at once," King roared. "Never show your face here again!"

Casey said nothing more and stomped from the premises, leaving King to finish the evening's business. The editor had little time for men of Casey's ilk, for he knew the supervisor to be a corrupt political figure. It was common knowledge that ballot boxes used in recent elections had been constructed with false sides, which could easily be removed to allow the depositing of specious votes. Many of the city's municipal officers were believed to have reached their various positions of power by employing such crooked methods. King intended to expose them all.

King seemed neither annoyed nor concerned for his safety when he left the office for dinner at five and scurried up Merchant Street toward his home. He walked with his head down and his hands in his pockets, lost in thought. He turned onto Washington Street and then Montgomery, following the planked sidewalk north. Meantime, Casey shadowed King's movements on the opposite side of the street, walking briskly to keep abreast of his prey while reaching for the Navy revolver in his coat pocket.

As King crossed Montgomery at the Bank Exchange Saloon and walked diagonally toward the Pacific Express office on the west side of the street, Casey moved in for the kill, rapidly closing the distance between himself and his oblivious target. When a horse-drawn carriage rumbled between the two men, King lifted his gaze and found a seething Casey blocking his path.

"Draw and defend yourself!" Casey screamed, shrugging off a long cloak to reveal the cocked revolver in his right hand. The gun roared before King could respond. The slug tore through King's left breast, passed through a lung and blew a hole through his back just beneath his shoulder blade.

"Oh, God!" he cried. "I've been shot!"

His knees buckled and he lurched forward, struggling to maintain his balance. He grasped frantically at his chest in a failed effort to plug the flowing wound. The horrifying spectacle sent men in top hats scurrying for cover behind passing horses and reduced several nearby women to screaming hysterics beneath their parasols. King stumbled into the Pacific Express office where he collapsed in a widening pool of blood.

Casey, smoking gun still in hand, remained standing in the street. Around him, morbid curiosity and the initial shock of witnesses quickly evolved into something sinister. "Hang him," one man yelled, pointing at Casey. "Hang him by the neck!" Another man lunged from the gathering crowd and attempted to wrest the revolver from Casey's grip, but the gunman refused to relinquish his weapon. "Run him up the lamppost!" another voice urged, reinforcing Casey's conviction that his sidearm had become a necessity. At that moment, three police officers shoved their way through the crowd and took Casey into custody. Having rushed to the scene upon hearing the news, a reporter from the *Daily Alta California* described the commotion:

> In less than three minutes, the street corner was densely packed
> with human beings, who were in a wild state of excitement, running
> in every direction, inquiring the cause of the assault, the condition
> of the wounded man, and the location of the prisoner.

Inside the Pacific Express office, startled employees helped King into a chair. Dr. R. K. Nuttall was the first doctor to arrive. He bent over the patient, loosened King's shirt and probed the wound with his finger in an attempt to ascertain the bullet's trajectory. Though in extreme pain, King remained conscious.

Outside, a multitude of people surrounded the building, pushing in so close that several windows shattered. Other doctors soon arrived and began debating the best course of treatment. Still bleeding profusely, King was moved across the street to an upstairs room in the four-story Montgomery Block—the city's first fireproof and earthquake-resistant building—at 628 Montgomery (where today stands the Transamerica Pyramid).

Twenty doctors busied themselves around King's bed and administered what each believed to be the best remedy. Pills were taken and elixirs sipped; doctors prodded the wound with curious fingers and sponged away the blood that continued to flow. King passed in and out of consciousness, his body temperature dropping and his extremities growing cold. Doctors rubbed his arms and legs to maintain circulation and placed a hot water bottle beneath the sheets. Mustard wraps were applied to his skin to restore a small measure of warmth.

Casey, meanwhile, sat on a bunk in the city jail at the Sacramento Street police station and pondered his fate. The irate rumblings of an angry mob could be heard beyond the drab, gray walls of the cell. The police had brought him here for his own protection, though how far the officers would go to guard him from an outraged citizenry remained to be seen. Word of Casey's whereabouts had spread quickly, prompting a crowd of thousands to march up Merchant and Washington streets before converging on the station house with guns and rope in hand. In case the armaments and accoutrements of hanging did little to convey their purpose, members of the mob shouted: "Hang the son of a bitch!" and "Take him out!"

Casey nervously glanced through the bars of the adjacent cell, where gambler and gunman Charles Cora sat rolling a cigarette. Cora had fatally shot United States Marshal William H. Richardson outside a Clay Street bank on November 17, 1855, following an exchange of harsh words several days prior when Richardson's wife referred to Cora's girlfriend—a known prostitute named Bella—in less than flattering terms. On the night of the shooting, Cora and Richardson had met for drinks at the Blue Wing Saloon on Montgomery to iron out a truce. A bottle of whiskey did much to put the two men in an amicable mood. They left the saloon on seemingly good terms and turned onto Clay Street, where Cora pulled a piece and blew a hole in Richardson's chest.

Cora had spent the months since lounging about his cell in relative peace, awaiting his murder trial. Now, he lit his cigarette in a state of extreme agitation, aware the mob would be more than pleased to seize two accused murderers for the price of one. "Casey," he chastised through the bars, "you have sealed the fate of us both!" But Cora need not have worried yet. Outside, a contingent of heavily armed officers had positioned itself around the station to halt the mob's mission of vengeance. At least for now.

———◆———

FEW PAID ATTENTION TO THE carriage that made its way down Washington Street after nightfall and turned into Dunbar Alley, behind the police station. Casey had been brought up from his basement cell to the building's rear entrance and armed with two pistols for his own protection should the mob attack and overpower his police escort. The plan, Sheriff Dave Scannell explained, was to transfer Casey under cover of night to the more secure county lockup at Broadway and Kearny. The sheriff kicked open the door and bundled

Casey—gripping pistols in both hands and surrounded by "a strong force of police officers and deputy sheriffs"—into the back of the coach. The sudden commotion in the quiet alley drew the crowd's attention. A wave of frenzied, jeering men and women flooded the small thoroughfare and encircled the carriage. Casey, imbued with boldness by the moment of bravado, waved his pistols at the crowd and threatened indiscriminate slaughter. The hackney driver snapped the reigns and forced the horses to cut a swath through the riotous tangle of people. Screaming its now familiar mantra of "Kill him! Kill him! Kill him!" the mob gave chase as the carriage veered out of the alley.

The county building stood about eight feet above the street, which had been sloped to form a ten-foot bank in front of the jail. A number of Casey's gambling associates, all heavily armed and obviously aware of the jail transfer well in advance, had taken up defensive positions around the building. "There they stood," recalled W. O. Ayers, a member of the mob, "a dangerous looking company, quietly looking down on the angry crowd that filled the street, and surged back and forth in its intense excitement."

As the enraged public surged toward the building, a lone figure scrambled up one of the jail's balcony posts. It was Tom King, brother of James. He turned to face the crowd on the street below, shouting, "Who will go with me and drag the murderer of my brother from that jail?" The crowd roared its approval and hissed violently when an armed officer demanded that King climb down. King did as he was told and, upon the advice of friends, bundled himself into a waiting carriage and left the scene. The mob stayed and demanded that Casey be dragged from his cell and lynched on the spot. The ruckus only intensified when a company of volunteer soldiers, bayonets polished, turned the corner of Dupont Street. Members of the mob initially cheered, believing the infantrymen had come to reinforce the public's ranks—but the jubilation did not last long.

The platoon numbered twenty soldiers and took up position in front of the jail and on the roof. They were reinforced by troops from the California Guards, First Light Dragoons and National Lancers. "This did not please the crowd," reported the *Alta*, "who howled, groaned and uttered many imprecations upon the band of those who would interfere with the administration of justice to a culprit." Not even Mayor Van Ness, who arrived at the jail shortly after 6:30 PM to restore some sense of civility to his city's streets, garnered any respect. He addressed the crowd from the jail steps:

> I desire to say to you that you are here creating an excitement which
> may lead to some occurrence this night, which will require years to
> wipe out. You are now laboring under a great excitement, and I
> advise you to quietly disperse, and I can assure you that the prisoner
> is safe and let the law have its course, and justice will be done.

The people could have hardly cared less; they booed him back into his carriage.

THINGS REMAINED JUST AS CHAOTIC back at the crime scene.

"The various streets all about the fatal corner were now completely filled with persons," wrote one witness, "all of whom seemed to imbibe the excitement almost to frenzy." The doctors tending to their patient were joined at seven by King's wife, who sat by her husband's side and stroked his forehead. The wound was eventually bandaged. Shortly after ten, having received a heavy dose of morphine, King drifted off to sleep.

The crowd outside the Montgomery Block building now reportedly numbered ten thousand. One news scribe noted:

> The streets as far as the eye could reach seemed to be filled with
> persons, either rushing to the scene, or hurrying away on some
> errand connected with the affair. Every building in the vicinity was
> alive with humanity, and the whole presented one of the most
> thrilling and exciting scenes we have ever seen.

Rope barriers were stretched across the street to prevent the multitudes from entering the building. Thousands had also gathered outside the *Bulletin* offices, where updates on King's condition were posted every half hour. As night settled heavy and tense on the city, word rippled through crowded streets that justice would soon be at hand. Such a belief was not passed down by any high court or law official, but in a single sentence men now whispered to one another: "The Vigilance Committee has organized."

The committee—a collective of private citizens turned vigilantes—had been born in 1851 out of the lawlessness that swept San Francisco in the wake of the Gold Rush. The city's small police force, many of its officers being men of questionable moral character, did little to prevent crime. The committee adopted a charter, promising to maintain "the peace and good order of society, and the preservation of lives and property of the citizens of San Francisco." It had then dispensed its violent brand of justice for two months beginning on July 9, arresting wrongdoers, convicting them in trials and hanging them in very public places to set an example. Such justice was not uncommon on the frontier, where the institutions of civilized society—such as courts, jails and basic laws—were corrupted by crooked officials or not yet fully established. A citizenry tired of rampant crime welcomed the harsh campaign waged in the name of justice. The committee disbanded that September, after just a few months of activity, satisfied that criminals now knew the score.

Even in its dormant years, the committee had remained organized in the event an act of brutality necessitated quick and savage retribution. Its signal to gather was the mournful tapping of the bell at the Monumental Engine Company near Clay, Kearny and Dupont streets. Now, hours after Casey's fateful pull of the trigger, as the city's clocks tolled a restless midnight, the clang of the vigilante bell echoed through the streets yet again. The members gathered under the leadership of William T. Coleman, one of the city's most highly respected merchants, and quickly set up shop in a grain warehouse at 41 Sacramento Street.

"A Committee of Vigilance, organized by our citizens, men of the first standing in society, members, mechanics, professional men, was called together on Wednesday," the *Bulletin* reported. "The Association held their session from an early hour in the morning until late at night. They enrolled, we are told, upwards of three thousand names."

The committee assumed a militaristic air. Its members fortified the grain warehouse and surrounded the building with sandbags stacked ten feet high. They christened their base of operations Fort Gunnybags and placed cannons on its roof and those of surrounding buildings. Armed patrols kept guard at all hours of the day, while the small San Francisco police force remained power-less to intervene. Committee members, over the next three days, organized themselves into military companies armed with rifles and bayonets. They appealed to the citizenry through newspapers, urging everyone to join the cause. One man out for blood voiced his opinion:

> As a law-abiding man, under ordinary circumstances—a husband and father of a wife and children—and as one who has large inter-ests here, and who wishes to make this his home, I appeal to you to show the gamblers and shoulder-strikers and the world that a felon from a State Prison cannot shoot down an innocent man in our streets, and go unpunished. Go into the Pacific Express office and see upon the floor the life-blood that has flown for you, and swear upon that blood that it shall be avenged.

Stoked by the media, emotions continued to run high. Nearly every city paper voiced its support for the vigilantes. Tom King took the helm of his brother's *Bulletin*, which ran articles touting the greatness of its stricken founder and voiced on the front page the vengeful sentiments of its readers. Within two days of the shooting, the paper had received more than a hundred letters from readers urging the Vigilance Committee to act. "Several of our carriers inform us that yesterday, at almost every door on their routes, the ladies were waiting to see them to enquire into the state of the health of Mr. King, and that the little girls ran half way across the street, asking the same question," reported the paper on Friday, May 16. "One lady enquired, 'What is to be done about that villain, Casey? If the men don't hang him, the ladies will!'"

The lone exception among the cries for blood was the *San Francisco Herald*. In a column the day after the shooting, the paper took a low-key approach and abstained from any rabble rousing:

Motives of delicacy, needless to explain, force us to abstain from
commenting on this affair; but we could not justify ourselves in
refraining from the most earnest condemnation of the mob spirit
last evening. We refrain from expressing an opinion as to the affray
of yesterday. If Mr. Casey be guilty, let him be punished. If he be
innocent, we will express our conviction to that effect, though all
the world were against us. But let him have a fair trial.

Being the lone voice of objectivity, however, proved costly for the paper.
By the following day, its pages had already been reduced. "It appears that
either the language or the views of a paragraph in the Topics of yesterday's
Herald gave offence to a number of persons in this city, who immediately signi-
fied their displeasure by withdrawing their advertisements and subscriptions,"
the paper reported, explaining that 212 readers had cancelled their subscriptions. Many residents were now threatening to boycott any business that considered purchasing advertising space in the offending sheet. "The number of
other further evidences and sovereign displeasure and discomfort on the part
of the disaffected," the paper sadly declared, "we have not space to narrate."

Gov. J. Neeley Johnson, summoned by Mayor Van Ness, arrived by
steamboat from Sacramento Friday night to quell the madness. After setting
up office in the Continental Hotel, he summoned Committee Leader
Coleman to his suite to discuss the situation. What, the governor asked, did
the Vigilance Committee intend to do? "Just what the Committee of 1851
accomplished," Coleman replied. "To see that the laws are executed and a few
prominent criminals do not go unpunished; to drive some notoriously bad
characters out of the state; to purify the moral and political atmosphere, and
then disband."

Sheriff Scannell had organized about a hundred men, known as the Law
and Order Party, to stand in armed opposition against the vigilantes. Control
of the group was offered to future Civil War great William Tecumseh
Sherman, a major general in the state militia, who had been tasked by the

governor to restore order to San Francisco. Sherman appraised the situation and declined the governor's request, realizing the Vigilance Committee outnumbered any force the state might be able to muster. When Johnson requested federal troops, he was bluntly refused.

On the morning of Sunday, May 18, four days after the shooting, the Vigilance Committee sprang into action.

On the roof of Fort Gunnybags, there hung a large steel triangle that served as a bell; its monotone clang served as a muster call for all committee members. Throughout the morning hours, the makeshift bell tolled, summoning men clad in dark blue uniforms and armed with rifles bearing bayonets. The men of the Vigilance Committee, numbering twenty-six hundred in all, were organized into twenty-six companies. They began to march at noon. Their boot-clad feet stomped in unison up Sacramento Street, toward Montgomery, as they made their way to the county jail. Thousands of curious onlookers crowded rooftops, lined the streets and gazed out windows as the procession passed. "The entire summit and upper slopes of Telegraph Hill were densely crowded with a multitude of spectators, who were anxiously watching the scene below," recalled committee member W. O. Ayers, "for the square bounded by Broadway, Kearny, Vallejo and Dupont Streets was closely invested by armed men, who had marched to their station with military step and order."

Brandishing rifles, shotguns and pistols, the citizen army took up position in front of the jail. They stood ten-men deep and formed an open-ended square, placing in its center a four-pound artillery piece mounted on two wagon wheels with its muzzle aimed at the jail's facade.

At 1 PM, Coleman and Marshal Charles Doane, head vigilante, approached the jail and knocked upon its doors. Sheriff Scannell appeared at the jail entrance and surveyed a scene bristling with firepower. He engaged Coleman in brief but animated conversation. Coleman demanded Cora and Casey be turned over to the vigilantes, but Scannell refused. Coleman did not mince matters. "Mr. Scannell," he said, "we give you five minutes and no more. If, at the end of that time, the two men are not surrendered, we shall take them by force; the doors of the jail will be blown open, and you will be taken, Mr. Scannell, as well as Casey and Cora."

Scannell retreated back inside the jail and scurried to Casey's cell, where he found the prisoner pacing the floor. Casey knew the situation to be bleak, but was not prepared for Scannell's news.

"What?" he shrieked. "Are you going to give me up?"

"James," said Scannell, admitting defeat, "there are three thousand armed men coming for you, and I have not thirty supporters about the jail."

"Not thirty!" Casey said. "Then do not peril life for me. I will go."

There followed a brief moment of madness: Casey pulled from his coat a dagger he had stowed away in his underwear and threatened to plunge the blade through his heart rather than be taken alive. Members of the committee assured Casey in his cell he would be treated like a gentleman and not dragged through the streets like an animal. Outside, the five-minute deadline was about to elapse. "When about five seconds off the fifth minute remained," recalled Ayres, who had taken up position fifty yards from the jail on the south side of Broadway, "the door was opened." Casey, shackled at the wrists, was led from the jail, flanked on either side by Coleman and Doane.

He showed no signs of fear as his captors marched him through the crowd to a closed carriage at the corner of Dupont and Broadway. Two armed committee members helped him into the hackney, its curtains drawn, and closed the door. The rattle of the carriage wheels and the rhythmic clop of hooves was all that could be heard as the carriage moved at a funereal pace away from the jail toward the committee's improvised fortress. "The silence of the city seemed to me something frightful, something unnatural, a silence that could be felt, like the darkness that fell upon the land of Egypt," recalled one witness, "but I suppose it was only the effect of my imagination." The carriage returned thirty minutes later, and the committee members demanded the prisoner Cora also be turned over to them. Scannell, realizing he had no choice in the matter, again acquiesced and released the gambler-turned-killer into the custody of the vigilantes.

ON TUESDAY, MAY 20, 1856, the *Daily Evening Bulletin* reported:

DEATH OF MR. KING

James King of William died this afternoon at half-past one o'clock. He expired without a struggle, apparently suffering no pain. For the previous three hours, he was not fully sensible.

The mournful tolling of church bells signaled King's demise. The bulletin boards outside the city's newspapers—with the exception of the *Herald,* reported the *Bulletin*—"all bore the black insignia of death." Within the hour, black ribbons draped city trees and hung from nearly every balcony. From one end of Montgomery Street to the other, crepe fluttered in the evening breeze. "Hundreds shed tears as they promenaded the public streets," wrote the *Bulletin*'s reporter, "and many were perfectly speechless with grief."

Two days had passed since Casey's seizure by the Vigilance Committee. When word of King's death reached the prisoner in his cell at Fort Gunnybags, he shed any pretense of courage and dignity. The color drained from his face and he developed a severe tremor. The timing could not have been worse, for the Vigilance Committee was in the middle of trying him for attempted murder. In the severely biased proceedings, Casey was denied outside counsel, forced instead to select members of the committee—the very people who wanted to see him hang—to serve as his defense.

No question surrounded the outcome. The jury, comprised of committee members, found both Casey and Cora guilty of their respective crimes. Cora took the news in stride, while Casey fell to his knees, pounded the floor with his fists and cursed his fate.

King's body was placed on public view at five that evening, allowing the thousands who crowded the streets around Montgomery Block—the building where he died—to bid him a final farewell. The mourners entered the building through the Montgomery Street entrance, filed through the room where King lay and exited onto Merchant Street. "For some time, the line of persons anxious to view the body extended from the door of the room to as far as Clay Street," reported the *Bulletin*, "and until a late hour at night their line was unbroken. Many ladies availed themselves of the opportunity to pay a last visit to their departed friend, and many, many left the room with tearful eyes."

A horse-drawn hearse retrieved King's body and brought it to the Unitarian Church on Stockton Street. King's wife and six children sat in the front pew as pallbearers took up position on both sides of the altar. Following a solemn anthem by the church choir, the Reverend Cutler ascended the altar and addressed the large gathering of mourners. "With a bold pen he assailed giant evils," Cutler said. "With an unshrinking, unfaltering hand he probed the general corruption; with hard blows he struck at the stronghold of inequity and crime; and with unsparing criticism he unmasked villainous character—and it is for this that he now lies before us motionless and a corpse."

Following the May 22 ceremony, a procession of nearly six thousand people and a string of carriages more than a mile long followed the hearse, drawn by four gray horses, from the church to Washington Street. It turned slowly onto Montgomery and made its way up to Bush and Lone Mountain Cemetery, where the body was interred. Roughly twenty-five thousand people lined the sidewalks and crowded rooftops along the route. Captains aboard ships in the Bay ordered flags lowered to half-mast. The *Bulletin* reported:

> Every trade, avocation and profession was represented, and natives of almost every clime were marching in the ranks. Silently, thoughtfully, sorrowfully, they walked behind the corpse—strangers, most of them, to this person while living, but friends of the principles he advocated, and mourners now at his funeral. Even the lowly African was there, trudging along with tearful eyes and saddened heart, for he remembered that Mr. King when alive plead [sic] most eloquently for all who were oppressed and unfortunate.

King's widow had carried herself with dignity up until the burial when, according to one witness, "nature gave way and she was lost in an agony of grief."

WOODEN PLATFORMS, LIKE PLANKS ON a pirate ship, extended from two top-floor windows at Fort Gunnybags. Workmen busied themselves with cable and pulleys throughout the morning, making sure the two platforms—actually makeshift gallows—were each strong enough to support the weight of a man. It was just shy of one in the afternoon. While the burial was being performed at Lone Mountain Cemetery, Cora and Casey were being prepped for execution. Cora married his prostitute girlfriend, Arabella Bryan, an hour before the scheduled hanging. The Reverend Maraschi performed the ceremony. Casey, as he had done since his initial incarceration, paced his cell. He had spent the previous night in the company of the Right Reverend Bishop Alemany, but the holy man's words brought him little comfort.

Thousands filled Sacramento Street between Front and Davis to witness the grim proceedings. Cannons and caissons kept the crowd a hundred yards distant from the site of execution, while committee members armed with muskets kept an eye on the more than eight thousand people who assembled for the spectacle. At a quarter past one in the afternoon, Cora and Casey stepped onto the platforms, the nooses dangling from two beams above their heads. Cora betrayed no emotion as the rope was fitted and maintained his composure; Casey cried out for his mother.

The rope was slipped around Casey's head and his eyes were covered. His knees buckled as he stepped to the fatal spot, prompting two men to extend their arms from the window and hold him steady. Someone out of view pulled a lever and collapsed both planks. The two men fell five feet before the ropes snapped their necks. Cora died without so much as a spasm. Casey's body twitched violently and then was still. The bodies remained dangling for an hour to accommodate the viewing public. The ordeal was done. "Both victim and assassin," declared the *Bulletin*, "sleep equally the sleep of death."

The *Bulletin* summed up the life of its founding editor in prose that made no attempt to be subtle:

Behold! Fellow citizens—it now floats over his remains. In triumph see it kissing the winds of heaven and lending every air that passes, the perfume of its sanctity. Under it he fought many a dangerous battle, dared to the death combat many a powerful foe. Who can forget his holy ways? No Crusader ever engaged Mussulman beneath the walls of Jerusalem with sterner resolution, and more glorious chivalry, than he did the dastardly pests, that for years past have hovered like carrion-crows over the decomposing elements of California Society.

In the end, the shooting of King and the frenzy that followed served a purpose that far outweighed any moral crusade. When the *Bulletin* hit the streets on the afternoon of Friday, May 23, a notice to readers on its front page declared: "We are happy to be enabled to say that our regular circulation has increased, within the last seven days, to upwards of six thousand five hundred copies. This is the largest circulation among regular subscribers that the *Bulletin* has yet obtained."

In this environment, where bad news was the best news and a printed word could mean serious injury or death, another young newspaperman would rise above the journalistic din. The public would not love him as it had the *Bulletin*'s founder, but he would engage the wrath of his paper's readers and soon have all of San Francisco caught in the crossfire.

His name was Charles de Young. As a boy of eleven with a burgeoning interest in newspapers, he undoubtedly followed the drama of King's death. He wouldn't have known the events were foreshadowing his own dubious end. Like King of William, de Young would wield his pen with Napoleonic fervor, assailing politicians, the rich and his rivals with unabashed glee. He would claim he was doing it for the betterment of San Francisco. Some agreed, while others saw only a self-seeking glory hound who plumbed the depths of poor taste in the name of circulation.

His paper, initially dismissed as an inconsequential theater sheet, would become one of the nation's largest metropolitan dailies: the *San Francisco Chronicle*.

1

YOUNG BLOOD

AN APPROACHING STEAMER, WITH ITS news of other places and much-needed goods, generated plenty of excitement when it landed in San Francisco in 1854. On the decks, passengers lined the railings to gaze upon the young city and its undeveloped backdrop of rolling hills. Incoming vessels dropped anchor off North Beach, and the passengers were rowed to shore as crowds of people blackened Telegraph Hill and witnessed the influx of San Francisco's new denizens.

On board were the de Youngs, a family with an obscure history draped in sordid rumor. Some have suggested they were descended from French aristocracy and came to San Francisco from New Orleans after losing their lot in Texas. A less flattering version of the family story identified the de Young boys as offspring of Cincinnati merchants who ventured west to avoid military conscription. But such theories paled in comparison to one tale that

maligned Mother de Young's character and questioned her sexual morality—
that she was a madam and former prostitute from St. Louis. The rumor, whatever its origin, lingered for years and caused much carnage.

The facts of the de Young family history are not so tawdry. Michael de
Young emigrated to the United States from the Netherlands, arriving in Baltimore in January 1813 at the age of twenty-one. He made a living as both a
jeweler and the manufacturer of tortoiseshell combs (though, in later years,
his son would insist his father was an important East Coast banker). In 1827,
he met French native Amelia Morange and took her hand in marriage. De
Young and his young bride moved to New York—where Amelia's family
lived—sometime in the mid-1830s. He worked there as a merchant until
packing up in 1838 and moving westward with his wife and their two young
daughters, Virginia and Clara. The family bounced around, living in Texas,
Louisiana and St. Louis. Everywhere, Amelia was admired for her beauty and
proficiency at the piano. "Mrs. DY very much accomplished," noted the diary
entry of one acquaintance, "and deserves a better looking husband."

Sometime in the late 1840s or early 1850s, de Young moved his family,
which now included eight children, to Cincinnati and sought employment in
the dry goods trade. They lived in Ohio until 1854, when the sixty-three-
year-old de Young and his forty-five-year-old wife boarded the *Tecumseh* with
their large brood, intent on settling in California. Patriarch Michael did not
survive the journey; he died of apoplexy aboard the steamer.

Charles de Young—born in Natchitoches, Louisiana, on January 8,
1845—was nine when he and his family first set foot on San Francisco soil.
Amelia moved with her children—five daughters and sons Michael Henry
and Gustavus, in addition to Charles—into humble lodgings and drew
meager wages as a seamstress, relying on her sons to assist in providing for the
family. Burdened by such responsibility, Charles scoured the streets in search
of work—but he didn't mind, for he worshipped his mother. It was an idolatry
that in later years would become the stuff of news and murder. "His love for
his aged mother was something phenomenal," a *New York Times* correspondent later wrote, "and to the day of his death it certainly strengthened."

In the 1850s, San Francisco, still a city of gamblers and whiskey dealers,

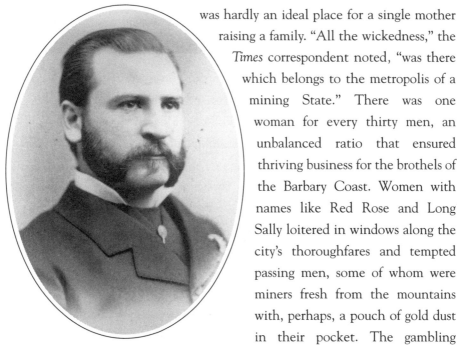

Charles de Young, founding editor of the
San Francisco Chronicle, whose love for his
mother would ultimately lead to gunplay
and murder
[PHOTO COURTESY OF THE CALIFORNIA HISTORY ROOM,
CALIFORNIA STATE LIBRARY, SACRAMENTO, CALIFORNIA]

was hardly an ideal place for a single mother raising a family. "All the wickedness," the *Times* correspondent noted, "was there which belongs to the metropolis of a mining State." There was one woman for every thirty men, an unbalanced ratio that ensured thriving business for the brothels of the Barbary Coast. Women with names like Red Rose and Long Sally loitered in windows along the city's thoroughfares and tempted passing men, some of whom were miners fresh from the mountains with, perhaps, a pouch of gold dust in their pocket. The gambling houses, crowded at all hours by inebriated roughs not afraid to riot, stayed open on Sundays. More than a dozen large halls for cards and dice were open for business. Winnings were paid in silver and, oftentimes, gold nuggets. "It was among such elements as these," the *New York Times* later reported, "when Charles de Young passed those years of his life when a man's character is principally formed."

Charles found work selling and folding various newspapers. The nature of his job required he associate with the more rough-and-tumble members of society, often frequenting saloons and gambling houses to hawk the daily editions. His character remained incorruptible despite the early exposure to whiskey and tobacco. Moreover, witnessing the guttural existence of San Francisco's drunks and card sharks instilled in Charles an everlasting hatred of gambling. The pitiful display of grown men rendered useless by drink, slumped over card tables or lying facedown in the mud-strewn streets, resulted in a strict adherence to sobriety. Once older, he occasionally enjoyed a glass of wine or liquor, but never to excess. Surrendering to such immoral cravings would have disappointed his mother. Recalled one contemporary:

> Whatever may be the opinion entertained of his subsequent career, it is certainly not to be wondered at that he grew into manhood with peculiar notions of morality, and, looking upon human life as of comparatively no value whatever when weighed in the balance against an insult to Californian "honor."

Although Charles de Young was two years older than his brother Michael, he looked—according to one account of the day—at least ten years younger. His eyes were an impenetrable black, but his gaze was more attentive than piercing. His short and medium-built body possessed boundless energy, evident in movements that were "quick and spasmodic." He rarely sat still, retiring to bed late at night and rising before dawn. His look became increasingly severe as he matured. He grew a thick, black mustache, which he complemented with bushy side-whiskers and an ever-present black silk hat. He took great pride in his looks, often consulting mirrors to ensure his appearance met the high standards he set for himself. "If he had any weakness at all," a reporter later noted, "it was vanity with regard to his personal appearance."

Charles, driven by ambition, matured quickly. He continued to sell and fold newspapers until 1856, when he was hired at age eleven as a compositor for the *Weekly Gleaner*, a newly launched Anglo-Jewish newspaper run by a rabbi named Julius Eckman. A compositors' union had been formed several years earlier, ensuring a fixed salary for all members. Michael and Gustavus joined their brother in this endeavor and, together, learned the basics of typesetting.

By the early 1860s, Charles had left the *Gleaner* behind and was plying his trade at the *Alta*. His first independent foray into newspaper publishing was an eight-page rag that reported the daily happenings within the city's public schools. The paper sold well and earned him the respect of the Board of Education. From there, he started the *Holiday Advertiser*, a short-lived enterprise, before launching the paper that would secure his place in journalism history.

"The starting of a paper was Charles de Young's idea," Michael wrote in

Michael H. de Young in his office at the *Chronicle*
[PHOTO COURTESY OF THE CALIFORNIA HISTORY ROOM, CALIFORNIA STATE LIBRARY, SACRAMENTO, CALIFORNIA]

1875. "I had been in other newspaper enterprises and, at first, I declined to go in with him, but we launched the enterprise together." It began with a borrowed twenty-dollar gold piece from the pocket of William C. Hinckley, a retired sea captain who had settled in San Francisco some years earlier and made his fortune in real estate. He was also the de Young family's landlord at 422 Bush Street. Michael, at the urging of Charles, had requested the loan for the intended purpose of starting a newspaper. Having taken a keen interest in the fatherless boys, Hinckley happily provided the initial capital and wished the brothers luck. "This was the fund that started the *Chronicle*," Michael wrote, "and the only money we ever borrowed to make it a newspaper."

MORE THAN A DOZEN DAILY and weekly journals—including the highly touted morning papers *Alta California* and *Call*, and the established *Bulletin* and *Examiner* in the evening—waged a fierce ink-and-paper war for circulation in San Francisco. It was a conflict dating back several years and humble in its beginnings. Initially published in Monterey in July 1846, the small, poorly printed *Californian* was California's first newspaper. Its editor, a Kentuckian named Robert Semple, had come to the territory in search of a wife. After striking out on the Monterey Peninsula, Semple decided to try his luck in Yerba Buena, the settlement of six hundred people that would eventually become San Francisco. Already being published in the region by a Mormon hailing from New York was the *California Star*, which debuted in January 1847 as a four-page weekly. Through the *Star*'s editorials and columns, publisher Samuel Brannan preached the Mormon word. "But for the discovery of gold," noted one early historian, "San Francisco might have been a Mormon town and California a Mormon territory."

The *Californian*, and its small-time rivalry with Brannan's *Star*, was short-lived. The discovery of gold in January 1848 prompted Semple to close shop on May 29 and head for the hills in search of riches. "The whole country," wrote Semple, "from San Francisco to Los Angeles, and from the sea shore to the base of the Sierra Nevada, resounds with the sordid cry of gold, gold, gold." Gold fever having plucked off its staff one by one, the *Star* also ceased operations two weeks later. "The town," observed one witness, "was thrown into intellectual darkness."

Within several weeks, Semple found the riches he so desired, forever quit the newspaper trade and sold his printing equipment to Brannan. Soon deciding he'd also tired of the news business, Brannan sold his operation to a young printer named Edward Kemble and left to make his fortune in the mercantile trade. Under its new ownership, the revitalized *Star* grew in size and, in January 1849, changed its name to the *Alta California*. The challenge of finding individuals immune to the lure of gold to work at the paper proved difficult, and forced the *Alta* to publish only occasionally. Not until the emergence of the *Pacific News* several months later did the *Alta* begin publishing three days a week. In December 1849, both the *Alta* and *Pacific News* became dailies in an effort to stifle the competition put fourth by the new *Daily Journal of Commerce*. The following year saw the San Francisco newspaper market explode with the publication of the *Evening Picayune*, the *Herald* and the *Courier*. Ink now flowed freely.

Papers ranged in price from fifteen cents to a quarter. News stories combined reporting with aggressive editorializing. Reporters imbued each story with their own sense of humor or moral indignation. Objectivity was a casualty of fierce competition as each paper sought to enthrall the city's burgeoning population with stories of crime, corruption and the debaucheries of high society. Reporters roamed the streets like rival gang members, many with the reassuring weight of a sidearm against the hip. For their work, reporters earned roughly fifty dollars a week—a decent salary for the day. Correspondents who reported the sometimes blood-soaked happenings in the mining camps earned up to twenty-five dollars for every thousand words.

Murder was the news industry's bread and butter in those early days. A tale of killing always received priority coverage and was seldom cut or held to make room for copy of a less dramatic nature. "This was the reader's daily food for the mind," remarked one reader. "The newspapers had a style 'all their own,' suitable to this cosmopolitan mass of humanity on the border-land of civilization."

In the 1800s, much like today, sex and violence sold newspapers.

———◦———

THE DE YOUNG BROTHERS ENTERED the fray with confidence. With the captain's advance, they paid two weeks' rent at William C. Harrison's printing office at 417 Clay Street. They purchased two stands of type and a large redwood desk, and put money down on one week's worth of in-house printing services. With a contract in place to publish theatrical advertisements, the paper debuted on Monday, January 16, 1865. The brothers' self-penned salutation was almost impish in its wording, resplendent with the enthusiasm and self-assuredness of youth:

We make our politest bow, with one hand upon the left side of our
blue and green plaid waistcoat, one foot being thrown gracefully
forward in the operatic managerial style, and our glistening new
sombrero held negligently resting on our left hip bone. We incline
smilingly toward our friends, the public, and announce our prospec-
tive intentions with regard to the *Daily Dramatic Chronicle*, asking
them to take the tiller of our fate into their own hands, knowing as
we do, that with such pilots the favoring breeze of success will fill
our sails, and give us a clear sea.

We shall do our utmost to enlighten mankind in *esse*, and San
Francisco en *posse*, of actions, intentions, sayings, doings, movements, successes, failures, oddities, peculiarities, and speculations,
of "us poor mortals here below."

The *Daily Dramatic Chronicle* measured ten by fourteen inches. Its four
pages were light on news but heavy on advertisements and theater programs.
All four columns on the front page were devoted to selling the latest in vene-
real disease remedies and tickets to a local vaudeville house on the northeast
corner of Kearny and Clay streets, featuring the popular Fairy Sisters in a
three-show performance, concluding "with a Non-descript, Fantastico,
Morceau of Absurdity, arranged expressly for this House, entitled THE
GROTTO NYMPH." Several quirky briefs peppered page two, including one of
a somewhat randy nature headlined "Pretty Girls":

We do not think that any city in the United States, proportion to the
number of its inhabitants, contains as many beautiful and tastefully
dressed "sweet sixteens" as San Francisco. It does our heart good to
walk along Montgomery Street on a bright afternoon, but woefully
spoils our appreciation for our usual corned beef and cabbage.

Under the headline "Sad Accident," a news item of a more dramatic
nature followed:

During the performance of the "Yellow Dwarf" at Worrell's Olympic on Friday night, one of the masked fiends unwittingly knocked Miss Sophie Worrell down with a stuffed club. She remained insensible for some time, but we are happy to say this worthy young lady was not seriously injured and will appear to-night as usual.

The paper's one major news story was of the death of Whig Party politician Edward Everett, whose two-hour speech at Gettysburg on November 19, 1863, was forever eclipsed by a two-minute address by President Lincoln.

Because, in those fledgling days, the paper could not afford the services of the Associated Press, the brothers would collect dispatches from across the country at the local Western Union office and reword them, injecting more flare into the language. This budget-minded approach to national coverage would soon establish the *Chronicle* as a serious journalistic contender.

The paper immediately became Charles de Young's passion. He was the engine behind its creation and oversaw every aspect of its publication, investing in that debut issue a Herculean effort. He managed its business concerns, obsessed over every word and went in search of advertisers. A steaming mug of coffee was his constant companion as he sat at the large redwood desk, papers scattered about him. It took five days to put that first issue together, during which time he slept a total of thirteen hours. Vain he may have been about his appearance, but there was no hiding his exhaustion. His hair was ruffled and his eyes bloodshot. His sleeves were often rolled up to his elbows and his hands stained with ink. When the debut issue finally rolled off the press, fatigue forced Charles de Young to the floor.

"The *Chronicle*," the brothers declared in that first edition, "will find its way every morning, in all the restaurants, saloons, hotels, reading rooms, stores, boats, cars, among the large private residences, making it the best advertising medium on the Pacific Coast." It was a lofty goal that was not immediately realized. In the name of economy, the brothers folded and distributed the paper themselves. They ran about town each afternoon, delivering what they could to hotels, restaurants and saloons. A number of papers were left daily at the box office of the Worrell Olympic vaudeville house. "We did as much work as we could ourselves to keep expenses down and make the paper a success," Michael wrote.

The brothers scoured smoke-filled card rooms and saloons at night in search of discarded copies of their paper to resell. They surveyed the aisles of the Worrell Olympic, picking up issues trashed by audience members and left trampled on the floor. Back at the Clay Street office, they set to work. They dried pages damp with beer and shook them free of cigar ash. Papers were smoothed and pressed flat on the large, redwood desk and then mailed to "hotels in the interior," where news from the civilized world—no matter how dated, singed or crumpled—remained a valuable commodity.

The *Chronicle* made an impression with its sly mix of social commentary and sordid observations, allowing the de Youngs to pay Captain Hinckley back his twenty dollars at the end of week one.

Notebook in hand and pencil at the ready, Charles de Young worked the streets in search of gossip and debauchery. "He was enterprising, shrewd, and, above all, successful," one paper later reported. "But, at the same time, he was cruel and unscrupulous so far as his public business as a journalist was concerned." One quip that characterized the *Chronicle*'s youthful joviality appeared a week after the paper's debut:

> On Sunday morning last, as we were peregrinating in the vicinity of
> Starr King's church, a very fashionably dressed young lady swept
> majestically by us (by the way, ain't all the little girls getting dignified,
> though), on her way to Sunday School, and as she gracefully raised
> her skirts to pass through the gateway, we noticed, accidentally, of
> course, a hole in the heel of her stocking. She probably knew of it
> Saturday, but remembered the Sabbath and kept it *hole*-y.

The follies of girls and their stockings earned guffaws in parlors and bar-rooms, but did nothing to enhance the paper's credibility. A little more than a month into their new endeavor, the brothers published an article headlined, "ASTONISHING":

So far as we have been able to learn, no new daily or weekly paper appeared yesterday, and none of the old ones deceased. This is remarkable. In San Francisco we average three new journals per week, with about the same number of deaths.

———————

THE MORNING OF SATURDAY, APRIL 15—four months after the *Chronicle*'s debut—seemed like any other when Michael de Young dropped by Western Union Telegraph on Montgomery Street, between Commercial and Sacramento. Entering the office, de Young found the wires thrumming and the operator, General W. H. Carpenter, in a frenzied state of excitement.

"Have you heard the news?" Carpenter asked.

"No," said de Young, "I haven't."

"Lincoln has been assassinated!"

Carpenter, a green eyeshade sitting lopsided on his head, thrust a dispatch at the young newspaperman: "Washington April 15. Gen. H. W. Carpenter: His Excellency President Lincoln was assassinated at the theater last night." The immensity of the news momentarily rendered de Young speechless, but the consummate journalist in him restored his senses and propelled him into action.

He committed details of the killing to memory as they buzzed across the wire, then dashed to the newsroom. The city's morning papers had already gone to print, meaning the ragtag *Chronicle* now had the chance to severely trounce the competition. "I ran to the office to put the news in type. We got out an extra [edition] and sent it around town, distributing it free at all the business houses, offices and places of public resort," Michael later recalled. "Then I got the telegraph company to give me all the news there was. We kept on issuing extras during the day." The brothers published three extras that afternoon.

As the front page was solely dedicated to theatrical advertisements—the paper's main source of revenue—the story ran on page two under the headline "DEATH OF THE PRESIDENT." The brothers' lead on the story meant the morning papers had no chance of catching up, and they also beat the evening papers by several hours. "The excitement," Michael de Young remembered, "got to be tremendous."

Charles sent Michael to gauge public reaction to the news. Crowds were gathering in the streets and massing outside the city's other papers, demanding additional details. One particularly vociferous gathering had assembled outside the offices of the *Democrat Press*, a two-year-old paper that had been sympathetic to the Southern cause. Outraged by such an editorial policy, Warren C. Butler, a foreman at the U.S. Mint on Mission Street, stepped from the crowd and assailed the paper for taking sides against Lincoln during the war. Another man in the crowd echoed that sentiment and dropped the name of every San Francisco newspaper aligned with the Southern rebellion. "Down with traitors!" cried a voice in the audience, sparking a sudden frenzy of violence.

Four men immediately charged the doors of the *Democrat* and hurried up the stairs to the empty second-floor newsroom. With no one to oppose them, they set to work destroying what they could. Some desks were overturned; others were hoisted and thrown through windows. Rowdy crowds in the street below cheered beneath a shower of broken glass as office furniture dissolved in splinters, and cases of type were scattered and trampled on. The *Daily Alta California* covered the unfolding drama:

> The extras issued from the offices of the *Alta* and the *Bulletin* furnished the details of the terrible event with such circumstantiality that nothing was left upon which a hope might be based either of exaggeration or mistake. At once the shops were everywhere closed. All business was suspended. The bells tolled, and the emblems of mourning were everywhere displayed.
>
> Then the public wrath began to kindle; soon it burst forth into a consuming conflagration, threatening the destruction of everything reasonable in its path. The offices of certain obnoxious publications were entered and their types and presses thrown into the street.

Satisfied its work at the *Democrat* was complete, the mob marched to the Clay Street offices of the weekly *News Letter*—a pro-South publication run by British editor Fred Marriott—and repeated the performance. The paper had openly gloated some years earlier when the Royal Navy broke a Union blockade and delivered arms to Southern rebels. Rioters now stormed the *Letter*'s newsroom with stomping feet and swinging fists. Every desk tossed through a window was again cause for violent celebration. The police, who were slow to mobilize and eventually turned out in modest numbers, could do little to soothe the mob mentality.

The rampage continued. "I followed the mob from behind, taking items," Michael de Young later wrote. The cheering, chanting masses descended upon the weekly *Monitor*, the city's leading religious paper, which had taken neither side during the conflict. Its neutrality mattered little to a riotous crowd caught up in the thrill of destruction. Angry men stampeded through the newsroom, splintering furniture and scattering supplies. The same office building just happened to house the French weekly *L'Union Franco Americaine*, which also fell victim to the roving maelstrom. The paper would never recover. The police could do nothing but follow in the mob's wake and make note of the damage. The *Irish News* and the pro-Union *Voz de Mejico* in the building next door were severely maimed. Neither paper would publish again.

Next on their hit list was the pro-South *L'Echo de Pacifique*. But, to get to those offices, one had to pass through the *Alta* newsroom. As the *Alta* reporters and staff readied themselves for combat (some ripped the legs off chairs and desks for use as makeshift clubs, while others wrapped blocks of metal type in handkerchiefs and wielded them like medieval weapons), an *Alta* editor named MacCrellish stuck his head out a window and addressed the crowd. "We, up here, are not inclined to permit any one to pass through our editorial offices on such an errand," he said. "We suggest that you people go elsewhere, and hurriedly." The *Alta* successfully barred its doors, preventing mob entry to its newsroom and that of *L'Echo*.

The *Occidental* presented a less formidable target. The paper's miniscule budget meant there was little for the mob to destroy, but they trampled what they could before turning next to the offices of the *Bulletin*. "If opportunity could have been had for reflection," reported the *Bulletin*, "the majority, at least, of the citizens concerned in this attack would have seen that such violence in the eleventh hour of the country's trouble, when all danger from disloyal presses is at an end, was not the best expression for heartfelt sorrow over the death of a good man."

Police Chief Martin Burke belatedly realized his small department was out of its depth and called for Army intervention. Word quickly reached Major General Irvin McDowell of the Department of California in his headquarters on Washington Street. With his sidearm in its holster and Provost Marshal Major Alfred Morton in tow, McDowell strolled to the *Bulletin* offices to address the seething crowd.

"Gentlemen," he said in a booming voice fit for a man of his rank, "your course today was very wrong but it was natural, and in interfering with the affairs of the press you have but anticipated me, and have perhaps saved some trouble. However, you must disperse at once. The Army will now take over." The crowds dispersed as the clanging of City Hall's fire bell summoned two thousand troops from the Presidio. Soldiers took up positions in the shattered newsrooms, while others stood watch over the offices that had managed to escape the carnage. "This is a protective measure," the general told reporters, warning residents and the press not to incite further devastation. "Any paper so offending, or expressing any sympathy in any way whatever with the act will be at once seized and suppressed."

The de Youngs reported the events in their paper on Monday, April 17, under the headline "IRREGULAR JUSTICE":

> There are some things which we cannot openly commend, though
> we may deem them commendable. Individuals and communities,
> are sometimes impelled by the irresistible impulses of just resent-
> ment, to acts which though not "lawful," they feel instinctively to
> be "right" . . . Each case of this kind must be judged by itself
> according to its own particular circumstances. On Saturday last, the
> people performed certain acts of "irregular justice," which though

not sanctioned by the courts will not be severely condemned by even the most moderate and law-abiding citizens.

The *Chronicle* had scored its first major coup and established itself as a significant journalistic commodity.

BY THE MID-1860S, MINERS, hucksters and the boringly respectable had bolstered the population of San Francisco, the largest city in the West, to sixty thousand. The women wore European fashions and carried French parasols, but there were still plenty of unpaved streets to dirty their dresses, and barrooms—such as Dick and Harry's Thunderbolt Saloon—to offend their sensibilities. "Every one who can, lives here, at least part of the year," wrote one visitor to the city, "and miners, when out of work, come here to spend their money and enjoy themselves."

The Thunderbolt, at 938 Kearny Street between Jackson and Pacific, was a frequent advertiser in the new *Chronicle*. Run by Harry Bolte and "Plum Dick," the establishment built its reputation on wine, oysters, lagers, billiards, free concerts and girls. Its advertisement played up the latter:

Haste away boys—do not tarry;
Go and see bold Dick & Harry,
Take a drink and hear a tune
At the Thunderstruck Saloon
Big Kate and Little Kate—
Lots of pretty girls there wait;
Eyes bright, handsome, flashing fire
Has the beauteous, bright Homeyer . . .
Hanchat graceful as a swan,
Has bright eyes as ever shone;
Fair Johanna all adore—
If not enough girls, we'll get more.

Establishments like the Thunderbolt catered to the city's flourishing literary scene. "At the time of the commencement of the *Dramatic Chronicle*, there existed in San Francisco a set of Bohemians we don't see today," Michael wrote. "These men were Bohemians in every sense of the word. They had no club or fixed places of abode and their nightly rendezvous was in Faust's Hall at the corner of Clay and Kearny streets where they got beer and German food."

The *Chronicle* also fostered the city's burgeoning literati, as its colorful reportage drew a number of aspiring authors to the paper's cramped office. One journalist in particular set up shop in the paper's newsroom within a week of its opening. "Mark Twain, for the privilege of desk room with us to write his famous *Carson Appeal* letters, contributed squibs to the *Dramatic Chronicle* and made his headquarters in our office," wrote Michael. "About six months after the starting of the paper, we began to gather around us a lot of those Bohemians who figured in the early history of California journalism and later become famous . . . These people hung around the *Dramatic Chronicle* office and made it a sort of headquarters where they could borrow $5 when 'broke' and contribute the products of their brains to the *Chronicle*."

Within a month of their paper's first issue, the brothers claimed a circulation of two thousand readers and increased the *Chronicle*'s size by three inches in both width and length. Four months later, the paper's circulation had climbed to five thousand in the wake of Lincoln's assassination. Now squarely established and with revenue coming in, the brothers had contrived a system to maximize their readership. Recalled Michael:

> We adopted a system of publishing the *Dramatic Chronicle* about 10 o'clock in the morning, get the criers around the business part of the town and then hold back until just 12 o'clock when we would spring it on the big restaurants, around the market where the principal eating houses were. Here, the business men and others went for lunch and at 12 sharp, or a little after, when the eating houses were full, we would go through them and put a *Chronicle* on every table . . .

There were criticisms on public men, crisp references to important events, shots at conspicuous people, and other such information all in condensed form. The result was that everybody around town, merchants, club-men and others, looked for the *Dramatic Chronicle* every day to see what our writers were saying.

Despite their growing success, the brothers could not yet afford to pay staff writers, relying instead upon the talents of the city's Bohemian set. Future poet Bret Harte, then a clerk at the Mint, and others who enjoyed the paper's anti-establishment spirit—among them James Bowman, Robert Greely, Prentice Mulford and Twain—imbued the *Chronicle*'s pages with a rebellious attitude. The Clay Street office became a de facto writer's sanctuary, where those with literary aspirations met to smoke and apply their talents. In the evening, Charles and Michael would sit and review the East Coast papers with their Bohemian friends, discussing the strengths and weaknesses of each publication. "The publication of squibs from these bright pens," remembered Michael, "attracted more attention to the *Chronicle* and made us known throughout the whole community." (The brothers, unfortunately, did not have the foresight to give these writers bylines.)

A gentleman named Tremenhere Johns penned theatrical critiques for the brothers. Not adverse to drink, Johns had imbibed his fair share when he unwittingly fired the opening salvo in the *Chronicle*'s first public feud by slamming the casting of the rotund Matilda Heron in the title role of the svelte Camille at Tom Maguire's Opera House on Washington Street. "Johns, after drinking his usual bottle, wrote a most fearful criticism," wrote Michael. "He was willing to concede she was a great star since she had size, figure and weight, but it was an imposition on an honest critic to force him to fit her into the role of the fragile and consumptive Camille."

The review outraged Maguire, the self-described "Napoleon of the Stage." Maguire had been a New York hack driver before he landed a job tending bar in one of the city's many Bowery joints. (He won the affections of his future wife, Emma, in such an establishment after pummeling a foul-mouthed hoodlum in a vicious, biting scrape.) By 1846, Maguire owned the bars on the second and third floors of New York's Park Theater and found, much to his surprise, that he enjoyed theater life. When news of California gold reached New York in 1849, he and Emma packed their belongings and headed west. They reached San Francisco that year and opened Porter's Hill, a saloon and gambling house on Portsmouth Square. In October 1850, he opened the Jenny Lind, the city's first full-sized theater dedicated solely to drama.

By the time of the *Chronicle* critique, Maguire's widespread theater empire included playhouses in Sacramento, Stockton, Sonora, Marysville and Virginia City. "Though an ignorant, illiterate man, he possessed wonderful energy, but he could not brook opposition," Michael wrote. "It was a bold thing for penniless young men to start in and criticize a field and fight the man controlling it." In response to the review, Maguire immediately barred "the damned paper" from the Opera House and the Academy of Music on Pine Street, which he also owned.

The de Youngs retaliated by assaulting Maguire in print, tying him to an unsavory partnership with a future state senator, Timothy McCarthy, then the proprietor of a gambling saloon that adjoined Maguire's Opera House. Denizens of the saloon, in which Maguire was a silent partner, entered the Opera House through an entrance in the barroom. "The result of Maguire's interest in it was that the gamblers attached to his saloon had entrée to the theater with their prostitutes and mistresses," according to the de Youngs' story, which detailed a debauched enterprise of gamblers, prostitutes and sexual practices. "The thing was notorious, disgustingly so. A respectable woman could not attend the theater without some prostitute coming and sitting beside her. We called public attention to the fact that the aisles were always crowded with the gamblers and the best seats monopolized by these women of the town."

The accusations did not stop there. The *Chronicle* charged that, behind the Opera House stage, scenes of disturbing immorality played out on a nightly basis. Actresses, including stars and those of a lesser caliber, were routinely "assaulted, drugged and outraged." Rendered limp by narcotics, the women were unable to deflect Maguire's sordid advances. His needs satisfied in the most heinous way imaginable, Maguire had no problem passing the used women off to others beneath the stage.

"We always took advantage of these things and wrote them up," Michael recalled of their quest to defame Maguire, "denouncing the whole moral atmosphere of the house. At first the effect was nil but in time it began to work."

Maguire tried to sink the de Youngs by launching seven theatrical newspapers over a period of several years to compete directly with the *Chronicle*, but the plan only met with failure. Thus, the conflict continued, reaching new lows of rascality and mischievousness. "The foundation of the *Chronicle* was really laid in Maguire's fight against us," Michael wrote. "It was a big thing for us all the time."

Wanting to strike Maguire where it would really hurt—in the pocketbook—Charles once again turned to Captain Hinckley, the paper's initial benefactor. Hinckley's extensive real-estate holdings included a large parcel of land on Bush Street—a perfect location, Charles believed, for the building of a new theater. "In the prosecution of our fight against Maguire," Michael wrote, "we kept calling upon the citizens to build a decent theater in San Francisco." Hinckley, now well into his advanced years, was initially inclined to dismiss the proposal as a young man's dream. But he eventually relented, saying he would be willing to rent Charles the land if a suitable property manager could be found.

Trusting de Young's business acumen, Hinckley gave him permission to start a rumor that capitalists were eyeing the Bush Street property with the intent of building a brand-new opera house. "This statement we manufactured to create a sentiment in that direction," Michael wrote. "We then consulted a real estate broker here—one of the first in the city—by the name of Hoogs, of Hoogs, Madison & Company. Mr. Hoogs had the confidence of prominent capitalists and he stirred around to see if he could get a lease of this property of Hinckley's." Described in one account as "undoubtedly a brave Roman," Octavian Hoogs signed a twenty-five-year lease on the property at $1,000 a month—with an option to buy—and set about building the California Theater.

Charles de Young spared Maguire further drubbings from his poison pen, but asked the new theater owners to prohibit the "Napoleon of the Stage" from ever stepping foot on the new premises. "If these gentlemen allowed Tom Maguire ever to put his fingers on that theater, he would ruin it as he had ruined his own," Michael de Young later explained. Taking the advice to heart, the California's owners negotiated a lease "in which it was distinctly understood that they would never let, sublet or indirectly allow Tom Maguire to have ever any connection with the theater."

Heavily promoted by the de Youngs, the California Theater opened on January 18, 1869, and helped bring about the collapse of Maguire's empire. The former "Napoleon of the Stage" returned to New York and died there a broken man in 1896.

2

SON OF A PREACHER MAN

THEY CAME FROM MILES AROUND—the wholly devout and the non-believers—to hear the boy wonder speak. Isaac Kalloch, just sixteen in the summer of 1847, was delivering his debut sermon, an enthusiastic lambasting of sin titled "Prepare to Meet Thy God." Pale skinned and with a thick mane of hair the color of Hellfire, Kalloch, the son of a preacher, was already known for his vocal prowess. His hometown of East Thomaston (now Rockland), Maine, had embraced the temperance movement six years earlier, prompting many townsfolk to empty their wine jugs and instead drink water. Kalloch became leader of a temperance club for the town's morally straight youth. He routinely decried in public the evils of intoxication and the devil's milk, enthralling audiences with his fierce delivery and a voice that boomed like God's own thunder.

Kalloch reviewed his hand-scribbled notes as the eager and curious crowd filed into the Baptist church in South Thomaston. They crowded the benches and fanned themselves, tolerating the cramped conditions and the wretched New England heat just to hear the boy's golden voice. The invitation to speak had been extended by the church's pastor, who just happened to be Kalloch's Uncle Joe. The boy exuded calm as he mounted the pulpit, brushing a thick lock of red hair from his forehead. He gave his notes one last glance before slipping them between the pages of his Bible. He cleared his throat and opened his mouth. One witness recalled:

> Everyone knew him and the audience, which filled the room, included a sprinkling of non-churchgoers, and even deists and atheists. None daunted, Isaac read the sermon, which denounced their principles in the most daring manner, the flood of his own eloquence being enlivened by some sublime passages of Milton. It was a notable performance . . . and the fame of it spread.

HE WAS BORN ON A Sunday—July 10, 1831—to Amariah Kalloch, minister of the First Baptist Church of Thomaston, and the young and pretty Mercy Hathorn Kalloch, a nineteen-year-old who now shared her birthday with her first born. The relationship between mother and son would prove fleeting, for she died of Asiatic cholera when Isaac was no more than a year old. She succumbed to the illness only after ensuring her child survived the 1832 epidemic, which Americans had initially watched from afar as it swept through Europe with grim consequence before hitting New England's coastal towns. Isaac would grow up with no memory of his mother. Six months after Mercy's death, Amariah married the daughter of a local caulker. He continued tending to his pastorate, increasing the size of his South Thomaston ministry from sixty-nine people in 1830 to four hundred worshippers within two years, a stunning testament to the power of his oratory.

In 1832, East Thomaston, a mere four miles away, was home to a new church in need of a dynamic preacher. Amariah answered the call and claimed the pulpit for the next fourteen years. For Isaac, East Thomaston—

with its dark woods, open fields and a rocky shoreline lapped by the waters of Penobscot Bay—provided an ideal setting for treasure hunting and other adventures crafted by imagination. Adventure and the Kalloch name enjoyed a close bond: The family bloodline cut a bold swath through the battlefields of the American Revolution. One great-uncle wreaked havoc against the Royal Navy while serving on an American frigate; another carried a musket in the Continental Army and did the same again as a senior citizen when war with England again broke out in the War of 1812. Tracing the family lineage back further, one stumbled across stories of valiant campaigns against Indians and rousing adventures on the untamed frontier.

Isaac's life would also prove adventurous, though not in the same manner.

Isaac often traveled with his father to revivals in the backwoods of Maine. Ministers shrieked and howled, while audience members—befuddled with awe and their love for all things holy—wept and raved in tongues. Amariah, states one account, "was one of the best practitioners in the business." He would pace the stage, his hands lifted toward Heaven, his voice a soulful bass that convinced even the most desperate sinners there was hope to be found in the words of Christ.

As a boy, Isaac would watch the proceedings and take note, favoring delivery and emotion over theatricality. He was aware from an early age that the power to speak meant the power to sway and command. The sermons of Charles Grandison Finney, a man considered by many to be America's foremost revivalist, also influenced the boy. Men of Finney's caliber were often guests at the Kalloch household, where Amariah engaged his visitors in theological discussion and debate.

All these things shaped within Isaac a forceful personality not easily intimidated, one that came to the forefront when he opened his mouth to speak. Such was Isaac's success as a youthful public orator that Amariah realized his son had a gift that required nurturing. Amariah wished for Isaac to follow in his footsteps and become a Baptist minister, and Isaac's rousing performance at the South Thomaston church only strengthened that desire.

Isaac's education had involved classes at a private school in Camden and an academy in East Thomaston. It was at Camden that Isaac met another student—one of startling beauty—named Laura Flye. With hair the color of midnight and skin that looked like ivory, she stole more than a passing glance from numerous admirers. Isaac was naturally appreciative of Laura's stunning physicality. Not yet sixteen, he, too, had become quite the specimen, standing nearly six feet tall and boasting a muscular physique. The two young people developed a mutual attraction and courted as teens do—but the relationship would prove to be an on-again, off-again exercise as each fulfilled educational obligations and pursued a personal course. Neither one could imagine then that they would, in a few short years, find themselves embroiled in a scandal that would enthrall all of New England and have newspaper editors frothing at the mouth.

Isaac was the first in his family to attend college. Amariah financed his son's education by taking a better-paying job in April 1847 as minister for the First Baptist Church in Augusta. Amariah's new position doubled his salary to $600 a year, allowing Isaac, in the fall of 1848, to enter Colby College. Isaac's freshman year, an onslaught of courses in Greek and Latin, was notable only because he managed to get himself expelled. In the ensuing years, rumors suggested he was removed from the school because of his enthusiasm for all things carnal. One gentleman, speaking with a critic of Isaac Kalloch years later, claimed to know all about Kalloch's alleged sex-crazed youth:

I know nothing of Kalloch's later career; but I am very familiar with his earlier days. We, my wife and I, lived in the same house with Amariah Kalloch, Isaac's father, in Rockland, M[ain]e. Kalloch (Isaac) was the only son by Amariah's first wife; he was about 12 or 14 years old of age when we lived together. When Ike was about fourteen years of age, and when the family were living in our home he was caught in the act of * * with a girl younger than himself. Later, he was expelled from college. Our families then separated. Amariah accepted a call in Augusta, ME, to which town my wife and I also went, I having procured a position in a hotel. Isaac was sent to another college. One Saturday night while I kept hotel, Isaac put in an appearance, with a young lady *** and also a college chum, who was likewise accompanied by a young woman. These four had a roaring good time, drank wine and played cards until late after midnight. They then retired, using two beds. The next morning Isaac received a message from his father, asking him to preach in his stead, as he himself was sick. Isaac there upon came up to me, and in a confidential whisper, he told me "that he could preach the *** off the old fellow." This shows you what kind of a man he is. Later Isaac went to the church in Rockland, in which his father had preached. Here, he again found out the little girl with whom he had been caught as a boy, and left Rockland.

Such insinuations, whether true or not, would plague Kalloch for most of his life. In fact, it was Isaac's sense of humor, and not his alleged nymphomania, that resulted in his expulsion after he stuck a notice on the school bulletin board declaring classes had been canceled for the day. The news quickly spread, infecting many of the school's eighty students with a sudden need to let loose. Alcohol was consumed in vast quantities and behavior typical of drunken college students ensued.

It did not take long for the Colby faculty to realize they had a problem. Not only were classes half empty, but a number of students had taken it upon themselves to march around campus, blowing horns and singing songs in their inebriated revelry. It was fun while it lasted, but sobriety brought with it the discomfort of a hangover and the pain of expulsion. Isaac, unfortunately, had not done a good enough job disguising his handwriting and was promptly kicked off campus. Amariah, who sat on the school's board of trustees, pulled some strings and managed to get his son readmitted. Isaac, now eighteen, returned to his classes in the fall of 1849, but decided to drop out several weeks later and find his own way.

ISAAC WAS ENTIRELY ALONE BY his nineteenth birthday, as Amariah had died chasing a dream.

When word of California gold reached Maine in early 1849, Amariah had initially resisted the siren call of possible riches. He watched from the pulpit as his congregation shrank, its members pulled away by a force not easily countered by words and prayer. Amariah at last gave in and set his sights on El Dorado in late 1849. He purchased passage for him and his wife on the brig *Perfect*, which braved the seas off Cape Horn and delivered the couple to California's shore in May 1850.

Having survived the voyage in good health, it seemed all the more cruel that Amariah contracted yellow fever shortly after his arrival in Sacramento. Instead of taking the time to convalesce, he pushed on with his journey, eager to reach Placerville and stake his claim. He arrived in Gold Country determined but shattered by illness, and died a month later on June 16—a Sunday. His wife, suffering the same affliction, passed away several days later.

Word of Amariah's death took six months to reach Isaac. By then, Isaac had married, taking the hand of a sea captain's daughter named Caroline Philbrick on November 19, 1850, in Waterville, Maine. The two had known each other since childhood. She was two years older than Isaac and would prove to be fiercely loyal in her matrimonial role. By the time Caroline took the Kalloch name, Isaac had officially entered the ministry. He became the pastor of the small Baptist church once administered by his father and set about starting a family. In September 1851, the couple became parents to Isaac Milton Kalloch, the first of four children.

Kalloch, like his father, was a dynamic presence in the pulpit. His fiery hair and rapturous voice commanded attention. Despite what one might consider the soft nature of his job, Kalloch exuded a staunch masculinity, weighing in at 220 pounds. He had a muscular build with a slim waist and a chiseled upper body that put the stitching of his shirts to the test. The quaint country church with its wooden steeple and planked walls painted white was too small for such a vibrant personality. As it had in his younger years, word of Isaac's blistering oratory spread and drew large crowds.

When he wasn't eliciting a glorious "Amen!" from his congregation, he was penning literary reviews and essays for the local *Lime Rock Gazette*. Perhaps he sipped from a tumbler of whiskey as he pondered what to put on the page, for the idealism of his youth had surrendered to a more grounded view of morality. His support of the temperance movement had been washed aside by a fondness for whiskey—a fact that would come out later in less than flattering circumstances.

WORD OF THE YOUNG BACKWOODS preacher who drew large crowds soon reached the trustees of the Tremont Temple and piqued their curiosity. The Boston church was in need of a new public figure, one capable of restoring its dwindling congregation and fattening its thinning coffers. Convinced Isaac had the force of personality and the faith to pull it off, the temple trustees offered him the job and a yearly salary of $1,000. Isaac accepted.

"He was regarded," noted the *New York Times*, "as a most promising and wondrously devout youth." He arrived in Boston on June 20, 1855, and proved an instant success. His sermons were a creative blend of theology and poetry, interweaving biblical discussion with the words of Milton.

At the intersection of Tremont and Beacon streets, the Tremont Temple—three stories high and massive in design—had the capacity to seat thousands. Ticket booths stood on either side of the temple's main entrance and hopeful congregants lined up hours in advance to gain admittance. Once allowed in, the eager masses pushed their way past the temple's expansive lobby and up the eight flights of stairs in a rush to grab seats in the Main Hall. Beautiful stained-glass windows diffused the outside light, bathing the temple's interior in a spectrum of heavenly colors. It made for spectacular viewing and gave the impression that God himself played audience to Kalloch's sermons.

"Kalloch's fame grew rapidly," one paper reported. "Crowds were turned away on every occasion for want of standing room." The demand for Kalloch was not merely limited to the confines of his new pastorate, and soon the lecture circuit beckoned. His popularity enabled him to charge up to fifty dollars for an address, which he often did, depending on how far he had to travel. His lectures and his sermons often embraced a political theme, and it was not uncommon for the young preacher to use his considerable talents to bolster the Abolitionist cause.

Kalloch's attitude toward slavery had been shaped when he was just six by an incident in his hometown. In the spring of 1837, the schooner *Boston*, captained by his future father-in-law, Daniel Philbrick, had set sail from Rockland with a shipment of lime rock destined for Savannah, Georgia. When the vessel reached its destination, Philbrick hired shipwright James Sagurs to repair the *Boston*'s leaking hull. Sagurs, in turn, charged one of his slaves—a twenty-two-year-old carpenter named Atticus—with the task. Atticus proved a master craftsman and earned the respect and friendship of the *Boston*'s crew, who so enthralled the young slave with stories of their home state that when the ship set sail, Atticus secretly stayed on board. (It remains uncertain whether the crew played any role in the stowaway plot.)

Sagurs did not take kindly to northerners absconding with his property. He rented a vessel and took off in pursuit of what he deemed to be rightfully his, armed with two Navy pistols and a violent temper. Once docked in the North, Sagurs went in search of the sheriff and had an arrest warrant issued for his runaway slave. The *Boston*, meanwhile, had reached its home port several days prior. The ship's mate, Edward Kelleran, having taken a liking to the stowaway, invited Atticus to his home. Atticus was something of a novelty in Maine as people of African descent were not a common sight. The townsfolk took an immediate liking to their new resident. They offered him paying jobs and, when Sagurs showed up in a rage, they pretended to be ignorant of the runaway's whereabouts.

Sagurs was not a timid man. He began a systematic search of the town with a sidearm holstered to each hip and the backing of Deputy Sheriff Piper. He pounded on doors and asked questions, but his search efforts were only met by quizzical stares and shrugged shoulders. He finally offered a twenty-dollar reward to anyone who came forward with information, and two individuals caved in for a quick buck. Atticus, hiding in a local's barn, was approached by the traitorous duo and promised safe escort to the local stop on the Underground Railroad. They delivered him instead into the custody of Sagurs, who had promised to "skin that boy alive" should he ever catch him. At the dock, an angry crowd lined the water's edge and verbally assailed Sagurs as he dragged a shackled Atticus aboard his Georgia-bound vessel.

The incident made a great impression on the young Kalloch, who remained forever aligned against the evils of slavery. As an adult, he roared from his Boston pulpit, igniting the Abolitionist cause with fiery words. Some critics complained the young man's sermons were more political than theological, but such criticisms mattered little to the temple trustees. The masses were paying good money to see Kalloch, and the controversial nature of his sermons meant more publicity for the church. Kalloch was now playing showman to the largest congregation in the United States. The trustees upped Kalloch's salary to an impressive $3,000 a year, which ensured their Golden Boy would stay put and allowed him to purchase a well-appointed home at 3 Holley Square on Burroughs Street.

Things seemed to be going well for the Reverend Isaac Kalloch, until the night his past came to visit.

3

A Tarnished Halo

A RAVISHING SIGHT, HER RAVEN-BLACK hair fell just beneath her shoulders and framed a face the color of delicate china. A crucifix on a chain rested just above the swell of her breasts—quite noticeable in the elegant lace-fringed gown she had worn for the occasion. A heavy snow was falling on the afternoon of January 5, 1857, and flakes glistened against the black fabric of her dress as she entered the Kalloch residence. The effect was quite startling, or so thought Isaac, who stood in the foyer to meet her alongside his wife, Caroline, and six-year-old son Milton.

The visitor was Laura Flye, the young lady with whom Kalloch had been infatuated during his Camden school days. She had since married, finding comfort and prosperity with J. F. Stein, a respected Vermont businessman. Alas, Mr. Steen was away on business and unable to accompany his beautiful wife on this trip to Boston. A shame. The Kallochs had kindly offered her a place to stay, as she planned to remain in town for a series of concerts by famed pianist Sigismond Thalberg.

Also a guest at the Kalloch house that night was the Reverend David Thomas, a Baptist evangelist from Ohio. If only Isaac had spent the evening pursuing more ecumenical matters, engaging Thomas in some droll conversation, his life may have taken a different turn. Instead, the events of that January night would hound the reverend for years to come and firmly establish his bawdy reputation.

That evening at dinner, between mouthfuls of food, Kalloch spoke of "Heroes and Hero Worship," topics he planned to address that night with the East Cambridge Lyceum. The invitation to speak had been extended to him just prior to New Year's Day, along with a promised payment of fifteen dollars. Now, leaning back in his chair with a full stomach, Kalloch asked those at the dinner table if they cared to attend his speaking engagement. Thomas said he had other business to attend to, and Caroline preferred an early night. That left Laura, who accepted with much enthusiasm. Delighted, Kalloch excused himself from the table to make some last-minute arrangements.

Kalloch donned his coat in the hallway and ventured into the snow. He trudged from his house in Hollis Square to a nearby livery at 7 Harvard Street, run by Edward Gould, Jr., and arranged for a sleigh to pick him up at 6 PM. Driver John Reynolds arrived at the prescribed hour and knocked on the door. Kalloch and Laura emerged from the house, the warm glow from the lanterns within spilling soft light on the snow-covered lawn. As the couple climbed aboard the carriage, Kalloch informed Reynolds he was giving a speech in East Cambridge—a mere half hour away—and wished to review his notes before taking the stage. Was there a hotel in town where he might work in private? Answering Kalloch's question in the affirmative, Reynolds jostled the reins and gently snapped the steed on its rump.

Kalloch's carriage pulled up in front of the Lechmere House hotel shortly before 6:30 PM and was greeted by co-proprietor Ephraim P. Bailey. A jubilant man of hefty proportions, Bailey opened the carriage door and bade his two guests a warm welcome. What happened next is of much dispute, as a full account has never been conclusively established. The following account is based on the testimony of those who were present that night.

"I am giving a lecture this evening," Kalloch allegedly said as he disembarked behind his female companion. "Can you give me a private room upstairs for myself and my wife, as I wish to look over my lecture before going to the church?"

"We have a room, but it is not yet warmed," Bailey said. "If you could wait a few minutes, I will have a fire built upstairs."

Kalloch nodded and, with his "wife," retired to the hotel's dining room while the maid readied parlor chamber No. 12 on the second floor. The lecture had been scheduled for 7:30 PM, thus giving Kalloch roughly an hour to kill beforehand. A weak fire crackled in the dining room's hearth and offered little warmth as Kalloch and Laura settled side-by-side on chairs pulled close to one another. Laura in particular stood out in the minds of witnesses. "The lady was dressed in black," remembered Margaret Griffin, the wife of one of the establishment's landlords. "She had on a black dress and a black bonnet. She was very pretty. Her complexion was between light and dark. She had curls, and her eyes were dark blue." Subsequent media accounts would christen Kalloch's mystery woman "the Lady in Black."

It just so happened that Mrs. Griffin had plans to attend Kalloch's speech that evening. Upon hearing the guest of honor had made an unscheduled stop at the hotel, she went to the dining room to ensure everything had thus far met with his satisfaction. She found Kalloch and the pretty woman she believed to be his wife sitting very close to one another in front of the hearth. The flames had all but died.

"I guess there isn't much of a fire, is there?" Mrs. Griffin said, nudging the embers with a poker.

"Oh yes," Kalloch chuckled, "there's plenty."

Mrs. Griffin smiled, somewhat perplexed by the reverend's response, and sat at a nearby table to sip a cup of coffee. She noticed that Kalloch's "wife" kept to herself and avoided eye contact. Kalloch and his significant other engaged one another in quiet conversation—their tone was intimate, so the words they shared reached Mrs. Griffin as an inaudible mumble despite her best effort to eavesdrop. Kalloch's companion allowed herself a giggle just as Bailey entered the dining room to inform them parlor chamber No. 12 was ready. He led the couple upstairs and watched as they disappeared behind the bedroom door. Fifteen minutes passed before the servants' bell in the lobby jangled, summoning Bailey back to the couple's room. Kalloch answered Bailey's knock, peering around the edge of the door and flashing a quick grin.

"Can you furnish me a glass of warm whiskey, without letting anyone know about it?" Kalloch asked.

Bailey, thinking it a strange request from a minister, went downstairs to the barroom, mixed a shot of whiskey with hot water and sugar, and delivered the concoction to Kalloch's room. He entered without knocking and found Kalloch and the woman sitting by the fire. The woman's discarded furs were strewn across the bed. Bailey put the drink on the bureau, left a bill for five dollars and scurried back to the reception lobby.

In the dining room, Mrs. Griffin finished her coffee and retreated upstairs to primp herself for Kalloch's speech. Her bedroom just happened to be next door to parlor chamber No. 12. As she sat in front of her dresser, putting powder on her nose and dabbing her cheeks with blush, she couldn't help but notice the giggling coming from the adjacent room. Curious, she sneaked into the hallway and placed her ear against the couple's bedroom door.

"I couldn't hear anything distinctly from the hall," she later recalled, "but I could hear them talking in a low private manner."

Discarding all taste and propriety, she retrieved a chair from her bedroom, stood upon it and sneaked a peek through the transom above the couple's door. The two of them sat in the glow of a roaring fire; the gas lamps in the room were turned down low.

"How can I help from loving you?" Kalloch was saying. "My love will be everything to you—or nothing."

The "Lady in Black" remained silent and tenderly stroked his arm.

"There is no comfort to be taken in this world, anyway," Kalloch sighed, his shoulders slumping under some invisible burden.

"What would they say if they knew we were here?" the woman asked.

"How will they know?" Kalloch responded. "Do you think I would be so corrupt as to tell?" He paused momentarily to blunt the edge in his voice. "I must get to my papers for fear some of the folks might come up. I told them I wanted a room to look over my lecture, for me and my wife. They think you are my wife."

The woman laughed and pinched Kalloch's cheek. "How do I look?" she asked.

"How do I look?" he countered. "You haven't got to stand up before an audience, which will be asked, after they get home, what sort of a looking man it was who talked? What was the color of his hair? And so on."

In the hallway, Mrs. Griffin made an effort to stay calm as she watched Kalloch move in for a kiss. Having been in the hotel business for only two months, she had not yet developed a regular habit of spying on her guests. She would later claim this was the first time she had been so intrusive. She blamed her actions on the so-called "Mrs. Kalloch's" behavior, stating she wished to know why the woman had seemed so subdued in the dining room.

———

NOT MORE THAN A MILE away, the Reverend F. W. Holland sat in the study of his modest parsonage and pondered the small table set with tea for two. He glanced at the clock on the wall and then at the note in his hand, delivered only minutes ago by a sleigh driver from Boston. The note's contents had left the reverend feeling somewhat aggrieved. It seemed the Reverend Kalloch had stood him up.

Holland had met Kalloch shortly before the New Year at a gathering of the Young Men's Association in Boston. Speaking at the assembly had been Eli Thayer of the New England Emigrant Aid Company, which was busy with its efforts to colonize Kansas. Kalloch had introduced Thayer to the stage and so impressed Holland with his commanding presence and thunderous delivery that, at the end of the evening, Holland approached Kalloch to invite him to speak before the East Cambridge Lyceum. Kalloch accepted and agreed to meet Holland for tea an hour before the engagement.

Now, back in the parsonage, 6.30 PM had come and gone. Holland again stared with some annoyance at the note, its message scribbled across the page in a sloppy scrawl. Kalloch had excused himself from tea. He was apparently too "occupied" with his lecture notes to make use of Holland's hospitality.

———————

AT LECHMERE HOUSE, MRS. GRIFFIN continued her covert surveillance. The clandestine couple had finally disengaged their lips and turned back to the task at hand: the lecture. Kalloch got up from his chair and walked toward the bedroom door.

"I really must get to my notes," he said.

Mrs. Griffin hopped off her chair, dragged it back to her room and shut the door. She heard Kalloch leave his room and descend the stairs. She finished applying her makeup and ventured down to the sitting room, where she found the reverend chatting with Bailey. "Mrs. Kalloch" joined them a few minutes later and murmured a half-hearted greeting. Her presence loaned a noticeable weight to the atmosphere, which strangled the conversation. Somewhere, a clock ticked. Mrs. Griffin, attempting to act normal, cleared her throat and commented on the weather. Bailey blew his nose. An eternity had almost passed when Kalloch announced that he and his traveling companion had better get going. He didn't want to be late for his speech. No sooner had the couple beat a furious path to the front door than Mrs. Griffin divulged the reverend's sordid secret.

Kalloch arrived at the local church shortly before 7:30 PM and took a seat near the pulpit. A bitter Rev. Holland approached and, without salutation, reminded Kalloch he had promised to come to tea. Kalloch offered a curt apology and turned his attention to a sheaf of paper in his hands. Holland took the stage and introduced Kalloch to an audience of several hundred people, then took his seat in the front row. At 7:38 PM, Kalloch stepped to the podium and began his speech. He talked for the better part of two hours, pummeling his fists in the air, jabbing his finger for emphasis and enveloping the crowd with his exuberance.

The members of the audience, upon Kalloch's final thunderous word, leapt to their feet in adoration and clapped vigorously. Kalloch dabbed his forehead with a handkerchief and took a bow. He left the stage and found Holland loitering in the wings with a post-lecture invitation to tea. His brow still glistening, Kalloch politely declined. He was in a hurry, he explained, to return home but would be honored if Holland graced the Kalloch residence with his presence sometime soon for dinner.

The two men shook hands and went their separate ways. Holland—his opinion of the Reverend Isaac Kalloch somewhat soured—returned to the parsonage. Kalloch and the "Lady in Black" hightailed it back to Lechmere House. Kalloch would not see Holland again until the trial.

Once back at the hotel, Kalloch and Laura retreated quickly up the stairs to the sanctity of their parlor chamber. They bypassed the barroom where Ephraim P. Bailey sat on a stool nursing a drink. Over the rim of his glass, he saw the couple hurrying through the lobby. Although Bailey knew full well the reverend's licentious secret, he decided to initiate his own investigation. He sneaked up the stairs and crouched outside the couple's door, listening for the sounds that generally accompany carnal behavior, but there was no creaking of bedsprings, no breathless moaning. Taking a page from Mrs. Griffin's book of appalling behavior, Bailey retrieved the chair from Mrs. Griffin's bedroom and placed it in front of Kalloch's door. He climbed on top and peered through the transom.

"There was a bright gaslight in the room they occupied," he recalled. "I saw Mr. Kalloch sitting in a chair near the fireplace. He was perhaps six feet from the door over which I was looking. I could see the back part of the lady. She was sitting on his right knee. The lady's left arm, I think, was around his waist. They were talking in a low tone of voice. They were kissing, too. They did it quite a number of times, I should say."

It made for great viewing.

"What do you suppose your wife would say if she knew where you were?" the woman asked Kalloch, nuzzling his neck.

"What would your husband say if he knew you were here?" the reverend guffawed, casting a keen eye toward the bed.

The woman followed Kalloch's gaze and shook her head. The bed, she said, would make too much noise. Kalloch suggested the floor. The woman removed herself from Kalloch's lap and kissed his forehead. She stepped to the bureau mirror and removed the holding pins from her hair, which fell in a dark cascade around her shoulders. Kalloch smiled his approval, took two pillows from the bed and tossed them somewhere near the fireplace. Their arms around one another, the couple sank to the floor and out of view. All Bailey could do was listen to the frantic rustling of clothes being removed in a hurry. And then he heard Kalloch speak.

"How does it feel?" the reverend inquired.

The woman whispered something inaudible.

"Well," Kalloch said, "don't hurry."

Bailey wondered if watching a man of the cloth partake in such devilish delights might itself be a sin. He continued his spying for several minutes as he contemplated the question. Deciding it wasn't, he went in search of someone with whom he could share this unique experience. He scuttled downstairs and came across local hack driver Samuel R. Giddings, waiting for a fare in the lobby. Giddings swung by Lechmere House as many as thirty times a day, looking to make a buck. On this occasion, he got to look at something else. Bailey could hardly contain himself as he detailed the carnality unfolding upstairs, and Giddings rushed up to witness the scene.

"I went upstairs as quick as I could get my boots off," he said. "I got up on the chair and looked through the crack but couldn't see anything at first. Then I saw a man get to his feet from the floor. His pantaloons were unbuttoned and his shirt was outside his pants."

Giddings then felt a tugging on his trouser leg and looked down to find Amos—who served a dual purpose as co-proprietor and Mrs. Griffin's husband—begging to share the chair. Every hotel employee working that night—with the exception of the maid—had now viewed the happenings in parlor chamber No. 12. The two men watched Kalloch tuck in his shirt and straighten his hair, and gawked as the woman dabbed herself clean with a handkerchief, adjusted her stockings and tried in vain to hand-iron the creases in her dress. When the woman put on her bonnet and Kalloch his coat, Amos realized the show had come to an end. He dragged the chair back to his wife's room and, with Giddings close behind, retreated to the lobby.

The reverend's heavy footfalls came thumping down the stairs just minutes later. Neatly dressed and showing no obvious signs of exertion, Kalloch found Bailey leaning behind the dull, mahogany bar and paid him for the whiskey and accommodations. Bailey thanked him with a broad smile.

In the sitting room, the reverend's "wife," wrapped in furs and a scarf, joined Kalloch as he waited for Reynolds to arrive with the sleigh for the ride home. The two seemed perfectly content, blissfully ignorant of the maelstrom that would soon erupt around them.

———◆———

THE RUMORS BEGAN CIRCULATING AROUND Boston within days. The story, vague in its details, was passed along in whispered tones. It seemed a rather robust gentleman who bore more than a passing semblance to a certain preacher at the Tremont Temple had been seen at an out-of-town hotel—an establishment not generally the kind frequented by discerning gentlemen and women not their wives. It took little more than two weeks for the rumors to find their way into the *Boston Times*, a scandalous rag that cared little for accuracy. In its issue dated January 23, the paper quoted several anonymous sources, printing the most salacious of details. Kalloch, out of town to schedule a lecture tour, could not be reached for comment.

He returned to Boston two days later, just in time to be mauled by another story in the paper. The *Times* interviewed Ephraim P. Bailey and Samuel R. Giddings, both of whom freely admitted to spying on the reverend and his lady friend in the privacy of their bedroom. There was also mention of a whiskey drink being served. The salacious story gave the paper's circulation a healthy boost, and other publications followed suit. Kalloch was being tried and convicted in a frenzy of tabloid ink. Before long, the clergy followed suit. The same day the second *Boston Times* article ran, the highest echelons of the city's Baptist clergy met and demanded Kalloch come before them and explain himself.

Kalloch appeared in front of Boston's Baptist elite within hours of his return to town and, still exhausted from his journey, suffered a grueling inquisition. He conceded the Lechmere House was an establishment of the devil.

He admitted to ordering a whiskey drink, explaining a doctor had prescribed weakened spirits to combat an ongoing throat ailment. He also acknowledged taking a woman—merely a friend—to his hotel room, but insisted his behavior had been anything but lecherous. Powerful political enemies, he said, were attempting to destroy his standing in the community.

The committee members decided the *Boston Times'* reputation as a scandal sheet was enough to cast doubt on the whole miserable affair. Clearing Kalloch of any wrongdoing, the committee released a statement for publication. The *Times,* it declared, "is a filthy sheet, which has given itself an infamous notoriety as a scurrilous defamer of good men's names . . . We, as a church, have full confidence in Rev. Kalloch's integrity, and will rally around him with renewed affection." All fifteen Baptist churches in Boston endorsed the statement.

On Sunday, February 1, Kalloch delivered a sermon at Tremont Temple, aptly titled "Slanderers and the Consequence of Their Guilt—Particularly Backbiters, the Most Contemptible of All Slanderers." Ruminations in the press, Kalloch declared, "had caused vile men at the corners of the streets to point fingers at me, and good men to look askance." A crowd of more than two thousand people eager to hear Kalloch's booming repudiation of the charges made against him packed the temple to capacity.

Kalloch's words did little to stem the onslaught against him—in fact, they only further infuriated those who believed the reverend to be a deviant. The press continued to ravage his reputation, demanding an investigation into the blasphemous affair and urging those with the power to do so to indict Kalloch on the severest charges possible. In Vermont, a paper revealed the object of Kalloch's illicit affections to be the beautiful—but unidentified— wife of a Brattleboro resident whose association with high society all but guaranteed her innocence.

Whether Kalloch was innocent, however, remained a matter for the courts to decide. On February 14, the Grand Jury of Middlesex County indicted the reverend in the Court of Common Pleas, East Cambridge. The indictment read:

Isaac S. Kalloch, late resident of Boston, in the County of Suffolk, in the Commonwealth of Massachusetts, on the 5th day of January in the Year of our Lord 1857, at Cambridge, in the county of Middlesex and Commonwealth aforesaid, did commit the crime of adultery with a certain woman whose name is to the jurors unknown, by then and there having carnal knowledge of the body of the said woman, whose name to the jurors is unknown as aforesaid, the said Isaac S. Kalloch being then and there a married man, and then and there having a lawful wife alive other than the said woman whose name is to the jurors unknown, and the said Isaac S. Kalloch and the said woman whose name is unknown, not being then and there lawfully married to each other.

News of the indictment reached Kalloch in Rockland, Maine, where he was visiting his sister. Eager to restore the luster of his reputation, he ventured back to Boston and turned himself into authorities. He pleaded not guilty when brought before a judge, posted a $2,000 bond and immediately began planning his defense.

Naturally, he had no idea the trial to come would sensationalize all of New England and have lingering repercussions for decades to come.

4

IN JUDGMENT

ON THE MORNING OF TUESDAY, March 31, 1857, a crowd gathered outside the Court of Common Pleas for Middlesex County, all waiting to catch a glimpse of the defendant. Women wore the best their wardrobes had to offer, while men turned out in top hats and coattails. Reporters lined the stairwell leading to the courtroom, scribbling even the slightest detail in their notebooks. "The number of gentlemen connected with the press . . . was larger than we have noticed on any previous similar occasion," wrote the *Boston Times* reporter. "The anxiety of the reporters to furnish their reports expeditiously to their respective newspapers was worthy of praise."

Shortly before 10 AM, Kalloch entered the courtroom with defense attorneys Richard H. Dana, Jr., and Charles R. Train at his side. "He appeared rather pale, but was entirely composed," noted one reporter. "Taking a seat beside his senior counsel, he exhibited his indifference of the proceedings by beginning to clean his fingernails." In securing his defense team, Kalloch had spared no expense. Senior Counsel Dana was a star of sorts, having established a name for himself in 1840 with the publication of *Two Years Before the Mast*, the bestselling account of a sailor's life at sea.

The forty-one-year-old Dana, like Kalloch, was something of a maverick. Following an attack of the measles his junior year at Harvard, Dana dropped out in 1834 and enlisted as a sailor aboard the brig *Pilgrim*. He spent the next two years roughing it on the waves, braving a voyage around Cape Horn and keeping notes of his adventures in his journal—upon which he would base his popular book. He returned to Harvard after his maritime quest and graduated with a degree in law. Although he specialized in maritime law, Dana, who was nothing if not shrewd, undoubtedly realized the inherent publicity of the Kalloch trial would translate into book sales.

Prosecuting the case was District Attorney Isaac S. Morse, who hoped to advance his career with a high-profile victory. The defense, however, had an ace up its sleeve. He sat in the front row, dressed in a dapper black suit and bowler. The man, not recognized by any of the reporters crowding the public gallery, had accompanied Kalloch and his attorneys into the courtroom. He shook Kalloch's hand and slapped him reassuringly on the shoulder before Kalloch took his seat at the defense table. The well-dressed gentleman was none other than Mr. Stein—husband to the "Lady in Black"—who had absolute faith in his wife's fidelity and Kalloch's innocence. So aggrieved was he by the charges brought against the reverend and the slandering of his wife's reputation that he had agreed to testify for the defense.

At 10 AM, after Judge George Partridge Sanger banged his gavel and declared court in session, Morse approached the jury box to deliver his opening argument. The courtroom fell silent as the prosecutor addressed foreman Philip Russell and the other eleven men sitting in judgment. "Gentlemen of the jury," he said, "we are about to commence the trial of a case of great interest, not only to the party deeply concerned in it, but to the public at large." Morse spoke eloquently, banging his fist on the jury box for emphasis as he laid out the people's case. Eyewitness testimony, he said, would place the defendant and his anonymous lover (she had not yet been named in the press) in that upstairs bedroom at Lechmere House. "Evidence will be produced, showing that the landlord went and looked into the room . . . and saw what he considered improper intercourse between the parties inside the room." He then hastened to clarify, lest someone get overly excited: "I do not expect to show you, gentlemen of the jury, what occurred inside the room in every particular detail. I can show you that the defendant and the lady were both on the floor, and in a certain position."

Morse shot a glance in Kalloch's direction, hoping to see some outward sign of discomfort. There was none. The defendant leaned back in his chair and continued picking at his nails. He maintained this appearance of nonchalance even when Morse called Ephraim P. Bailey to the stand. It was Bailey's testimony that first gave the proceedings an air of perversity. Over the next day and a half, the co-manager of the Lechmere House, and one-time saloon owner, detailed how he spied on Kalloch and the mystery woman after they retired to the upstairs bedroom. Bailey relayed the manner in which the woman slipped the bonnet from her head and removed the combs from her hair, and how Kalloch took a pillow from the bed and tossed it on the floor. "She went near the spot where the pillow was thrown down," he said. "I saw her in the act of lying down on the floor. Her back was towards me. After she got down, he got down in the same place."

All heads in the courtroom turned in Kalloch's direction.

Bailey told Morse he went downstairs after seeing all he could. "I next saw Kalloch when he came into the barroom through the office and told me he wanted his bill," Bailey said. "I told him it was five dollars. He handed me a ten-dollar bill and I handed him back a five. He then said, 'I guess I'll take another whiskey skin!' I made him a warm one and he drank it at the bar and then he passed out into the sitting room."

Next, defense attorney Train began his cross-examination. He opened by asking the witness if he had ever been charged with indecent exposure. The smirk on Bailey's face disappeared. "I never heard it reported that I had exposed my person," he stammered. "I never heard the charge made by anybody—I would recollect it if I ever heard it."

Train's questions delved into Bailey's past sexual proclivities and the defendant's attempts to keep them under wraps. "Did you not offer a man one hundred dollars to keep quiet about that charge?"

Bailey shook his head. "I never offered a man one hundred dollars in money if he would keep quiet about that very charge," he said, which may have made some courtroom wags wonder if Bailey had bought silence with some other amount.

Train pushed forward his interrogation and attacked the veracity of Bailey's statement to investigators. Through his questioning, Train accused the witness of exaggerating the salacious details of Kalloch's behavior in his statement to the *Boston Times*. Bailey denied any such thing and insisted he had no idea the events of January 5 would be splashed all over the paper's front page. Bailey went on to say that when two trustees of Tremont Temple arrived at Lechmere House to examine the crime scene, he exercised restraint in his narrative. "They came over to see me and wanted to hear all about the occurrence," Bailey stammered. "They wanted to see the room, and I showed it to them. I did not narrate to them everything that transpired. I told them I would not tell them all, for it was a matter which I did not wish to come out."

Train, unmoved, took Bailey to task over the exorbitant price the witness had charged for a whiskey. Why, he asked, was Kalloch made to pay five dollars for such a libation? Bailey cast a forlorn look in the defendant's direction. "I charged him five dollars to protect the reputation of my house," he said. "I would not have made the affair public if it had not been leaked out by someone else. Five dollars is not enough to purchase my house for purposes of prostitution." Laughter rippled through the public gallery; even Kalloch seemed slightly amused. He smirked at Bailey's testimony and once again turned his attention to a bothersome nail.

The prosecution next called Samuel Giddings, hack driver, to the stand. Giddings's testimony was in very much the same vain as Bailey's, though it managed to draw an audible gasp from spectators when he divulged more lurid details about the tryst. He described peering into Kalloch's bedroom and watching the reverend button up his pantaloons and straighten his disheveled shirt. "Mr. Kalloch had his cap and coat on, and the lady was at the glass, arranging her hair," Giddings said. "Her bonnet was off. She came from the glass and they spoke together. After a minute or so, he left the room."

When Morse asked the witness to describe in detail what happened next, the defense objected, but was overruled. In the witness stand, Giddings glanced uneasily at the jury. He cleared his throat and fidgeted with his tie. With another prompting from Morse, Giddings answered the question. "After Mr. Kalloch left the room, the woman turned round facing me," he said. "She took her handkerchief from her pocket and, with it, wiped her private parts. She stood about five feet from me. She then put on her furs, cloak and shawl, and left the room. I then left and went down to the barroom."

Kalloch shifted in his seat as a low groan made its way through the courtroom. Reporters jotted the testimony down in their notebooks and wondered whether such wording would even make it past their editors. And, on that rather sordid note, court recessed for the day.

ON THE THIRD DAY OF trial, Thursday, April 2, a *New York Times* reporter wrote:

> The trial of Mr. Kalloch was resumed in Cambridge this morning. The defendant occupied a seat beside his counsel. He exhibited a confident mien and shook hands with many friends.
>
> A plan of the room occupied by Mr. Kalloch and his female companion at the Lechmere House was exhibited to the jury. Three witnesses were then examined for the prosecution, but their testimony was merely relative to the defendant's presence at the Hotel, and in the Lecture Room, and threw no new light upon the criminal charge.
>
> The Prosecuting Attorney then inquired of defendant's counsel if they intended to hold him to prove that on the 5th of January last, Mr. Kalloch was a married man, having a lawful wife other than the woman in his company at the [Lechmere] House.

The question Morse posed to the defense was really a dare. If Dana refused to meet Morse's challenge, it would show a lack of confidence in his own case. The courtroom fell silent save for the scratching of pencils on paper as reporters took frantic notes. "I do not decline to answer," Dana said, "but desire a little time to consult with my associates."

"It is my desire that if they wish, the counsel would consult together," Judge Sanger said, "and expedite this trial as much as possible."

Dana thanked the judge and leaned across the table to whisper in Train's ear. The two men conferred with Kalloch in hushed tones. Kalloch sat and nodded, seemingly satisfied with his attorneys' counsel.

"The question is a most extraordinary one to ask us at this time and to admit two material facts," Dana said, rising to his feet. "Before this trial began, I was written to by Mr. Morse to know if Mr. Kalloch would admit that the woman who was at the Lechmere House was not Mrs. Kalloch. My client was willing to admit long before the trial that he was a married man, and that the woman who came to the Lechmere House was not his wife." Dana now turned to his client and placed a hand on Kalloch's shoulder. "Mr. Kalloch is pleased to inform the Court and jury that he is a married man, and that as soon as the foul, disgusting lying details of his trial are closed, his wife will be in Court and sit by his side. She will be put upon the stand and state that she is not the woman who went to Lechmere House. This is the admission, Mr. Morse, and you are welcome to it, if you like the way in which it was given."

A satisfied Morse called several more witnesses—all of whom testified that Kalloch was indeed seen with another woman at Lechmere House on the night in question—before resting his case. The judge promptly called a recess.

When court reconvened at noon, Kalloch strode to the defense table with his wife by his side. "Her appearance caused considerable sensation," wrote one Boston reporter. "She was dressed in black throughout; and many thought they beheld the identical 'lady in black.'" Caroline Kalloch sat in the public gallery's front row, her hands clasped in her lap and her gaze fixed firmly on her husband, who turned frequently in her direction to offer encouraging smiles.

One of the first witnesses called by defense attorney Train was J. Warren Merrill, a perfume wholesaler in Boston, who also served on Tremont Temple's board of trustees. When word of Kalloch's lecherous activities began making the rounds, Merrill and fellow trustee Thomas Richardson were dispatched to Lechmere House on January 20 to investigate. The two men had met with Ephraim P. Bailey and found him to be a rather repulsive individual. "We told him we had heard stories prejudicial to Mr. Kalloch's character, and told him that we heard the reports came from him," Merrill told Train from the stand. "He said he was not aware that the stories came from him."

"And what did you say to that?" Train asked.

"I told him I should expect to see the story in the newspapers in a few days," Merrill said. "He was reluctant to tell me anything. He said he was afraid it would hurt the reputation of his house, and that was low enough already—everybody knew."

Train allowed himself a smile and urged Merrill to continue amid guffaws from the gallery.

"He said he was trying to make the house a strictly first-class hotel," Merrill said. "I told him we were not members of Mr. Kalloch's church, neither were we officers of the law; we were simply trustees of Tremont Temple, and, as Mr. Kalloch was in a certain sense in our employ, we had a right to know if the reports were true."

Merrill continued, testifying that Bailey told him he had spied on Kalloch in the upstairs bedroom. "I then asked Mr. Bailey if he saw Mr. Kalloch do any unlawful act," he said.

"How did he answer?" Train asked.

"He said no," Merrill said. "I then asked him if the bed was tumbled. He said they knew too much for that. He said if they had done anything unlawful, they had done it on the floor. I asked him if he saw them on the floor, and he said no. I asked him how he knew they were not man and wife, and he said he did not know—but he did not believe they were."

Merrill testified that, when pushed for additional details, Bailey pleaded ignorant and said others had seen more than he had. "He said he thought we had better let Kalloch know the story was out, so that Kalloch might escape,"

Merrill said. "I asked him if he thought that was the way to let criminals go. I asked Bailey if he thought Kalloch was the right kind of man to go around preaching, and he replied that he did not think it was the just thing. He said that Kalloch gave him a five-dollar bill and that was evidence of his guilt."

Court adjourned on that note until nine o'clock the following morning.

ON FRIDAY, APRIL 3, THE defense launched an earnest attack on the credibility of the Lechmere Hotel's staff. Train called Mrs. Margaret Griffin, wife of Lechmere House co-proprietor Amos Griffin, to the stand. The witness testified that she married Amos in November 1855 and spent the wedding night at the Fountain House Hotel in Cambridge. "I was there before I was married," she said. "We stopped overnight, but I did not occupy the same room with Mr. Griffin. I slept that night with Mrs. McQuestion, my niece. She was in room No. 26."

The attorney nodded and walked slowly to the defense table. He pulled a ledger from a stack of evidence and asked Mrs. Griffin if she would recognize her husband's handwriting. The witness nodded. Train approached the stand and handed her the leather-bound volume, which he identified as the October 1855 Fountain House registry. He pointed to an entry for the night in question and asked Mrs. Griffin to read it out loud. She scanned the page with a creased brow and quivering lower lip. "Amos and lady," she read. "Room No. 27."

From the public gallery, there came a collective gasp. Mrs. Griffin, her pre-marital sin now part of the public record, lowered her head and scurried from the courtroom as the defense called character witness Thomas Frye, a physician and ten-year resident of Rockland, Maine. "I've known Mr. Kalloch for twenty-one years. I boarded at his father's house," Frye testified. "Mr. Kalloch's general character for chastity and purity of character is good. It was good until this charge was made against him."

Train took a seat and left his witness to the mercy of a relentless Morse. The prosecutor sprang to his feet and asked Frye if he ever heard rumors regarding the defendant's sexual tendencies.

"I may possibly have heard reports against the defendant's chastity," Frye said, looking away from Isaac. "But I never heard any reports that were reliable. I heard the same that is remarked about all ministers."

Morse smiled and leaned against the jury box. "Did you ever hear any reports against the chastity of Mr. Kalloch previous to the fifth of January?"

Frye said nothing. He opened his mouth to answer, only to close it again and stare at his lap as though searching for an appropriate response. "I have heard reports touch his character," he said, punctuating the statement with a deep sigh. "I cannot tell you when I first heard these reports. I will swear I have not heard reports for five years past."

Asked if he ever heard rumors of Kalloch visiting "houses of ill fame," Frye answered in the negative, but could not do the same when asked if Kalloch had ever availed himself to the pleasures of another man's wife. "I have heard that he had criminal intercourse with a woman," Frye said, and relinquished her identity when asked for a name. "The lady's name was Mrs. Ballard—I think it was about three years ago."

Morse pressed home his attack and asked Frye once more if he ever heard Kalloch's moral character called into question. Frye looked at Kalloch and glanced at the jury before settling his defeated gaze on the prosecutor. "I can't say that I never heard anything said against his character for chastity," he said.

Train moved quickly to repair the damage. He called to the stand Joseph Farwell, a Rockland resident and brother of the just-maligned Mrs. Ballard. "I have known Kalloch for twenty-one years, and I knew his father," Farwell said. "Kalloch was as well known in Rockland as any man there. I've heard rumors touching upon his reputation for chastity—but his reputation was good, notwithstanding the rumors."

During cross-examination, Morse sought to capitalize on his recent gains and asked Farwell how many times he'd heard Kalloch's behavior brought up in conversation. "I could not tell how many times I have heard Kalloch's character talked about," the witness answered. "It is so many times, that I cannot recollect."

The defense found little humor in the comment.

A HANDFUL OF ROCKLAND RESIDENTS testified as to Kalloch's good standing in the community. Yes, rumors regarding the defendant often surfaced, suggesting the occasional sexual conquest of a married woman, but such gossip was given little credence. Through it all, J. Frank Stein—husband to the "Lady in Black"—sat behind Kalloch and listened to the most sordid of testimony without so much as a grimace. He ignored the curious stares of others when details of his wife's supposed indiscretion spilled forth on the stand.

On the fifth day of trial, Dana—taking a turn for the defense—stood before the jury box and called his star witness. "I live in Brattleboro, Vermont," Stein testified. "I am the husband of Mrs. Laura Stein. I received an invitation from Mr. Kalloch for my myself and wife to come to Boston." Stein said he had been unable to accept Kalloch's invitation because of business obligations. He did, however, encourage his wife to take the trip. "She returned in one week," he said. "She is now very sick with consumption and is confined to her bed most of the time."

Dana asked if Mrs. Stein would be able to testify as to her role in the current controversy.

"I think it would be extremely dangerous for her health to be submitted to the examination and cross-examination necessary to secure her deposition," Stein said. "Her family physician told her she must not go."

The testimony was far from sensational, but what Stein said was beyond the point. His appearance itself was key to Dana's strategy, as the beleaguered husband's willingness to testify for the defense was a powerful argument in favor of Kalloch's innocence. Dana thanked the witness for his time and took a seat to watch the cross-examination.

Morse rubbed the bridge of his nose in thoughtful contemplation and made a theatrical show of pondering his first question. "Tell us," he said, "how you met your wife."

"I first knew Ms. Flye in Camden," Stein replied, smiling at the memory. "It was about nine years ago. We married in 1851 at East Abbington, Massachusetts, where she had resided about six months."

Was the witness aware of his wife's relationship with the defendant? Morse asked.

"I did not know she was acquainted with Mr. Kalloch," Stein said in a defensive tone of voice. "I first heard of it last summer. She informed me in a letter from Damariscotta, Maine." Morse next asked Stein if Kalloch was a friend, for the two had seemed quite chummy throughout the trial. Stein said he had only met the defendant in February, when he paid a social visit to the Kalloch residence. Asked to elaborate on his wife's condition, Stein replied, "My wife is pretty sick. She is able to converse, but cannot converse in a loud tone of voice. She has been failing for a year past." Then Morse, finished with his questions, excused Stein from the stand.

The defense next called Dr. Dickenson, its final witness and the Stein family physician, who testified Mrs. Stein would not survive a turn in the witness box. "She has bleeding at the lungs, and I think a journey would be quite dangerous to her health," he said. "I think it would still be more dangerous to put her on the stand."

Morse, who found Mrs. Stein's absence more than convenient for the defense, assailed the doctor with questions regarding his patient's immobility. "She does not go out doors," Dickenson said. "She has been feeble whenever I have seen her . . . I have advised her in regard to her mode of life, diet, etcetera." Morse continued his assault, asking Dickenson to recall distant dates and various treatments and medicines prescribed. The doctor prattled off answers and shifted uncomfortably in his chair. As Morse continued his cross-examination, Dickenson's face took on a pallid hue and a light sweat glistened on his brow; his voice developed a sudden stammer. The doctor began to sway in his chair, as though balancing on the precipice of unconsciousness. "At this point in the cross examination," noted one spectator, "the witness was taken suddenly ill."

Morse ceased his questioning and seemed unsure of how to proceed. When it became apparent that Dickenson—either putting on a convincing act or actually suffering a legitimate attack of some kind—would not recover, Morse angrily dismissed him from the stand. The doctor seemed to regain just enough strength and balance to stagger from the courtroom.

Dana rose and said the defense had presented its case. The judge scheduled closing arguments for the morning of Monday, April 6, and recessed court for the weekend.

———◦———

"THERE CAN BE NO QUESTION but that the public interest in the Kalloch trial is on the increase," the *Boston Times* reporter wrote for the Monday late edition. "Long before the time for commencing the trial this morning, the inner avenues leading to the courtroom were densely packed, and it was found necessary for the reporters and others having business in the Court room to enter by the private door."

Judge Sanger entered the courtroom at nine, banged his gavel and asked the prosecution and defense if all evidence had been submitted. Both Morse and Dana answered in the affirmative. "Mr. Dana," he said, "you are at liberty to address the jury." Dana stood and approached the jury box.

"Faith in human nature, faith in the virtue of man, faith in the purity and chastity of woman, is as essential to a sound and just judgment, as suspicion and distrust are fatal," Dana said, his hands clasped in front of him as if in prayer. "Let us believe the wives of New England are faithful, that the marriage bed of New England is not defiled, that our daughters, our sisters, our wives are pure, that the men of New England are not base, and that a dark blot is not to rest upon our history today."

He paused for effect, allowing the jury time to consider the immensity of its pending decision.

"Gentlemen! What is the charge here and who is the criminal?" he continued passionately. "The crime of adultery is not merely uncleanness, fornication, it is the breach of the marriage vow, it is the violation of an obligation, the destruction of that security upon which our very social system itself rests." Dana slapped an open palm on the jury box and launched into the facts of the case, picking apart the testimony and targeting various witnesses for their denigratory comments. "The Government has not produced a single witness from Camden or Rockland or Boston to show the defendant had not a good reputation. With all the resources of the Commonwealth at

their command, after searching every bad tavern, after hunting over the cata-
logue of the Baileys and Griffins of Rockland, they cannot find a man base
enough to come here and express a doubt as to the reputation of Mr.
Kalloch."

Dana pulled a handkerchief from his coat pocket and dramatically
dragged it across his mouth. It was the prosecution's position, he argued, that
Kalloch went to the Lechmere House to commit his infidelity under a cloak
of secrecy. But such a theory, he roared, was ludicrous. The stable owner who
rented Kalloch a carriage, the coachman and the aggrieved Reverend Holland—who still harbored a grudge at being stood up over tea—all knew
Kalloch to be at the hotel. "Is not this most astonishing?" Dana said with
mock theatricality. "He has many virtues, many shining talents, but I do not
think laying a plot for crime is his forte."

Surely, the twelve men now sitting in judgment could not condemn the
defendant based on the testimony of such low individuals as summoned by
the prosecution, Dana said. "If there ever was a man leprous all over with
lechery, it is Ephraim P. Bailey," Dana said, then recapped Bailey's testimony
and own questionable history. "What says Bailey? That he saw the lady take
out her combs and look in the glass while discussing the question with Mr. K.,
whether it should be the bed or the floor. That is the way. It was no sudden
yielding to temptation, the way dark, the current swift, with no time for
thought . . . Bailey could not understand, with his unsophisticated mind, how
a man and woman could be in a room together for fifteen minutes without
committing adultery."

Dana had now come fully alive. He paced before the jury box, arms
pointing and gesticulating. The charges against Kalloch, he said, were simply
not believable. He turned and faced the public gallery, motioning to Mrs.
Kalloch and Mr. Stein. "His wife, who sits by his side, believes he is innocent.
The husband of the lady, coming from the confidence of her dying chamber,
knows he is innocent."

He turned again to face the jury and assail the testimony of the other
hotel employees. Amos Griffin and his wife lacked moral standing for

sleeping in the same bed a month before their wedding. Giddings, the Cambridge hack driver, was also a wretch. He had testified that he saw Kalloch buttoning up his pantaloons, but Dana suggested the defendant had merely buttoned up the lower two buttons of his coat. "To a vulgar and suspicious mind like Giddings', that might be conclusive, but to us it amounts to nothing," Dana said. "And as to the lady arranging her hair, I would like to ask whoever heard of a lady being in a room ten minutes, where there was a looking glass, without arranging her hair?"

Dana made his final plea. "The defendant is in your hands," he said, adopting a solemn tone. "It is in your power—but you will not do it—to send him away a convicted criminal. Give a verdict, gentlemen, which shall satisfy yourselves that you have looked at this case in the faith of men who do believe in virtue, who do put confidence in the chastity and purity of the women of New England, and in the virtue of her sons. In rendering that verdict, allow me again to suggest to you, you will be within the line of your duty. And if a man keeps within the line of his duty, it will give him peace at the last."

Dana mopped the sweat from his brow and returned to his seat, exhaustion manifesting itself in a deep sigh. He had spoken for three hours and forty-five minutes.

All eyes turned expectantly to Morse, who, in his closing argument for the prosecution, implored the jury not to disregard the testimony of Bailey and Giddings. "If the evidence was not true," he said, "then the witnesses for the government are the vilest villains who ever drew breath." He wondered out loud whether the defense had conspired to destroy the reputation of certain witnesses. "Let us forget today that Mr. Kalloch is a minister of the Gospel," he said, "and judge of him simply as a man. If he really has committed the crime of adultery, let him be punished. If he holds the sacramental cup in one hand and a whiskey skin in the other, let him suffer the penalty of the law."

He turned and faced the defendant. "Consider, for a moment, the whole tenor of the story. A strange man and a strange woman came into the hotel and sat down in a private room. How should the people in that house have known the lady with him was his wife [unless] he had told them she was?" he said, his voice rising. "How could they have known that she was not his wife if [the man and woman] had not indulged in some conversation that caused them to suspect something? How did they know that he had a wife at all? All the facts offered here go to show that the story of Bailey and Giddings is true."

At this point, court recessed until nine the following morning. The *Boston Times*, reviewing Morse's performance, gave the prosecutor a glowing review:

> Mr. Morse's argument, thus far, is spoken of as being very powerful, and must tell upon the jury. He has reviewed the evidence of the witnesses for the government with a master hand, and the sophistry of the senior counsel for the defense has vanished like dew before the morning sun.

Morse resumed his argument when court convened early on the morning of Tuesday, April 7. Returning to his argument's key theme, he said it made no sense that witnesses would conspire against Kalloch and accuse him of such reprehensible behavior unless it was true.

"The defense say that Mr. Stein thinks his wife is innocent," he said. "It makes no difference what he thinks." He reviewed the testimony of those called as character witnesses by the defense. All of them, he bellowed, heard rumors regarding Kalloch's sexual appetite. A Baptist minister serving the true calling of God surely did not need others "to prove his previous good nature." He now moved to the center of the courtroom and thrust a finger at Kalloch. "If he has stolen the livery of the Court of Heaven, to serve the Devil in, and committed the crime of adultery, let his ministerial robes be torn from him," Morse crowed, banging his fist in an open palm. "Let him be placed where he can no longer go about like a wolf in sheep's clothing, and make our firesides desolate."

As Morse returned to his chair, he shot a spiteful glance at the defense. It had taken him four hours to plead his case.

———◆———

AT NOON, THE JURY RETIRED to consider its verdict. Crowds hung about the courthouse eagerly awaiting the final judgment. "At twenty minutes past two o'clock, the Jury had not arrived at a verdict," wrote one newspaperman, "and they had permission of the Court to pause in their deliberations until after they had fortified their physical wants, and enlivened their minds by the discussion of a good dinner."

They deliberated through the night, unable to reach a verdict. Deadlocked, the jury returned to the courtroom the following morning and delivered the news. The final vote had been eight for acquittal and four for conviction. Morse fell back in his chair. Indeed, Kalloch—as portrayed through witness testimony—came across as both sinner and saint. The rumors regarding Kalloch's sexual aplomb suggested the reverend's reputation was not as holy as the defense claimed it to be. On the other hand, the moral character of the prosecution's key witnesses left a lot to be desired. It was hard to pick one over the other.

Although he had not won a rousing repudiation of the charges against him, the defendant seemed more than pleased with the outcome. A beaming Kalloch thanked his attorneys and returned to Boston with a reputation for licentiousness firmly in tow. The homecoming did not please everyone. "He returned as a dog to his vomit," noted one contemporary.

5

VIOLENCE AND VILLAINY

O N SEPTEMBER 1, 1868, the paper that began as a throwaway vehicle for theater advertisements and drama critiques transformed into something more viable. It was on that Tuesday the brothers de Young premiered the *Daily Morning Chronicle*. Explaining the latest step in the evolution of what had been his "little gratuitous advertisement sheet," Charles de Young wrote:

> A new era has commenced in the history of the CHRONICLE,
> which today enters upon a higher and wider sphere. We have made
> a great stride toward the goal which we have held steadily in view
> from the beginning, and we intended to do more than redeem every
> pledge we have given the public in the past. We propose to publish
> what will prove a novelty in San Francisco journalism—a bold,
> bright, fearless and *truly independent* paper.

The new *Chronicle*, wrote de Young, would not align itself with any political party nor take any "political interest" in candidates running for public office, whether it be for the presidency or county supervisor. He swore off allegiance to the state's powerful banking and railroad industries and dismissed the Republicans and Democrats as neither "great enough to frighten us or rich enough to buy us." From the twenty-three-year-old publisher's pen came more heady stuff:

> We shall be independent in all things, neutral in nothing. We shall
> assail with all our power, and with every legitimate weapon, all
> principles, measures, doctrines[,] parties and cliques that we regard
> as exercising an influence hostile to the best interests of society. But
> we propose to attack no individual unnecessarily.

The sincerity in that last sentence would prove questionable.

EARLY IN THE GAME, CHARLES and Michael de Young wanted to launch a daily newspaper with a general circulation. On January 16, 1867—nearly two years to the day after embarking upon their great adventure—the brothers had moved the *Daily Dramatic Chronicle*'s operation into a more spacious office at 606 Montgomery Street, near Clay. "We went into a large room there, bought an outfit of type, an imposing stone and put a counter in, also three or four desks for the Bohemians to lie around on," Michael remembered in later years. In front of the office, Charles placed a gold-leafed bulletin board upon which passersby could read the latest news. "Nothing would suit us but the ground must be of gold with the letters painted on," Michael wrote. "It was an important event with us. We were really prouder of that one-room office and that gold bulletin board than we have ever been since."

Once set up, the brothers hosted an open house, sending invitations to San Francisco's business and political elite. The open house proved to be a success. Those with invitations—and those who were simply curious—

crowded the office for the better part of the day, sipping from the large bowl of punch Charles had put on the front counter. The paper's small collective of Bohemians entertained visitors with their witty repartee, while the brothers busied themselves getting their name across. "What would be considered as nothing at the present day was quite an event then and everyone wanted to meet our brilliant writers," Michael wrote, adding, "we were still nothing but the *Dramatic Chronicle*." This would not remain the case for long.

From his office in the newsroom of the *San Francisco Daily Morning Call*, Editor in Chief Loring Pickering kept a weary eye on the *Chronicle* and the two young miscreants responsible for its creation. The *Call's* circulation of fourteen thousand was larger than any of San Francisco's other five dailies. People, however, were talking about the younger competition, and that made Pickering nervous. He had watched the *Chronicle* grow from its inception, maturing from a simple nuisance to an emerging threat.

"Though not dissatisfied with what we have already achieved, we have by no means reached the height of our aspirations," the de Youngs wrote on July 17, 1865. "Indeed, should we frankly declare in their full scope, the objects at which we aim, and clearly indicate the goal of our ambition, the statement might sound like a childish boast, and provoke the laughter off those who regard the CHRONICLE as 'a mere theater programme.' Time, however, will show whether our aspirations are inspired by an overwhelming presumption or by a just and reasonable ambition."

Pickering had initially dismissed the publication as a simple theater rag. Now, he wasn't so sure. Within two months of moving into their Montgomery Street office, the de Youngs had enlarged their paper to include three columns of additional copy and declared their purpose "by further enlargements, to make the CHRONICLE as big as the *Alta*—in case the public good shall seem to demand it."

The lads were making good on their threat. The *Chronicle's* ongoing feud with Tom "Napoleon of the Stage" Maguire had tongues wagging and readers anxious for the de Youngs' next vitriolic volley. Colorful writing and a sharp sense of humor buoyed the *Chronicle* and brought a sense of vitality to an otherwise musty field of competitors. The paper's youthful exuberance leapt from the page in offbeat meanderings such as this early piece headlined "HUMAN NATURE":

Human nature is a curious institution—especially feminine human nature. Yesterday, as we were perambulating the four-bit side of Montgomery Street (the west side) arm in arm with a well-known gentleman of the medical persuasion . . . we observed a plump, pretty looking lady approaching. Our friend no sooner caught sight of her, than he made an abrupt move to get on the other side of the street. "Let us cross over," he said excitedly, "I don't want to meet the woman. I attended her husband recently." "Ah!" said we innocently, "and you were so unfortunate as to have him die under your hands?" "Not at all," responded the man of pills. "On the contrary, I cured him, and she will never forgive me!"

In his office, sitting beneath a steel-gray cloud of tobacco smoke, Loring Pickering knew the de Young boys were trouble.

THE BORROWED GOLD PIECE FROM Captain Hinckley aside, sweat remained the primary investment that kept the *Chronicle* going. "At that time, we were doing most of the work ourselves," Michael wrote. "My brother used to set type. I used to set up the papers and [distribute] them. We did the folding and the mailing ourselves. We did as much work as we could ourselves to keep expenses down and the paper a success." The move into the larger Montgomery Street office earned them a reputation among those with fat wallets as "enterprising young men." Offers were soon rolling in from potential investors eager to see the de Youngs launch a daily newspaper. "The offers of these people attracted our attention to the fact that it would be good for us to change to a daily paper."

One man with an interesting offer was Loring Pickering, who decided the best way to destroy the competition was by offering it a job. He paid a visit to the brothers' Montgomery Street office one spring afternoon in 1867 with a plan he hoped would draw the two young stars into his orbit. Charles extended a hand of welcome and offered Pickering a chair in the corner of the small newsroom.

The *Call* editor removed his hat and placed it on his knees, drumming the brim with his fingers while Charles summoned Michael. The two brothers sat and eyed the opposition, wondering what reasons lay behind Pickering's visit. The elder newspaperman cleared his throat and laid out his plan. Pickering told the brothers he wanted to purchase the *Call* from its current owner and place the brothers in charge of the operation. It would, he said, "make it a great paper." The brothers declined the offer after brief consideration, saying they had no interest in making other people rich. They bid a flustered Pickering good day and escorted him from the office. Pickering skulked back to his newsroom, still not realizing how clearly the de Youngs had mapped out their own course of action.

IN THE WAKE OF PICKERING'S departure, Charles de Young stared about his newsroom. The four desks were presently empty, though a Bohemian could wander in at any moment, take a seat and produce some witty squib for publication. What the paper needed, Charles intoned, was a regular staff—and not one that subsisted on booze and tobacco.

As the months slipped by, the brothers pushed forward with this plan, first hiring as their London correspondent the popular playwright and author Anna Cora Mowatt. "As we had not yet a daily paper," Michael wrote, "she commenced working on the little *Dramatic Chronicle* and wrote dramatic letters from [London], which attracted a great deal of attention."

Charles de Young next hired Henry George to serve as the daily's "principal" editor. In 1865, George was an out-of-work printer with a wife and two children at home. One day, desperation had forced him to approach a well-dressed stranger in the street and plead his case. "You must believe me," he said. "I'm a printer out of work. My wife is at home with a new baby—our second son. The doctor says she and the baby are starving. If they don't get food, they will die. I must have five dollars."

The stranger eyed the miserable man with his outstretched palm and tattered clothing, thinking he possessed a certain dignity despite his ragged appearance. His shoulders remained upright, and a look of seething determination burned in eyes rimmed with grime. "You sort of impress me," the stranger said, reaching into his billfold. "Here's the five." The stranger continued on his way, not realizing the look of determination in George's eyes had actually been the homicidal glare of a man on the edge. George later wrote that had the stranger ignored his plea, he would have throttled the man dead. After enduring several years working in the trenches of various newsrooms, George went on to achieve fame in 1879 as the author of *Progress and Poverty*, which sought to explain the existence of poverty in an age of economic and industrial growth.

Rounding out the *Chronicle* staff were Frank N. Cross, as the city editor, and a New York correspondent.

To help finance plans for their new venture, the brothers sold the *Dramatic Chronicle* to John Wight, who resigned from his job as bookkeeper at the *Bulletin* to assume his new role as publisher. He renamed the paper the *Dramatic Review* and went into business as John Wight and Company. "The 'Company' was ourselves," wrote Michael de Young. "Fearing the daily enterprise might not be a success, we held on to the dramatic field, thinking we might possibly go into the business again." The brothers need not have worried. Still bachelors, they lived with their mother and brought home roughly $1,500 a month in salary. The brothers felt confident they had stashed enough money away by 1868 to launch their assault on the daily market. They rented offices on the southwest corner of Clay and Sansome streets, outfitting the space with type and printing materials, and hung a sign above the door. It read, "The Daily Morning and Evening Chronicle."

On September 1, the *Chronicle* rolled off the press as a daily. It claimed a debut circulation of 8,000, charged five cents a copy and sent Loring Pickering into a rage. "The CHRONICLE," wrote Charles de Young in that first issue of the paper's new incarnation, "enters upon a new stage of its existence."

PICKERING SUMMONED THE DE YOUNG BOYS to his office shortly after the new *Chronicle* launched. The brothers rolled down and buttoned their shirtsleeves, donned their hats and strolled to the *Call's* office, where they found Pickering at a large desk with the *Chronicle* spread out before him. He bid the brothers a cold salutation and told them to take a seat. The two sides stared one another down across the no-man's-land of Pickering's desk.

"You have made a great mistake in starting a daily newspaper. You were making money in the dramatic field, and it was very foolish of you to start it," Pickering said, jabbing at the *Chronicle* with his finger. "If, however, you continue as you are and make no attempt to acquire telegraphic news, I will not interfere with you." The "telegraphic news" that so concerned him was dispatches from the Atlantic and Pacific Telegraphic Company, a combine of the Union and Central Pacific railway lines organized to compete against Western Union. It was from these dispatches that the *Call*—now owned outright by Pickering—and the *Bulletin*, which he co-owned with two partners, drew their national coverage. He blew smoke from the corner of his mouth and leaned across his desk. "If you dare attempt to get the dispatches," he said, "I will crush you."

Charles's expression remained indifferent; he saw only fear in Pickering's threat. He glanced around the elder newsman's office, admiring the framed editions on the wall and wondered how long it would be before he acquired a workspace of similar size. He donned his hat and faced his foe. "The reason we do not have telegraphic news is because we cannot yet afford it," Charles said, heading for the door with Michael in tow. "But as soon as we can, we'll get the dispatches and take the chance of you crushing us."

Charles left the office prepared to fight, though he realized his situation was precarious. He could no longer rely on Michael visiting the Western Union office each morning to memorize the odd dispatch that buzzed across the wire. The brothers were now publishing a seven-column paper with an evening edition issued at three in the afternoon and sent into the mountainous regions by boat and rail for next-day distribution. News of national import was vital to the paper's survival. Thwarting the *Call-Bulletin* telegraph monopoly, Charles realized, meant the *Chronicle* would have to start its own wire service.

"Shortly after," wrote Michael, "we started a press association, taking in the *Alta, Sacramento Report, Oakland Tribune* and a number of country papers, and began the transmission of telegraphic news from the East. As soon as we started in publishing this news, the fight between the *Chronicle*, the *Call* and the *Bulletin* began."

The lines of battle were drawn on very unstable ground, as at 7:53 AM on October 21, 1868, the earth moved, thrashing the city from east to west with alarming ferocity. The quake lasted almost a full minute and sent men, women and children—some wearing little more than their bedclothes—screaming into the streets. "Many acted as if they thought the Day of Judgment had come," wrote one witness. A low rumbling ripped through the city "as if the mountains that form the backdrop to the city were laboring in pain." Noted one account:

> The scene that then ensued beggars all description—men, women
> and children rushed frantically forth in [*sic*] *en dishabille* in the
> streets, panic-stricken, and scarce knowing whither to turn for
> safety, and tremblingly awaiting what the next moment should bring
> forth.

Buildings buckled in the early morning haze, while the ground underfoot cracked like dry skin. The de Youngs had just settled behind their desks when the tremor hit, showering the office in plaster and dust. The windows in the small restaurant opposite the *Chronicle* newsroom imploded and covered early morning diners in glistening shrapnel. Charles staggered to his office door in time to see the firewall along Sansome Street come crashing down. "In the midst of our ruins," Michael wrote, "we set to work and sent the carriers, clerks and everything on two legs that could move, all over town to gather news and get out an extra."

The new daily's first extra hit San Francisco's ravaged streets at 1:30 PM. "EARTHQUAKE: THE SEVEREST EVER FELT IN SAN FRANCISCO," declared the headline above a six-column appraisal of the morning's carnage:

> Never in the history of San Francisco has so great a calamity befallen it as we have met with today. In the natural excitement of the moment, when the streets are so crowded with the affrighted populace and the people are crazed with terror, it is difficult to calmly write up the sad details or to find words in which to describe the scene of excitement and fear.

The *Chronicle* beat the competition by hours, utilizing, as it had with its coverage of Lincoln's assassination, the meager resources at its disposal. "It was accomplished under the most adverse circumstances, as we had to work in a perfect ruin," wrote Michael. "The printers had to set type out of boxes filled with plaster. The editors sat down among plaster and dirt, and the desks were covered with it." Three more extras rolled off the paper's press that day, chronicling not only San Francisco's ordeal, but also the chaos wrought in surrounding cities. The quake—its magnitude later estimated at 7.0 on the Richter Scale—killed seven people and injured thirty. "The *Chronicle*," the young editors later boasted, "had an opportunity to show what energy it could display."

That vigor was its primary weapon against the competition.

THE CHRONICLE HAD NEVER BEEN timid in criticizing its rivals. The paper routinely skewered the larger, more established dailies, scoffing at their coverage and questioning their journalistic integrity. The *Chronicle* looked upon the *Alta* as being grandmotherly, "a dear, good-knowing twaddler." The *Call* was routinely referred to as "the little *Call*" and assailed for what the de Young brothers saw as its inability to take a firm stance on any controversial issue. When the *Call* one day accused San Francisco of being a drain on resources that would soon leave California "as dry as a well-sucked orange," and the next day attacked those who dared question the measure of California's "wealth and resources," the *Chronicle* was quick to point out the flip-flop:

> It is evident that the catastrophe we had long been expecting has happened to the little *Call*. It has fallen off the fence twice, and committed itself to two diametrically opposite extremes of opinion . . . If the little fence-straddler can't keep its balance any better than that, its friends should see to it that it be tied on the fence, and that right speedily.

The writing skills of the *Call*'s staff were also called into question:

> The dramatic critic of the *Call* is an aspiring genius for whom the English language affords a totally insufficient vehicle for the conveyance of the thoughts, which sparkle in his wonderful brain until they burst into flame and burn bald spots on the top of his head.

The *Bulletin* was slammed for making news out of non-events. When the paper ran an article explaining how to prevent cholera, the *Chronicle* could not help but point out the disease was non-existent in the city:

> Not having any cholera to "prevent" ourselves, and not knowing of anyone else who has, we naturally read the item with an interest that we otherwise could not have felt. It is so blamed difficult, you know, to find an effectual preventative for cholera when there isn't any cholera to prevent.

The *Bulletin*'s penchant for such stories, the *Chronicle* argued, was sullying San Francisco's reputation. "Do somebody send up a bar of soap and a tub of hot water, and let the institution have a good bath," the de Youngs wrote. "It will make a dung-hill reputation of our tidy city abroad if it goes on this way! Oh, give it a good sousing—and hold it under awhile."

Loring Pickering, whose joint ownership in the *Morning Call* and *Evening Bulletin* made him a more than formidable challenge to the young upstart, did not take kindly to the abuse. The product of James King of William's moral crusade, the *Bulletin*—now co-managed by Pickering partner George Fitch— maintained a keen interest in the city's political machinations. It cast aside all timidity with bold reporting and sharp editorials. It only made sense that the *Bulletin* delivered the opening volley in Pickering's cannonade against the de Youngs, dismissing the *Chronicle* as worthy of little attention and labeling it "The *Daily Humbugger*."

The insult left the brothers incensed. "The *Chronicle* replied," Michael later wrote, "and it was a terrific one." The paper smeared Pickering and Fitch, portraying the two as con men and thieves. "We went through the early history and records of Pickering and Fitch," Michael recalled years later of their retaliation. "We branded Pickering for having robbed his partner, leaving the East and being followed on the plains and made to disgorge the money he had taken; also accusing Fitch of robbing the state government here." Pickering summoned the brothers to his office the next day. They arrived in good spirits but left their magnanimity at the door.

"What do you mean by that savage onslaught today?" he demanded.

"Mr. Pickering, we want you to understand for the first and last time that for every blow you ever give the *Chronicle* from this time forth, you will get two back," said Charles, bristling with power. "Our courses will be separate from this and our fight a bitter one, but you keep always in view that you cannot attack us with impunity. Boys though we be, we will fight you back every time."

Pickering failed to heed the warning and continued his assault. The de Youngs, likewise, responded with articles "equally as terrific," and the occasional act of rascality. The *Bulletin*, to meet its evening deadline, set its copy the night before. Knowing this, Michael de Young dropped by the paper's pressroom and handed the foreman a sheet of copy. The foreman, accustomed to late content being dropped off by random strangers, thought nothing of the delivery, set the necessary type and fed it through the press. Reviewing the *Bulletin*'s first edition the following morning, Pickering nearly swallowed his cigar when he read on an inside page:

> This paper called the *Chronicle*, published by the de Youngs, has in today's issue a description of a prize fight in which our leading ministers are made to appear.

"Of course, there was nothing about the ministers in our prize fight story," Michael wrote, "but the *Bulletin*'s article sent everyone looking for a *Chronicle*. There they found a very good report of a real prize fight—and were naturally attracted to the *Chronicle*."

On August 16, 1869, the paper was rechristened as the *San Francisco Chronicle*. By the end of the year, its subscription list had reached sixteen thousand. Readers who turned to the *Chronicle* found a newspaper unafraid to tackle controversial issues. It exposed crooked politicians and the manipulation of stock prices. It lambasted big industry when necessary and rallied against monopolies, but it maintained a deep affection for all things tawdry. Charles de Young, who saw in the sexual misadventures of others a chance to promote his circulation, never shied away from tales of carnality.

Such stories prompted the rival *Examiner* to blast de Young and his newspaper as a "scandalous" publication. "How any decent man," the *Examiner* complained, "can allow such literature . . . to enter a household, numbering refined women and innocent children of either sex among its inmates, we cannot understand." Lending legitimacy to such criticism was an article in the October 17, 1869, edition of the *Chronicle* headlined "THE COURSE OF TRUE LOVE." The article detailed the dysfunctional married lives of San Francisco's social elite. The story's lead set the tone:

> Nearly one year ago—in December last, we believe—the shoddy and codfish aristocracy of San Francisco, and all the worshippers of the "golden calf," and all the throng of butterfly fashionables, whose god is Mammon, and all the gossips and toadies and hangers-on of

the vulgar rich, were in a great state of excitement about a "wedding in high life."

The wedding alluded to was that of August J. Bowie, Jr., son of a respected physician, and Elizabeth Friedlander, daughter of City Supervisor Isaac Friedlander, at the Friedlander mansion on Bryant Street. The article continued:

> San Francisco was all agog in anticipation of the great fashionable
> "event" of the season. Everybody who was anybody in the world of
> shoddy was invited. Vulgar people, who didn't pay taxes on
> $100,000, couldn't get an invite, and codfish was in all its glory.
> Among the impecunious hangers-on upon the outskirts of fashion
> there was weeping and wailing and gnashing of the teeth.

The couple had plans to travel the world, for they "yearned to eat frogs in Paris and macaroni in Naples." But the couple's honeymoon left something to be desired, as the hot Parisian nights brought out the philistine in young August Junior.

"Alas! Alas!" declared the *Chronicle*, "that the sweet illusions of youthful love are liable to be so speedily dispelled. Alas! That men are not all that romantic maidens dream them to be." The groom drank himself into oblivion, shared his marital bed with strange women and preferred the company of croupiers and card dealers to that of his wife. The couple had come to Paris with $300,000 in traveling money, which was soon frittered away:

> He went to "see the lights," while his pensive bride was left forlorn,
> to meditate upon the fickleness of man and the evanescence of all
> earthly bliss. He fell into bad company . . . who seduced him into
> play, high play, dangerous play. His luck was down on him. That
> $300,000 melted away like the snows of February beneath the sun
> of April.

A devastated Elizabeth sent her father by trans-Atlantic cable a horrific tale of debauchery and beatings, and begged him to send fare for a ticket home. The story somehow found its way to Charles de Young ten months after the fact and promptly appeared in his newspaper. The competition was aghast. "The most infamous article that has ever polluted the San Francisco press," opined a disgusted Benjamin Franklin Washington, the *Examiner* editor and a southern colonel. "We have no hesitation in saying that the man and malignant publisher of the *Chronicle*, together with his disreputable editorial associates, ought to be publicly flogged through the principal street of the city, and that they deserve to be kicked off the sidewalk by every gentleman." Charles shrugged off the public lashing and let his paper's expanding circulation speak for itself.

"The *Chronicle* was a success at the end of six months," Michael wrote, "but our capital had pretty much petered out. We had sunk $20,000 of our own savings." Foresight and a unique financial plan saved the paper from early ruin. "We traded upon our success and instead of selling a man a route outright, we sold him a route to be paid for at the end of six months if the *Chronicle* lived so long, at so much per subscriber and compelled them to make a deposit of from twenty-five to one hundred dollars," Michael explained, adding carriers were eager to own a stake in the venture. Ten thousand dollars in carrier dues replenished the paper's coffers at the end of six months and "saved us from financial failure."

6

BEATINGS AND LITIGATION

BY 1871, CHARLES DE YOUNG HELD the dubious honor of having been sued for criminal libel a dozen times, an impressive record even by San Francisco's gaudy standards. His list of enemies was long and varied, and spanned the city's social spectrum from Superintendent of Schools Richard H. Sinton to the Rev. Dillon Egan, a man the *Chronicle* denounced as a quack. Acquittals fortunately kept pace with indictments. The fact no one had yet beaten Charles or his brother in the street, or used either one as target practice, proved to be something of a miracle.

That would soon change.

WILLIAM T. HIGGINS, A MEMBER of the Republican County Committee, representing the Fifth Ward, was not an individual one would call timid. He once killed a hackney driver in a Kearny Street saloon, where a number of ruffians had gathered to settle bets made on a prizefight. He was subsequently tried for murder, only to be acquitted by a jury who deemed the homicide "justifiable."

Why anyone would mess with Higgins was of question. "Higgins is a man who weighs about 225 pounds," noted one contemporary. "Higgins possesses a powerful physique and presents an appearance by no means inviting for a personal *rencontre* to an adversary." On the night of May 8, 1871, Higgins brought his considerable bulk to bear against the 140-pound Michael de Young at the Lick House Billiard Hall on Sutter Street. The *Chronicle* had recently accused Higgins of playing shady politics, alleging that he and several close associates planned to "pack" the local Republican convention in August, muscle their way into positions of political power and seek monetary compensation from those who sought their assistance on various issues.

Higgins was not happy. Shortly before 9:30 PM, he darkened the hall's entrance with an ironwood club some two-inches thick clasped in his hand and strolled with violent purpose through the saloon. Intent on his game with George King, "a lamented son of James King of William," de Young paid no attention as Higgins descended the stairs leading to the billiard hall and spotted de Young hunched over a table in the northeast corner of the room. "I was just leaning over to make a shot," de Young remembered, "when Higgins approached me with a heavy cane. While in this attitude, the man's shadow fell on me and, looking up, I saw him about to strike."

De Young spun around, wielding his cue like a sword and raised it above his head. Higgins swung his bludgeon with murderous force and connected with the cue, which, made of ash and hickory, disappeared in a cloud of splinters. The startled newspaperman, clutching a piece of the broken stick in his right hand, charged his assailant and delivered a well-placed blow to the bridge of his nose. Higgins dropped his weapon and retreated on unsteady feet as de Young lashed out, beating the hulking menace about the head and shoulders.

Higgins, in his retreat, stumbled over a spittoon. The unpleasant contents splashed up his trouser leg and oozed across the floor. All the while, de Young kept swinging as a cheering crowd gathered around the two combatants. Higgins finally regained his senses, raised his right arm and stymied de Young's counterassault. He wrestled the shattered cue from the smaller man's hand and tossed it across the room. The two men clinched and staggered back against a table before hitting the floor. The spectators continued to whoop and holler as the unlikely gladiators struggled at the crowd's feet, pulling hair and scratching whatever they could.

On the street outside, Charles de Young was just approaching the Lick House to meet his brother for a scheduled game of billiards when he heard the enthused cries of the establishment's patrons. Wondering what entertainment he was missing, he quickened his pace and entered the saloon, which was now empty. He hurried down the stairs to the billiard hall, where he found his brother on the floor, straddling and flailing a man of much larger size. "At this stage of the proceedings," recalled one witness, "Mr. Charles de Young interfered and lifted his brother from off the form of the prostrate bravo."

Higgins scrambled to his feet and pulled an ivory-handled revolver from his right pocket. The crowd, so eager to linger only seconds before, now wasted no time in scattering. As Higgins raised the gun, it was seized by his friend Thomas Chandler, who yanked it from Higgins's hand. Higgins wiped the sweat from his brow and wiped the sleeve of his jacket across his bloodied upper lip. "You are a good friend of mine, you are, to take away my pistol," he said to Chandler, speaking his first words since the affray began. "If you are a good friend of mine, give me my pistol." Chandler denied the request. Both de Youngs, displaying an amazing sense of calm considering the circumstances, stood with their backs against a billiard table in anticipation of Higgins's next move. Higgins, his face bruised and battered, eyed the brothers and, realizing he had lost, nodded his head. Chandler took him by the arm and led him up the stairs. "I did not receive a scratch," Michael de Young wrote. "Nothing came of this, as I did not prosecute."

The story naturally made the front page of the following day's *Chronicle*. "GAGGING THE PRESS," shouted the headline, "Murderous Assault Upon One of the Proprietors of the *Chronicle*." The article struck an indignant tone:

It is not often that the proprietors of a newspaper have occasion to allude to attacks made on their persons. Vilification and abuse from jealous and unsuccessful rivals are often made on the newspaper itself, but assaults on the proprietor are rare. Yet there are men who believe that the publication of facts concerning their political trickery can be stopped by an assault on the owner of the newspaper publishing them; men who have so little respect for themselves that they stoop to cowardly personal attacks with cane and pistol.

Before attacking Michael de Young, Higgins had expressed his dismay by assaulting the brother of a *Chronicle* staffer. "On that occasion," the paper reported, "Higgins succeeded in knocking down an inoffensive attorney and brutally assaulting him, and then had recourse to his revolver, as usual, which he drew with the readiness that betokens practice in the 'draw.'" A witness wrestled the gun from Higgins's grasp, prompting Higgins to apologize to his battered victim and blame his actions on a lengthy soiree with a whiskey bottle. Such behavior, the *Chronicle* reported, would not deter the paper from its crusade:

> The CHRONICLE aims fearlessly to be the guardian of public interests. It will expose the wrong doings of the evil-minded; it will unearth every little scheme, which the manipulators might conceive.

It made for rousing, if self-indulgent, copy. If the article's author—ignorant of history—truly believed attacks upon newspaper editors were uncommon, his opinion would change in the coming months.

THE ARTICLE THAT RAN ON page one of the *Chronicle* on Sunday, July 2, 1871, seemed innocuous enough. His Britannic Majesty's frigate *Zealous*, after spending some time in port, was returning to home waters. "The afternoon parties, hops or receptions given by the officers have been the most successful entertainments of the kind in this pleasure-loving city of San Francisco," the *Chronicle* gushed of the festivities. "The ladies admire the officers, the officers admire the ladies, and civilians simply bow to fate and allow these irrepressible attentions to have their way."

News of the ship's pending departure struck a hard blow to the city's social scene, which was softened somewhat by word of a farewell gala. The *Chronicle* dispatched a scribe to cover the event and report on the "pretty girls and gallant officers." The resulting article's headline, "THE ZEALOUS HOP— WHO WAS THERE AND WHAT THEY WORE," would not be out of place in the celebrity tabloid magazines of today. The reporter dutifully made note of the guests in attendance, including "Mrs. McKinstry, another one of the 'ladies of South Park,'" who wore a silk, lilac-colored dress with dark trimmings. Her date also received some press: "'Sweet William' was attentive, and palm lingered in palm." The coverage came as something of a surprise to Mrs. McKinstry's husband, Judge Elisha W. McKinstry, of the Twelfth District Court, who had not been on board the boat that day. He let his displeasure be known.

At 3:15 PM on the afternoon of Monday, July 3, a few days after the gala, de Young stood in conversation with Frank McCoppin, the former mayor, on the corner of Clay and Montgomery streets, when a well-dressed man— walking stick at his side—came strolling up Montgomery. The man, a stranger to de Young, recognized the one-time mayor and stopped to shake hands. The two exchanged customary pleasantries before McCoppin turned and introduced the man, Judge Elisha McKinstry, to Charles de Young. "The Judge, who is known to be of an even temperament, became very naturally excited," the *Alta* later reported with some degree of haughtiness. "The mean and low attack on his wife had disgusted him as it had all right-thinking people."

A rush of blood to the head colored McKinstry's features a startling shade of red. He stamped his feet and stammered, the sudden rage having diminished his capacity to utter complete sentences. Charles, unsure what to make of the strange performance, took a step back just as McKinstry swung his cane. The weapon's arc of travel was wide and slow, allowing Charles time to raise his arms and block the attack. McKinstry swung again. Charles, nimble on his feet, sprung to one side and felt the rush of air as the cane missed his head by inches. The next blow struck de Young on the shoulder. Another one followed in quick succession. McKinstry had apparently found his range.

Several onlookers stopped to watch the bizarre spectacle of an elderly gentleman caning a young man in the street. A stunned McCoppin now intervened and stepped between the judge and his retreating target, who ran into the doorway of Hixon's carpet store. A few sound words from the former mayor convinced McKinstry to surrender his walking stick. Charles, having escaped serious injury, scurried off in the opposite direction and didn't look back.

The *Examiner* took great delight in de Young's public humiliation. The assault upon his person, the paper opined in a piece headlined "Partial Justice," was well deserved:

> For several years, a flash sheet aspiring to be considered a
> respectable journal, has managed to exist here, and, growing bold
> by impunity with which its assaults have been made upon private
> character, has quitted the role of the more sensational gossip and
> became a general slander . . . Growing more and more depraved, in
> its descent from the elevated plane of decent journalism, it seized
> upon vague rumors of matrimonial engagements current in society,
> and has repeatedly placed ladies and gentlemen in most painful
> predicaments, and, in some instances, has perhaps seriously
> impaired their future happiness.

A column of abuse ensued. *Chronicle* reporters were labeled "despicable minions," and their work was dismissed as nothing more than "journalistic lewdness." The article that incurred the wrath of Judge McKinstry was typical of the *Chronicle*, the *Examiner* argued, with its "customary number of low innuendoes and unwarrantable criticisms of ladies and gentlemen." It was a shame the judge was so enraged as to violate the very law he himself represented, the paper editorialized, but his actions were well understood:

We are pleased to discover that there is still enough of manhood left in our midst to punish the worthless creature who allows a so-called "public journal" to be defiled with a perennial stream of blackguardism poured out on persons in public and private life . . . On one point of the affair we have heard a unanimous expression of sentiment, and that is, a regret that Mr. McCoppin should have deemed necessary to interfere to prevent the well-merited castigation, which would have been visited upon the *Chronicle* fellow.

The *Examiner*, "being humane in disposition," said it was pleased Charles de Young escaped major injury. "We hope," the paper concluded, "he will profit by the lesson."

De Young's education in the school of hard knocks was only just beginning.

———o———

"I WILL LAND THESE DE YOUNGS in San Quentin yet!" So threatened Delos Lake, San Francisco's Criminal Municipal judge. The *Chronicle* had actively pummeled the judge in print for the better part of two years, blasting his judicial acumen and overall fitness to serve on the bench. "There was a great deal of animosity between us," Michael de Young remembered. "He sentenced a Frenchman for stabbing a man, whom [was] caught staying with [the Frenchman's] wife, for 25 years in the penitentiary, while another, who assaulted and nearly murdered a man, he let off with a light sentence. All these things we continually brought before the public."

Lake had failed, despite his best efforts, to silence the brothers. In 1871, School Superintendent Richard Sinton filed four separate criminal libel suits against the *Chronicle*. The *Chronicle* was in the habit of regularly slamming Sinton for what it perceived to be his corrupt and inept handling of the job. When the legal issues made their way into Judge Lake's courtroom, Lake made no pretense of impartiality. "It was a most peculiar trial," Michael wrote. "The judge ruled out everything he could that favored the defense, and evinced the

most bitter and relentless feeling on the bench." Lake argued with defense witnesses and mocked their testimony in front of the jury. When the prosecution
overlooked facts that might successfully send the de Youngs to jail, Lake
proved more than eager to point out the oversight and offer words of advice.

Charles and Michael sat alongside their attorneys and watched the
curious proceedings with a somewhat resigned demeanor. "It was one of the
most remarkable cases ever tried," Michael wrote. "When the clerk had
drawn the names of the jury and the twelve men were put in the box, we took
a remarkable position and declined to ask them any questions as to whether
they were prejudiced or not." What, under such circumstances, would have
been the point? In the end, the jury deliberated no more than ten minutes
before returning a surprising verdict of not guilty. The acquittal came despite
a closing argument from Sinton's attorney, who claimed anything other than
a guilty verdict would forever label his client a "bully and a blackguard"—
terms the de Youngs had employed to describe the school superintendent.
"When the jury rendered the verdict, there was great excitement," Michael
wrote. "Lake nearly fainted."

The de Youngs did little to improve the judge's attitude toward them in
the run-up to that year's municipal elections in November, when Lake ran on
the Democratic ticket against Republican-backed future mayor Judge M. C.
Blake. (Blake's nomination itself bore testament to the Chronicle's growing
power. Up to that point, the People's Party—a combine of leading merchants
who once dispensed harsh justice as members of the Vigilance Committee—
dominated city politics. "They always elected their officers," Michael
explained. "The Republicans never met and nominated a city ticket, as most
of them were in the People's Party—but the Democrats always did.")

Lake appeared on the ballot courtesy of a lawyer named Hoag, a fellow
Democrat who, at the party's convention, paid the ten-dollar nomination fee
and tossed the absent Lake's hat into the ring. The judge, who had considered
calling it quits amid the endless barrage from Charles de Young's pen, was not
pleased when he heard of Hoag's actions the next day. "You are a damn fool,"
he told Hoag. "I don't want the nomination!"

It was too late. Hoag couldn't get his ten dollars back.

The last thing Lake wanted now was continued exposure to public harassment from the *Chronicle*, which had attacked nearly every decision the man made since being appointed to the bench in 1869 by Gov. Henry Haight. When the People's Party met at their twenty-four-man convention in 1871, the de Youngs—having forgotten their early promise to remain politically neutral—showed up to rally the opposition against Lake, whom they described as "a passionate, vindictive and corrupt man, unfit to judge." Lake's supporters put $30,000 behind his campaign, to little effect. On election night, a large crowd gathered at the *Chronicle* office on Montgomery Street to await the results. "When (opponent) Judge Blake was found to be elected," Michael wrote, "the cheers were tremendous. Then, two weeks after that, Judge Lake attempted to shoot my brother."

Shortly after half-past three on the afternoon of Friday, December 1, 1871, Charles de Young was strolling on the east side of Montgomery, between California and Sacramento streets, accompanied by banker John McCombe. The two men were lost in conversation and unaware they were being watched. Lake had dropped by the *Chronicle* newsroom earlier that day with a solid whalebone cane in one hand and a pistol tucked into the waistband of his trousers. He asked to speak with the troublesome brothers, but a clerk told the annoyed jurist the two men were out. Lake left the building and took up position in the doorway of Barry and Patton's Saloon on the opposite side of the street. He pulled the brim of his top hat down low and lay in wait. When he saw Charles approach, he made his move. "I had no intention of shooting him, or anybody else," Lake said after the incident, "but I did intend to chastise him with my cane for the manner in which he treated me in his paper."

Like his brother, Charles was diminutive in size, weighing only a hundred and forty pounds. Lake tipped the scales at more than two hundred pounds and made full use of his considerable bulk when he charged, screaming, across the street with his whalebone cane raised above his head. He moved fast for a man of his size and took de Young by surprise, clobbering the publisher upside the head. De Young shrieked and backed into the street as Lake took another swing. The cane splintered across de Young's forearms, which he raised to cover his face, and sent him reeling. Lake lunged forward and struck again, only to be thwarted by de Young's surprisingly nimble footwork. The smaller man ducked and dodged to the side as one shattered half of Lake's cane whistled off course. The judge, by now, was "breathless with passion and exhausted by his violent efforts."

De Young, battered and nearly spent, crouched low and threw himself against Lake's knees. The two men tumbled to the street, kicking and flailing in the dirt. De Young managed to straddle his assailant but was quickly knocked aside. Lake scrambled to his feet, dropped his bludgeon and took several steps back. Retreating fifteen paces from de Young, Lake reached into his jacket and pulled the large-sized Southerner pistol from the waistband of his trousers. "I'm not armed!" de Young cried, reaching for the sky.

Lake pocketed his sidearm and retrieved a broken piece of cane, next attacking de Young's still unmarred face. De Young ducked and felt the cane cut the air above his right shoulder. The two men clinched and again hit the dirt. Lake, "a man of more than ordinary muscular strength," used his considerable heft to pin de Young. "And now," the *Chronicle* later reported with dramatic flare, "the real struggle for life began."

The pistol again appeared in Lake's right hand and discharged. The shot went wild, scorching the side of de Young's head before striking innocent bystander E. D Wheeler, a lawyer with the firm Wheeler and McQuaid, just above the left knee as he stood on the opposite side of the street. Wheeler yelped and fell hard. Lake, undeterred, now whipped de Young about the head with the pistol butt. "At length bystanders, who had hitherto been prevented from interference by fear of the pistol came to the rescue," noted one witness, "and, assisted by F. G Berry and Officer Riley, dragged off the infuriated assailant, who made final efforts to kick Mr. de Young as he was being removed."

Riley and another officer—alerted to the fracas by the resonating crack of Lake's firearm—escorted the judge to a nearby station house and charged him with assault with a deadly weapon, with intent to inflict bodily injury. His bail, set at $1,000, was paid by District Attorney Henry Byrne. Released from custody, Lake asked to be taken to Wheeler's home. Meanwhile, another officer escorted Charles de Young back to the *Chronicle* newsroom and helped dress the publisher's wounds. Lake's bullet had scorched a blazing-red trail along the left side of de Young's forehead. The judge's repeated blows with the pistol butt had left two nasty cuts on top of de Young's scalp. A large bruise had blossomed on his right arm and turned the skin a dark shade of blue.

Later that night, a *Chronicle* reporter knocked on the door of the Wheeler residence at 618 California Street. Upon being shot, Wheeler had immediately been placed in a carriage and rushed to his home. The wound, though serious, was not life-threatening. Mr. Wheeler, although in much pain and feeling "rather flighty" from the opiates pumped into his system, was expected to make a full recovery.

The *Chronicle*, naturally, played the story large with an eight-deck headline and a blow-by-blow account of de Young's "desperate struggle for life." It proved an opportune time to rub in Lake's recent electoral defeat:

> It may not become us to enlarge this affair, but leave our associates of the press to criticize and our fellow citizens to estimate it. While we congratulate ourselves that Mr. de Young has escaped this premeditated assassination, we may also be permitted to congratulate the community that Judge Delos Lake has not the opportunity to administer justice in our Municipal Criminal Court for four years.

Although the editors of the *Chronicle*'s two chief rivals—the *Call* and the *Bulletin*—had their own grudges with Charles de Young, they were hard-pressed to find anything positive in Lake's actions. The *Call* labeled the assault "a disgraceful attack." The *Bulletin* ran a lengthy editorial headlined "A Bad Example," and condemned Lake's actions:

> It was especially urged in favor of Judge Lake's re-election that his rigor in punishing offenses against life, property and order demanded his retention on the bench. He has himself officially declared that

shooting on the street, with or without provocation, was a crime that ought to be put down. Yet we find him initiating a street brawl, which terminates in his wounding two men with a pistol shot.

The occurrence in which he has figured will be quoted abroad to the reproach of the city and State, and cited as a specimen of border civilization, whereas it is simply a phenomenal exhibition of private passion, which is regarded with as much surprise and regret here as it would be anywhere in the world.

The case came before County Judge John A. Stanly on the morning of December 30, 1871. "There was very considerable provocation for the attack on Mr. de Young," Stanly said, "but since Judge Lake was at the time in a position of much trust and honor and one that demanded a greater degree of control over his passions, I cannot let him off easily." The courtroom spectators leaned forward, eager to hear the sentence. Lake stood at attention, his hands clasped behind his back. Stanly picked up his gavel and said, "I thereby fine him $300."

That the Grand Jury had indicted Lake on the original charge of assault with a deadly weapon with intent to commit bodily injury seemed to be conveniently forgotten. Lake retrieved his wallet from an inside pocket and pulled out a check already written and signed for the required amount. Case closed. It was, wrote Michael de Young, "one of the most outrageous farces ever seen on the bench . . . Years afterwards, Lake made up with my brother and myself and we continued to be very good friends up to the time of his death."

PUBLIC CONFRONTATIONS AND SCANDALOUS REPORTING did little to stunt the *Chronicle*'s growth in power and influence. The paper started publishing seven days a week on September 6, 1872, when the de Youngs rolled their first Monday edition off the press. "At that time," Michael recalled, "none of the papers in San Francisco, or the United States—as far as

I know—were published everyday of the week, but all suspended either Sunday or Monday—generally Monday."

The paper's growth only fueled the brothers' enthusiasm for a good fight. One such case occurred on an evening in 1873, when Charles de Young dispatched *Chronicle* reporter R. D. Bogart on a story from which he failed to return. "We started out and hunted day and night, but could not find him," Michael wrote. "He was always reliable so far as his work was concerned. In the course of two or three days, we got hold of a clue that he had been abducted." Bogart had been snatched off the street in front of the *Chronicle* office and dragged to the naval base at Mare Island. Navy Secretary George Robeson wanted Bogart brought to trial as a defaulting paymaster.

The *Chronicle* would have none of it.

"We raised such a row over it and fought him so bitterly that the result of the trial was never promulgated and Bogart was set at liberty," Michael later boasted. "Robeson did not dare to promulgate it. He saw the influence of the *Chronicle* and we went for him, so he simply set the man free."

On November 25, 1873, a citizens' committee of independent auditors confirmed the *Chronicle*'s circulation to be 30,106. The paper's readership, the de Youngs were pleased to learn, had finally surpassed the *Call* and *Bulletin*. The brothers expanded their publishing empire, supplementing their daily newspaper with the launch of the *Weekly Chronicle* on January 1, 1874. At the same time, it dawned on the de Youngs—perhaps somewhat belatedly—that numerous dangers accompanied their chosen profession. Both brothers now went about their daily business with Derringers strapped to their hips. Events would show neither de Young to be slow on the draw, though their aim left something to be desired.

7

UNDER FIRE

WHILE HUMBLE IN ITS BEGINNINGS, the feud between the *Chronicle* and the short-lived *San Francisco Sun* quickly shed all pretense of civility and blossomed into a vile exchange of personal insults and pathetic marksmanship. Rival newspapers celebrated the clash as "offensive emanation." At its core were, naturally, Charles de Young—by now no stranger to antagonistic behavior and violent reprisals—and Benjamin F. Napthaly, editor of the *Chronicle*'s competitor. Originally confined to print, de Young's simmering animosity toward Napthaly hit critical mass when the *Sun* questioned the sexual morality of de Young's mother in an ugly article dated January 31, 1874.

A small daily sheet derided by the city's more prominent publications as "a blackmail sheet," the *Sun* debuted on December 18, 1873. At its helm was publisher Robert F. Fitzgerald, a self-confessed rascal and perpetrator of numerous crimes. His previous publishing endeavor had been the *Independent Defender*, a lowly rag known for its anti-Catholic rhetoric, which he published with business partner B. H. Bennett. The *Defender* proved to be a short-lived enterprise, however, after Bennett discovered Fitzgerald was cooking the books, charging local businesses for advertisements and then pocketing the money himself. Outraged, Bennett fired Fitzgerald and denounced him in the paper for "cheating, stealing, swindling, devilry, diabolism, forgery, defalcation, robbery and other dishonest practices." In case anyone missed the point, Bennett also described his former colleague as "a thief, charlatan, forger, vampire, swindler, mountebank, defaulter and robber; a man of baseness, pure deviltry, infernal cunning, malignancy, concentrated villainy, bigamy, etc."

Fitzgerald, incensed, sued Bennett for libel, and the case went to court. At trial, Fitzgerald took the stand and—through the aggressive questioning of Bennett's attorney—ultimately confessed to being a man of debauched character, acknowledging that "the allegations of the defendant were warranted by the facts and history of my life and career, and that I have suffered no damage by reason of the publication or its circulation."

The "facts and history" of Fitzgerald's past were indeed salacious. On May 31, 1862, under the name Frank Wilson, Fitzgerald had married Jennie M. Chase in Lagro, Indiana. Five years later, on September 21, 1867, Fitzgerald—then known as Frank Emerson—married Arabella Wright in St. Louis, despite the fact his previous wife "remained alive and undivorced." Both ladies, naturally, were financially well-endowed.

Authorities eventually snagged the serial groom three months later in the town of Hannibal, Missouri, where the Marion County Grand Jury indicted him on charges of bigamy. A trial date was set for March 2, 1868, but Fitzgerald didn't stick around. Posting $800 bond shortly after his arrest, he jumped bail and hightailed it to Canada under the alias Oscar R. Payne. He established himself as a businessman in Montreal and, on October 27, 1871, co-founded the Montreal Manufacturing Company with partner Harry Noble, producing a line of pinchbeck jewelry, or jewels made with gold substitute.

The partnership did not last long. Noble appeared in court two months later and testified before a grand jury that Payne had robbed him and the company blind. Police nabbed Fitzgerald, alias Payne, on February 16, 1872. A four-day trial and quick conviction ensued, followed by one month's hard labor in the city jail. After serving his sentence, Fitzgerald fled the northern territory for San Francisco—a city he believed to be more congenial to a man of his character.

Perhaps not surprisingly, in the face of such evidence, the court dropped Fitzgerald's libel suit against Bennett. Never a man to mope for long, he soon attempted a rebound with the poorly received *Sun*. He would serve as publisher and handle the paper's finances. What he needed was an editor, and he found one in Benjamin F. Napthaly. Like Fitzgerald, Napthaly boasted a less than stellar reputation. "Napthaly is bright and smart," reported the *Evening Post*, "and if he had any moral sense he would have made a first-rate reporter, but he has none."

Napthaly was twenty-one years old when Fitzgerald sucked him into his corrupt venture. A San Francisco native, the young man had buried both his parents by his twelfth birthday. With no friends or family to take him in, the lad made ends meet by selling bouquets in theater lobbies and papers down on the wharves. He took up lodging in a boardinghouse on Brook Street, opposite Geary, and paid his own rent. On November 17, 1864, police knocked on the door and dragged the juvenile Napthaly off to the state reformatory for "leading an idle and dissolute life."

He remained incarcerated for a year and, upon his release, took a job at a wire factory at 412 Clay Street, only to lose it shortly thereafter to the city's influx of cheap Chinese labor. Napthaly, again on the street, returned to selling newspapers on the waterfront. It was his misfortune on the afternoon of October 1, 1866, to be conducting his business near a produce stand burgled by a group of marauding youths. Dockside police captured the gang trying to flee with armfuls of fruits and vegetables. Caught in the dragnet was Napthaly who, despite his innocence, found himself back in the state reformatory for another year.

He bounced from job to job when he got out, until wandering into the *Chronicle* newsroom on a May afternoon in 1869. Wearing clothes that were no more than rags, he presented himself to Charles de Young in the hope of landing meaningful employment. In the sixteen-year-old orphan, de Young saw something of his younger self: a brash young man seeking to make his way in the world. He took the teen on as a reporter, assigning him general office work on the side.

So eager was Napthaly for full-time employment that he worked at the *Chronicle* for three weeks without pay before de Young began slipping him six dollars a week. Napthaly worked the crime beat, becoming a daily fixture at the morgue, police court and city jail. He patrolled Dupont Street with notebook in hand, familiarizing himself with the denizens of area brothels. Sometimes the ladies congregating out front would holler, "There goes a reporter!" as the young muckraker sauntered past. He enjoyed the work and the lifestyle.

On Tuesdays, after the printers and reporters had been paid, they would hit the various gambling houses about town. In the *Chronicle* print shop at night, they often rolled the bones to make a few lucky bucks. "Sometimes," Napthaly recalled, "as soon as the *Chronicle* printers are paid, they commence shaking dice for small sums on the composing tables." Napthaly occasionally tried his luck to supplement his meager wage. He sometimes accompanied the printers to the Washoe Exchange, a saloon on the corner of California and Kearny streets, which offered the *Chronicle* pressmen a discounted meal after midnight.

He filed copy at the *Chronicle* for two years—eventually earning twenty dollars a week—before receiving a better offer from Loring Pickering at the *Bulletin*: twenty-five bucks a week to do the same job. Napthaly accepted and tendered his resignation at the *Chronicle*.

"I have helped you all along," an insulted Charles de Young said, the young reporter's resignation in hand, "and now you are going to desert me for the *Bulletin*."

"It's nothing personal," Napthaly said. "It's a matter of money for me—I really need that money."

De Young grunted and eyed Napthaly in silent contemplation. "I will give you twenty-five dollars a week," he finally said, "if you stay here."

Napthaly accepted de Young's counteroffer and told Pickering he would remain at the *Chronicle*. Pickering understood, but warned Napthaly: "You can go back, but Mr. de Young will discharge you before long. I will keep the place open for you whenever you want to come." Pickering's prediction proved accurate. Without a day's notice, de Young fired Napthaly within weeks for being a man of "bad character." De Young pointed out Napthaly's penchant for rolling dice, ignoring the fact that it remained common practice among his other employees. Perhaps de Young merely desired to teach the young man a lesson for even considering a job with the competition.

And so Napthaly jumped ship to the *Bulletin* and then to the *Evening Post*. There, he earned a reputation for frolicking with women of low character—even if the only evidence suggesting such behavior was Napthaly's habit of conversing with streetwalkers. "Very slight circumstances sometimes go to show the character of a man," the *Chronicle* later reported. "When a man is seen nodding to the prostitutes of Dupont Street, upon a street like Kearny, publicly and in open day, then he carries his acquaintance with them."

Napthaly insisted he was merely working his beat. But his arguments were wholly ignored and the reputation stuck. No self-respecting editor wanted to hire a "whoremonger" and, consequently, Napthaly found employment opportunities scarce—until Fitzgerald approached him in December 1873 to edit the *Sun*.

No one took the *Sun* seriously. The *Evening Post* wrote on February 2, 1874: "The thing could not, by any stretch of flattery, be called a newspaper."

Its intended purpose was not to inform the public, but to elicit cash from city businesses with which to line Fitzgerald's pockets. Already a self-professed lowlife, Fitzgerald employed a crude—but effective—business tactic to bilk the city's insurance companies: He ran advertisements for various firms regardless of whether or not they had actually purchased ad space, then presented companies with a bill and—if they refused to pay—threatened to print something damaging in the paper. One such victim was John Lander, an agent with the San Francisco branch of the Manhattan Life Insurance Company. In early January 1874, Fitzgerald walked into Lander's office and tried to sell him space on the back pages.

"I told him that I did not want to advertise," Lander later recalled. "I told him I was doing very little advertising and that I didn't care about it. Well, he didn't take that for an answer, but he went on and inserted one advertisement in the paper. At the end of the month, a bill came in the amount of $20. I sent the bill back and stated that I had never authorized the advertisement. Subsequently, Mr. Fitzgerald came in . . . He then said that he would probably insert something in the paper that would compel us to read it."

Several days later, Fitzgerald walked into the office of H. H. Blake, manager of the Continental Life Insurance Company, and pulled the same scam. As Fitzgerald pressured Blake for cash, Michael de Young just happened to walk in off the street to discuss the placement of a legitimate advertisement in the *Chronicle*. The *Sun* publisher fell silent and cast his gaze elsewhere as Blake hurriedly got up from his desk and pulled de Young aside.

"What's Fitzgerald doing here?" de Young asked, knowing full well the extent of the man's character.

"He's here to see me about advertising," Blake said. "He put my card in his paper and is presenting me the bill."

"Did you authorize the ad?" asked de Young, perhaps sensing a chance to slime the competition.

"I did not."

"I suppose, then, that's what you call a blackmailing operation."

Blake, after pondering it for only a short moment, nodded his head in agreement.

The result of that brief exchange and several follow-up inquiries about town was an editorial in the Saturday, January 31, 1874, edition of the *Chronicle*. Headlined "Birds of a Feather," the short piece outlined the crooked business practice and ravaged the *Sun's* credibility. The editor and publisher "of the vulgar little sheet" belonged in San Quentin, the *Chronicle* proclaimed, before continuing:

Fitzgerald, the publisher of the sheet in question, is, by his own confession, a thief, a liar, a bigamist, and, on general principles outside
of these classifications of his peculiar abilities, a scoundrel.

B. F. Napthaly, the nominal editor, is a graduate of the Industrial
School, a professional black-mailer, a hanger-on of the lowest gambling houses and dens of prostitution, and, generally, one of the
most degraded specimens of hoodlumism.

Although less than ten inches in length, the *Chronicle* hit-piece was a
scathing indictment of Fitzgerald's criminality. It also served to publicize the
Sun's existence, as the *Evening Post* subsequently reported: "This first-class
notice was probably the first information had by any respectable number of
people that there was any such sheet as the *Sun* in existence; but early in the
afternoon it began to be reported on the street that the *Sun* was out with a
reply to the *Chronicle*, which made all previous libels ever published in this
city seem tame and insignificant."

The *Post* did not exaggerate the facts.

The *Sun*'s retaliatory strike caused a sensation. "It showed the very lowest
depth human nature could sink," one reporter noted, "and the vilest use to
which type and ink could be prostituted." The article has since been lost to
time and the *Sun* is no more than an oft-overlooked footnote in San Francisco history, but, for one brief moment in 1874, it served as a catalyst to one
of history's most outrageous feuds.

Hearing of the *Sun*'s vitriolic response, Charles de Young dispatched one
of his reporters to scrounge up a copy. What he read sent him into an apocalyptic rage. Even by the day's low journalistic standards, the *Sun* piece was
ghastly. "Such an atrocious publication was probably never put in print
before," declared the rival *Post* from the sidelines. "For it not only charged the
most atrocious crimes and immoralities against the Messrs. de Young themselves, but included in its villainous sweep all the female members of their
family, not even sparing the gray hairs of the venerable mother, an old lady,

who, whatever be the faults of her sons, is respected by all who know her, and who has already seen her great-grandchildren. Words fail to describe the atrocious nature of this villainous attack, which ought not to even be alluded to in a respectable paper."

De Young's rage intensified further when a reporter entered his office and told him the *Sun* was preparing to print a second edition that evening. But Charles was not the only one lusting for blood. His younger brother Gustavus had read the article and decided to take matters into his own hands. He went to the *Sun* offices on Washington Street, opposite Battery, where he found Fitzgerald in the print shop, studying the plates for the second edition.

Gustavus spun the offending party around and knocked him senseless with a well-placed blow to the jaw. Fitzgerald staggered backward, one hand on his face, the other trying to grasp hold of something to maintain balance. Gustavus rolled up his sleeves and got down to business, delivering vicious combinations to the head and torso. Fitzgerald never had a chance. He crumpled bleeding to the floor as Gustavus drew his revolver and took close aim. Several pressmen had ducked out of the office to avoid their publisher's humiliation, but those who remained tackled Gustavus before he could pull the trigger.

After Fitzgerald crawled away, the pressmen let Gustavus up off the floor only to find themselves staring down the business end of the aggrieved man's Derringer. Dusting himself off with his free hand, Gustavus let the press stewards know he would hold them personally accountable if they printed additional copies of the *Sun*. With that, he exited the premises and strolled off down the street.

Not long thereafter, Charles descended upon the *Sun* offices, armed with a warrant for criminal libel, a police escort and the "paddy wagon." Minor chaos ensued as some *Sun* employees tried to scamper out the back door or hide under their desks. With de Young pointing fingers and screaming accusations, police charged through the building and slapped shackles on eight printers and typesetters. The unlucky bunch, protesting their innocence and hurling insults in de Young's direction, were bundled into the police wagon and hauled off to the city jail.

Satisfied the *Sun* was at least temporarily crippled, de Young focused his attention on trying to buy and suppress copies of the paper containing the vitriolic rant against his family. It proved an impossible task. "Such was the curiosity to see it," reported the *Post*, "that Saturday night newsboys were selling them for $2.50 a copy and, on Monday, were offering to let people read it for twenty-five cents a piece." Long before Monday rolled around, however, the eight men rousted in de Young's raid were freed when an "optimistic" bondsman posted $2,000 in bail for every one, only hours after their arrest. By the following morning, Sunday, February 1, it was generally known on the street that the printers were going to publish the article again. The disturbing news reached Charles and Michael de Young shortly before two that afternoon. The *Post* recorded the subsequent events:

> The police were immediately informed and with the de Youngs and
> a posse of officers proceeded to the composing-rooms of the *Sun* on
> Washington Street, battered in the doors, and there found one
> galley of the libelous article lying upon the imposing stone, and
> several printers around with their coats off, setting up the last of the
> article. There was a general stampede, and several escaped through
> the rear window upon the roofs of the adjoining houses, and made
> themselves scarce. The majority, however, were bagged and locked
> up in a room.

In total, the police—with the de Youngs again leading the charge— "bagged" six printers, three of whom had been arrested the day before. Fitzgerald, still recovering from the previous day's thrashing, had stayed away from the office that Sunday, trading blocks of type and printer's grease for the comforts of the Lick House hotel on the corner of Montgomery and Sutter streets. The pleasure of an afternoon drink in the establishment's wood-paneled bar, gently lit by ornate chandeliers cut from elegant crystal, soured when news of the police action reached his bruised and swollen ears. Fitzgerald took one last sip of drink, being careful not to further damage his fattened lip, and retired to his room to wait out the storm.

Napthaly, named in the libel warrant, had not been seen since one o'clock the previous morning. The *Daily Alta California* reported, "It is said that B. F. Napthaly, the author of the scandalous article, had first intended meeting the attack which he had invited, but on learning the de Youngs were armed to the teeth and searching the town in all directions, concluded that he would not venture abroad, but remain hidden." He was eventually nabbed just before 10 AM Sunday at his home and tossed in the city jail. It was not until the following day that guns would again come into play.

At 9 AM Monday, Napthaly appeared before Judge Louderback in the city's police court on Sansome Street. He waived his right to examination, had his bail fixed at $3,000 and was remanded back to his cell. Later that afternoon, upon putting in a request with Police Chief Theodore Cockrill, Napthaly received permission to leave the jail under the watchful eye of one Officer Mahen and go in search of a bondsman. The two men left the jail shortly before two that afternoon and proceeded along Sansome Street— between California and Bush—toward the British Bank of Columbia at the corner of California, where they turned down Battery. The sharp crack of a pistol shot stopped both men in their tracks. They spun around and saw Gus- tavus de Young, no more than six feet behind them, crouched in a shooter's stance with his smoking Derringer held out in front of him.

Gustavus cursed Napthaly's name as he cocked the weapon again.

Mahen pounced, throwing his full weight into de Young as Napthaly bolted. Mahen and de Young tumbled into the middle of the muddy street, Mahen yelping as the hot gun barrel scorched his left ear. An enthralled crowd gathered and gawked on the planked sidewalks. The two men exchanged several blows and a few vile words before de Young managed to claw his way out from underneath the officer and dash off in pursuit of his prey. Cursing and screaming Napthaly's name in frustration, de Young squeezed off another round. The *Sun* editor jumped, ducked and zigzagged, his arms flailing wildly. The shot went wide. Napthaly kept running and de Young kept cursing, cocking his Derringer again. Bystanders, now realizing the gravity of the situation, ran screaming in all directions for cover. Gustavus remained unfazed. He again assumed a shooter's stance, his legs bent slightly at the knees, the Derringer held at full arm's-length in front of him.

Walking his beat on California Street, a copper named Ryan heard the sound of gunfire and ran toward the commotion. He turned onto Battery and saw Mahen scrambling in the dirt, trying to reach de Young. Ryan charged the gunman from behind. He ran and dropped to his side in the mud, sliding into de Young with outstretched legs. De Young's feet lost contact with the ground and he toppled backward, landing with a bruising thud. Ryan clambered on top of de Young and began wrestling him for the gun.

A gentleman—later named in local papers as Mr. Wigmore—joined the melee on the side of the police, running from a nearby store and jumping into the fray without any consideration for his tailored suit. Officer Mahen resumed his role in the action and joined the writhing entanglement of bodies. "You ought to have let me alone," de Young screamed, lashing out with his arms and legs. But a knee to the groin and a fist to the jaw finally compelled Gustavus to surrender his weapon. Covered head to toe in mud, Officer Ryan hauled an equally dirtied de Young to his feet and marched him off to the city jail, "followed by an army of citizens," according to the *Alta*. Officer Mahen, meanwhile, chased down Napthaly.

The angry crowd, demanding the gunman be hanged immediately, followed Ryan and de Young up Merchant Street. Word of the afternoon's crazed events spread quickly, prompting several dozen uniformed officers to form a protective perimeter around the jail. Ryan led de Young inside, taking him to the prison keeper's desk, where he was booked on a charge of assault to commit murder. Forty newspapermen, all of them itching for a story, played audience to the proceedings.

Within minutes, Charles and Michael de Young had also arrived, having scurried over from the *Chronicle* office. The two stood conversing at the far end of the jail's main corridor near the cells, while the keeper recorded the charge against their brother. A rather shaken Napthaly and an exasperated Officer Mahen joined the party just moments later. The two men got no more than six feet past the jail's main entrance when they were swarmed by newshounds. At the other end of the corridor, Charles and Michael noticed the commotion and exchanged a knowing glance.

"Can you tell us what happened?" an eager reporter asked Napthaly.

"Well," the *Sun* editor responded, "the shots came so quick that I was stunned."

As Napthaly detailed the attempt on his life, Michael de Young walked casually down the corridor toward the congregation, his hand in the right-front pocket of his jacket. He curled his fingers around the handle of a concealed pistol and pushed his way past several police officers and reporters. Napthaly, engrossed in the telling of his story, remained ignorant of de Young's presence behind him. A reporter for the *Evening Post*, however, caught a glimpse of the sidearm.

"De Young drew out a five-shooter or six-shooter, apparently with a razed barrel, and made an effort to point it at Napthaly," Harry Larkins wrote for that evening's edition. "Had it not been for a man who stood between Napthaly and de Young, and an officer who just stepped up to him as he drew the pistol, Napthaly would probably have been shot." Looking over his shoulder, Napthaly yelped and turned pale at the sight of another armed de Young. He stumbled over his own feet, grasping hold of a nearby police officer to stay upright, and begged for protection.

Filling out paperwork with Gustavus de Young at the prison keeper's desk, Officer Ryan heard someone scream, "Look out! Look out! Look out!" He glanced up in time to see several officers manhandling Michael de Young with little concern for the infliction of injuries. They clawed desperately at his right hand, trying to pry the gun from his grasp. Huddled together in a clumsy physical altercation, the group of men fell to the floor, rolling on top of one another as Napthaly continued shrieking for protection. The officers were eventually able to get the better of the raging de Young and snatch away his weapon. They pulled him violently to his feet and slapped cuffs on his wrists. Deprived of more traditional armament, de Young tossed a few verbal grenades Napthaly's way as officers hauled him down the corridor toward an empty jail cell. In reporting what happened next, the *Evening Post* called it "a scene . . . beggaring description."

With his two brothers in custody, Charles de Young—who had stayed put while Michael went in for the failed kill—chose now to strike. He charged down the hallway, a savage barbarian scream passing through his snarled lips as he slammed into the terrified Napthaly. The force of the impact sent the *Sun* editor sprawling. Charles de Young reached inside his jacket and began advancing on his target, who desperately tried to crawl toward an open cell at the corridor's far end. "For God sake," Napthaly cried, "keep that man away!"

Captain Short, head of the city jail, sprang from the crowd of startled onlookers and wrestled de Young up against a wall.

"Give me your pistol!" Short demanded.

"I have none," de Young said. Short shoved his own hand inside de Young's jacket and pulled out what one witness described as a "very vicious-looking" revolver. "By this time," according to the *Evening Post*, "the prison resembled Bedlam broken loose. Men were crouching in corners. Behind the safe, women were screaming, the prisoners in their cells were tugging at their bars, and every face was blanched with excitement. The contagion spread outside, and a large force of officers was required to restore some semblance of order." Charles, meanwhile, was arrested and booked—along with Michael—on charges of assault with intent to do great bodily harm. Insult was added to injury when Short informed the de Young brothers that Fitzgerald, over the weekend, had named them in a criminal libel warrant for the *Chronicle*'s "Birds of a Feather" editorial.

The de Youngs and Napthaly were hustled by officers into their cells opposite the jail kitchen. Napthaly couldn't get behind bars quick enough. As an officer shepherded him past his three assailants, he turned on them. "For God's sake," he said, "give me a chance. There are three of you. Give me a chance—I'm not even armed!"

"You dirty liar! You had better arm yourself, Goddamn you, for I will shoot you on sight," Gustavus roared as he and his brothers were escorted to their dank accommodations for a short stay. They didn't remain there long. Later that afternoon, a judge set bail for the de Youngs at five thousand each, and all three of them filed the required bonds. They were released by day's end. Napthaly, asked if he cared to venture out one more time in search of a bondsman, opted to stay put for the night.

The following day's papers splashed the fracas all over their front pages. The *Daily Oakland News* summed up the thoughts of many when it reported:

A fine illustration of the tendency of chickens to come home to roost, is the tribulation of the *Chronicle*. Of course, the *Sun* article was as vile and scurrilous as words could make it, and had the persons attacked been other than the de Youngs, shooting would be none too bad for the author. But that the *Chronicle* people should raise such a howl at getting a dose of their own medicine is of a piece with the conduct of a joker who loses his temper at a witty repartee. The *Chronicle* has carried the reputation of a merciless scandal-monger, and does not deserve the least sympathy when one of its scholars returns a characteristic blow. The three brothers have made asses of themselves by their bluster and bad shooting. But they have also taught San Francisco the valuable lesson that it is not well to encourage blackguards by supporting these journalistic enterprises.

Napthaly tried his luck again that afternoon and secured three police officers to escort him through the streets on his quest to obtain bail. "He was not successful and returned to the City Prison, having run the gauntlet of Montgomery and other streets without having to withstand fire from the rear," reported the *Alta*. A second attempt later that afternoon also failed to procure the necessary bond for release. In actuality, this suited Napthaly—who reportedly told his jailers he enjoyed the safety of his cell—just fine. His desire for security only intensified the following morning, Wednesday, February 4, when he learned from two unlikely sources that the de Youngs were again gunning for him. The disturbing information came from two *Chronicle* reporters, R. D. Bogart and S. F. Sutherland, who had worked late the night before and witnessed Charles de Young ranting in the middle of the newsroom, demanding that Napthaly's blood be spilled. The two men said they'd come to warn Napthaly "out of a sense of friendship."

"The Messrs. de Young were greatly incensed against Napthaly," Bogart remembered. "My opinion was based upon the idea that when a newspaper editor attacks a woman's character without cause, he lays himself liable to very summary vengeance." Charles de Young, in fact, had gone so far as to instruct Bogart to cover Napthaly's Thursday morning court appearance "as there might be something extra" to report. More ominous was the fact that Sutherland's gun had mysteriously gone missing from his desk's top drawer the day before.

The news left Napthaly distraught. He was scheduled to appear in front of Judge Louderback at 9 AM and update the magistrate on his efforts to procure bail. Now, Bogart and Sutherland were telling Napthaly to flee the city once released. Charles de Young, they said, was a man to fear. The inability of his brothers to kill Napthaly had only stoked his rage. With a few more words of caution, the *Chronicle* reporters wished Napthaly luck and left him sulking on his cot.

Police Chief Cockrill summoned Napthaly to his office shortly thereafter and informed him that if he wished to make another attempt to procure bail, he could—the alternative being more jail time. "The libeler quaked in his boots as he heard this," the *Chronicle* later informed its readers in a somewhat exaggerated account. "The perspiration broke out all over him at the mere thought of going into the street, but finally the inconvenience of lying in jail for months to come overcame his dread of facing the gaze of honest men and consented to go. He stipulated that he should be carefully guarded and as far as possible be shielded from the indignation of respectable citizens by a cordon of police."

Thursday morning's *Alta* approached the story from a different angle:

THREATS TO KILL

The De Youngs Again Arrested

The de Young brothers—Gus, Charles and Mike—were again arrested yesterday evening by Officer Kearns on warrants sworn by B. F. Napthaly, charging them with 'threats to kill.' The complaint states that the deponent, Napthaly, believes that the de Youngs intend to kill him on the first favorable opportunity . . . Deponent further avers that his information and belief that threats have been made against his life by each of the brothers is based on intelligence from R. D. Bogart and S. F. Sutherland.

On the strength of this affidavit and accompanying complaint, warrants were issued against the brothers and they were required to file bonds in the sum of $4,000 each to answer the charge before the Police Court.

Again, the brothers posted bond and were released late Wednesday night. Napthaly also managed to secure bail from Ab Gentry, a man Napthaly admitted to being a gambler and something of a shady character. When he appeared early Thursday morning before Police Court Judge Louderback to post bond, onlookers packed the courtroom and crowded the hallway outside, for word of Napthaly's possible assassination at the hands of Charles de Young had made the rounds. Ironically, representing Napthaly as an attorney was Judge Delos Lake, the same magistrate who had attacked de Young with a cane three years before.

Despite the anticipated bloodshed, the hearing that morning passed without incident, and—at high noon on Thursday, February 5—Napthaly left the city prison a free but nervous man. Across the street, a *Chronicle* reporter followed "the libeler" and made note of his activities. "He paused in the prison door for a second and cast a quick, furtive glance up and down the street," the reporter wrote. "Seeing no one around, he bolted for Kearny Street and slunk around the corner like a dog with a bladder to his tail."

Napthaly weaved through the crowds with his coat collar turned up and the brim of his hat pulled down over his eyes. He walked quickly to the corner of Kearny and Bush streets, where he ducked into a saloon and ordered a whiskey. The *Chronicle* reporter followed Napthaly in and took a seat at a corner table. In the next day's paper, he detailed what happened next:

While there, someone came in who knew Napthaly, and, in order to have some fun, called out: "Nap, Gus is coming down the street!"

The wretch never waited even for his change. He shot out of the back door like a singed cat, and bounded over a fence ten feet high . . .

and into a dark, dingy alley from whence he sneaked out into Bush Street.

Although Napthaly sought to keep a low profile, the wheels of justice would prevent him from doing so. The various shooting and assault charges against the de Youngs were left to the higher courts, where—according to one veteran newspaperman—they were quickly "forgotten." But on Thursday, February 12, the de Young family's libel case against Napthaly went before the San Francisco Grand Jury. Over the next six weeks, attorneys for both sides paraded dozens of witnesses through the courtroom to share tales of Napthaly's debauched habits and the de Youngs' crazed behavior.

The details made for entertaining reading and were carried prominently by the city's major papers, including the *Chronicle*, which skewed its coverage to portray Napthaly as the lowest of life-forms. In the meantime, Fitzgerald—who had thus far managed to avoid the media's scrutiny—was dismayed when Judge Louderback tossed out his libel action against the de Youngs. "This does not hold water," the judge ruled. "The character of Mr. Fitzgerald being so infamously bad, by his own admissions, he is not susceptible to damage by libel."

The Grand Jury's take on the Napthaly–de Young debacle proved more surprising than Louderback's obvious ruling. On April 24, 1874, the thirteen-man panel decided the editor had done nothing wrong. Only ten members opted to indict, falling two short of the twelve-man majority needed to make the charges stick. Upon hearing the news, Charles de Young threw a tantrum. Though he knew he was lucky to not be sitting in a jail cell on charges of attempted murder, he was angry the law had betrayed him, denying him his one last means of vengeance. With that bitter fact in mind, he tempered his anger and focused on his daily duties as publisher—though the *Sun* and Napthaly's malignant words were never far from his thoughts.

———————

WHATEVER UNOFFICIAL CEASE-FIRE EXISTED BETWEEN the two newspapermen proved short-lived. After nearly a five-month hiatus, the *Sun* suddenly reappeared on the morning of Sunday, June 15, with evil intent. Emboldened by the Grand Jury's decision and a dire financial situation, Napthaly—with Fitzgerald's backing—had fired up the *Sun's* presses for an encore performance. The paper's reemergence would have likely gone unnoticed had it not been for the article running down the left-hand column of the front page. What the piece lacked in originality, it made up for in sheer audacity: There, for all the city to read yet again, was Napthaly's venomous article pondering the sexual proclivities of the de Young matriarch.

Later that morning, excited chatter in the *Chronicle* newsroom drew Charles de Young from his office. Several reporters were hunched over a desk, lost in animated conversation. When he saw the source of their amusement, the shade of crimson that flushed his cheeks and the snarl that curled his lips sent the reporters scurrying to distant corners of the room. Without saying a word, de Young stormed back into his office and retrieved a newly purchased Colt from his desk drawer. He grabbed his coat and white beaver hat from a hook behind his door and stomped out of the building. It was time to deal Napthaly the "miserable dog's death" that he deserved.

IT'S NOT KNOWN HOW DE YOUNG managed to find Napthaly that afternoon, but find him he did, shortly after the lunch hour. The *Sun* editor stood on the corner of Merchant and Montgomery streets, conversing with his close friend Charles Weightman, a fishmonger. De Young, storming up Merchant, saw his prey and moved in for the kill. He attempted a stealthy approach by running up behind Napthaly on the balls of his feet. For a June afternoon, however, de Young's choice of clothing—specifically his tall, white beaver hat—stood out. Weightman, noticing the strangely dressed man approaching with a gun in his left hand, tapped Napthaly on the arm and pointed in de Young's direction.

Taking advantage of this forewarning, Napthaly darted up Merchant Street toward Dunbar Alley, which ran behind the Hall of Justice and the city police department. De Young gave chase, his gun arm extended, his other hand holding his hat on his head. Napthaly reached Dunbar Alley and charged through the rear door of the police station, finding himself within a small office, where six uniformed officers sat around a table, playing a game of pinochle.

Napthaly tore through the building, running down hallways and in and out of rooms. He waved his arms and screamed, "I am unarmed, and he is after me again with a pistol!" The officers, for their part, saw little urgency in Napthaly's predicament and continued with their game. Still screaming, Napthaly scurried from the building, exiting onto Kearny Street, and disappeared into the crowd. De Young barged through the police station's backdoor seconds later and into the officers' game. He flashed a broad grin, holstered his weapon and—after watching the officers play a round—quietly excused himself and returned to the *Chronicle*.

He gave it another shot the following day.

During the early morning hours of June 16, several people reported seeing Charles de Young hanging around Washington Street, not far from the post office, wearing a heavy overcoat with the collar turned up and a wool scarf partially concealing his face. De Young knew Napthaly frequented the post office several times a day to send and receive mail.

Shortly before 11 AM, Napthaly walked out of the post office through a door that opened into an alley on the west side of the building and walked toward the street. Busy with his mail, he didn't see the figure leaning against the lamppost near the new Appraiser's Building on the other side of Washington. Oblivious, Napthaly crossed the street and continued walking in de Young's direction, passing within mere feet of his nemesis. Once Napthaly had passed, de Young drew his five-shot Colt and fired.

He missed.

"There was the usual excitement and scampering incident to an alarm of this kind," the *Alta* reported. Innocent bystanders ran and ducked for cover as Napthaly pulled from his jacket a self-cocking English revolver and returned fire. De Young ran across Washington toward the White & Bauer stationery store. Napthaly, refusing to turn his back on the *Chronicle* publisher, backed toward Battery Street and squeezed off another round. The bullet pierced the ground near de Young's feet, causing him to twist and spin his body around. A young girl, running for cover, fainted and fell flat on her face in the middle of the street between the two men—neither of whom paid any attention.

Napthaly ran to the northwest corner of Washington in the direction of the old Merchants' Exchange building and squeezed off another volley. Having recovered his balance, de Young leapt behind a lamppost for cover and returned fire. The round missed its intended target and instead tore through the right calf of thirteen-year-old Henry Mitchell, a messenger for the Western Union Telegraph Company who was on his way to the post office. A gentleman ran from a nearby store and dragged the young lad to safety.

De Young marched into the middle of the street with one shot left in his revolver. He challenged Napthaly, now hiding in the Merchants' Exchange building, to come out and face him. Police, however, swarmed the scene and slapped shackles on both men. It was just as well, for a large crowd was beginning to congregate, demanding both men be strung up. Pointing to Napthaly as police dragged him from the building, one man yelled, "Let's lynch him! We've had too much of this shooting in the streets!" Napthaly yelled back that he was simply defending himself and argued for the hanging of de Young. The duelists were bundled into the back of the city jail wagon and taken to see Police Chief Theodore Cockrill, "who welcomed them as old friends." A judge subsequently set bail at $15,000 each, the limit of a bail bond in a case of assault with intent to commit murder. Michael de Young arrived at the jail not long afterward and posted his brother's bond. "On leaving the prison, de Young went to the *Chronicle* office, whence he sent $100 to the parents of the wounded boy, Henry Mitchell, with a note in which he stated his intention to pay the expenses of medical treatment and cover the time that the lad may be laid up from the wound," reported the *Alta*.

Napthaly, meanwhile, decided the lodgings weren't so bad and opted to say behind bars for several days. At a preliminary hearing the following week in front of Police Court Judge Louderback, de Young testified that Napthaly had drawn first and initiated the gunplay. Lawyers for de Young called to the stand a witness named Thomas Ryan, who backed de Young's version of events. Napthaly, acting as his own lawyer, asked Ryan if he had discussed his testimony with anyone beforehand. Ryan said he had not. Nodding, Napthaly excused the witness and called *Chronicle* reporter Oscar Shuck, who testified he had discussed the case with Ryan in minute detail. The *Sun* editor called Ryan back to the stand.

"You heard what Mr. Shuck said?" Napthaly asked.

"All I know about the case," Ryan said, "is that you fired the first shot."

"You seem a bit confused," Napthaly responded.

"Well, I sort of am, at that," Ryan admitted. "I have taken about forty drinks so far today, but Shuck didn't pay for them. All I know about the case is "

"Stand down!" Napthaly roared.

Impressed, Louderback dismissed the charges against Napthaly but ordered de Young to stand trial. Mercy, however, would come from an unlikely source. Napthaly, who would go on to become a respected lawyer, became a good friend of the de Young family—much as Judge Delos Lake had. How the de Youngs made friends out of mortal enemies remains something of a mystery—perhaps it was their winning personalities. In Napthaly's case, he asked that Charles not be prosecuted, explaining that he admired the de Young brothers' gumption and their enthusiasm for a fight.

8

THE COMING MAN

THE REVEREND ISAAC KALLOCH'S TRIAL for adultery had caused much commotion along the East Coast. Newspaper publishers imbued with the entrepreneurial spirit made sure each day's testimony was transcribed for public consumption at a profitable price. The proceedings in their entirety were eventually published in pamphlet format and proved to be an instant hit, selling out multiple print runs. Kalloch tried to ignore the residual excitement and set about establishing something of a more normal routine for himself. He returned to Boston intent on resuming his pastoral duties and putting his legal woes behind him. It was a task not easily accomplished. The sordid details leaked at trial were the topic of conversation about town. Rarely, beyond the privacy of one's own bedroom, were such carnal matters even considered.

The reverend paid no attention to the stares from those he passed on the street and ignored the excited murmurs. Time, he believed, would erase the memory of his alleged transgressions. A jury had failed to convict him in a court of law. As far as he was concerned, the matter was closed. Other parties, however, harbored an entirely different opinion. Prosecuting attorney Isaac Morse was livid about his defeat; he had believed his case to be ironclad. The poison tide of Kalloch's behavior had flooded New England's moral high ground, Morse believed, defiling the region's good name and holy nature. No sooner had the jury announced its failure to reach a verdict than Morse began contemplating his strategy for a second go-around.

The public, stated one contemporary account, "believed there had been a gross miscarriage of justice." New England's reputation, the people believed, would remain sullied until Kalloch was placed behind bars, well out of reach of the fairer sex. The press agreed. The *New York Herald*, upon learning of Kalloch's mistrial, made public its disgust:

> Here we have three or four credible witnesses testify directly to the criminal processes which they had witnessed between this Reverend shepherd and one of the pet lambs of the fold; and yet he finds a jury to whitewash him, and a faithful flock who rush to his rescue and resolve that he is innocent as a child, and as clean in his high office as the apostle Paul. In this disgusting business at Boston the Reverend drinker of whiskey slings and the adulterer is exalted by church as a mode of temperance and as a persecuted enemy of purity . . . Hot whiskey, too, in spite of the liquor law, at five dollars a drink and no questions asked! Wonderful people, these Boston Puritans of Baptist persuasion.

Such editorializing only furthered Morse's determination to drag Kalloch back into a Cambridge courtroom. The press had sympathized with the prosecutor throughout the trial, noting he was a solitary figure aligned against one of the best litigators in the country. Yet, the prospect of damaging his reputation with another galling defeat must have made Morse uncomfortable.

To some in the community, however, the thought of another trial proved discomforting for reasons altogether different. Before Morse could make up his mind whether to try the case again, he was reportedly paid a visit by "men of most excellent intentions, but of doubtful wisdom," who were of the opinion that the perverse nature of the trial had already damaged the community's reputation. It might be best, these unidentified individuals suggested, if the prosecutor simply let the case go. Whether the episode is true or not, Morse did not seek a second trial and left Kalloch to pursue his pastoral duties.

The press, naturally, failed to leave it at that. Kalloch—and, more specifically, the holy man's propensity for the unholy—sold newspapers. Editors dispatched reporters to keep a careful eye on the tarnished minister. Reporters tailed him down city streets and made note of the establishments he frequented. If they were hoping to stumble across another controversy—and they were—Kalloch failed to deliver the goods.

The Tremont Temple, eager not to let recent events scare away congregants and dim its preacher's star power, voiced its unqualified support for Kalloch. One contemporary author expressed in caustic words his strong aversion to the temple and Kalloch's seemingly brainwashed followers:

> The weak-kneed brethren and lachrymose sisters received him again
> as the pastor of the fold, and, by resolution declared that "he had
> come out of the fire like pure gold, doubly refined." The man whose
> moral habiliments were all reeking with the filth, nastiness and
> disgusting details of a public trial for adultery, was forthwith ele-
> vated to the pulpit in God's House, a sight for young men and
> maidens to feed their imaginations upon. Great Heavens! What a
> sacrilegious position, to be sure!

Indeed, Kalloch's brethren and sisters rejoiced at his return. Temple trustees need not have worried about what impact the reverend's alleged escapades might have had on their institution. Upon mounting the temple's pulpit once again, Kalloch found himself preaching to a full house on a regular basis. Naturally, many filled the pews out of curiosity, eager to catch a glimpse of an infamous media sensation. They flocked to the temple by the thousands; those who couldn't get in lined the streets outside, hoping to hear the reverend's legendary voice filter through the temple walls. "The indictment being . . . rid of, and a second trial rendered impossible, he returned weeping to his congregation at Tremont Temple," noted one writer of the day. "Like Beecher, he was better qualified, he said, for the duties of the ministerial office, because of the ordeal through which he had passed. He could better sympathize with weak humanity." All the while, the media maintained its close eye on Kalloch, hoping his urges would overcome prudence.

And so things continued on this track for about a year until February 1858, when Kalloch—perhaps worn down by the endless media scrutiny and constant reminders of his past—decided a change of scenery was in order. The press proved more than eager to ponder the reasons for Kalloch's desire to move, for nothing could be straightforward. The man's every move, as far as the papers went, was the work of some dark impulse. Whatever Kalloch's true motives, the twenty-six-year-old minister tendered his resignation to temple trustees and preached his last sermon on February 14, 1858. Several days later, he was en route to Leavenworth in the Kansas territory.

———

THE EMIGRANT AID COMPANY, ORGANIZED four years prior, offered anti-slavery adherents from the Northeast incentives to settle the Kansas territory. A stout abolitionist, Kalloch had for years sermonized against slavery, so, when his friend and Emigrant Aid agent Charles Robinson (a man soon to become the first governor of Kansas) asked Kalloch to join him on the frontier and advance the abolitionist cause, Kalloch was quick to accept. He ventured to what were the untamed wilds when compared to his Bostonian surroundings and set about doing what he could for the movement. The work allowed him to escape the ever-present shadow of the "Lady in Black" that loomed large in the East.

He established his home on a patch of land overlooking the Missouri River, sermonizing against slavery and trying his hands at several new pursuits such as horseracing and cattle breeding. Certainly, Kalloch kept himself busy.

He took part in the founding of Bluemont Central College—an institution that would eventually become Kansas State College—by raising funds to finance the construction of a school building. When he wasn't fund-raising, horseracing or preaching, he spent time studying successfully for the Kansas bar. All this he did within five months of reaching the territory. Indeed, things seemed to be going well for the young man.

On July 5, 1858, his fortunes changed drastically. It began with a flicker and a wisp of smoke in a theater on the corner of Third and Delaware streets, devouring the wooden buildings like kindling and growing into a massive conflagration that nearly destroyed all of Leavenworth. Kalloch's home, along with more than two dozen businesses, went up in flames. Whereas only days before he had been a man on the make, he was now left with nothing in his possession but smoldering ruins. Perhaps it was just dumb luck—or perhaps the working of a higher power—but at the moment Kalloch's life went up in smoke, a message from Boston arrived: the trustees of the Tremont Temple wanted him back.

The temple had suffered in the absence of its star preacher. The coffers were empty and the pews only half-filled. The stand-in ministers lacked Kalloch's fire and theatrical thunder. One account states Kalloch's regular audience numbered more than two thousand people; that number shrank to eighty in the wake of Kalloch's departure. When the Tremont Temple's plea to return home reached him out there in the badlands, Kalloch was more than happy to comply. But the Kansas territory, in many respects, had been a reprieve for the young minister. The people there allowed him to do as he pleased, free of media scrutiny. Returning to Boston, where he had left his wife and son for their own comfort and safety, he would again be subjecting himself to the inquisitive eye of the press.

He shrugged off such concerns and again assumed the pulpit at Tremont Temple, his wallet made fat by a generous salary of more than $5,000 a year, which the trustees paid to ensure their star stayed put. "The man Kalloch had triumphed for the time," wrote one of Kalloch's many critics. "He had been forgiven, and installed once more in the highest place in the Holy of Holies. Now was the time to repent, eschew evil and learn to live righteously. He had passed through a terrible exposure—one that would have utterly crushed ordinary clergymen, and caused them to bow their heads in shame for the rest of their lives." Kalloch, on the contrary, exhibited the same confident mien for which he was known. His powerful oratory again replenished the temple's dwindling funds and bolstered the number of congregants.

In tending to the temple's business, Kalloch again opened himself up to controversy. "The sanctity of the temple," bemoaned one writer, "was not proof against his defilement." He often met with members of his congregation and counseled them in personal matters, but such ministrations—when done for the benefit of young and attractive women—riled the suspicions of those who still believed the minister to be morally corrupt. Perhaps it was inevitable that accusations, whether true or not, would eventually be made.

The temple's maintenance worker, a man named Hayes, stepped forward to say he was witness to improper behavior. It seemed the reverend, according to Hayes, was in the habit of meeting with his female congregants behind closed office doors until late into the evening. The accusation lacked the overt debauchery of Kalloch's Cambridge escapade and was more than likely much ado about nothing. Still, it was investigated. Called before the temple's board of trustees and asked to explain himself, Kalloch said he was merely performing his ministerial duties. As there was no evidence to suggest otherwise, temple officials considered the matter a non-issue—much to the chagrin of one New York paper:

> The Committee thinks it was indiscreet of Brother Kalloch to receive a young lady in his private room, and remain alone with her till so late an hour; but they have no doubt that, as Kalloch asserts, she was in a state of mind which required immediate private conversation on the part of her pastor. What self-sacrifice, devotion!

Kalloch could see the storm clouds gathering and began pondering his next move. The smartest course of action seemed to be another out-of-town adventure, although he had been back in Boston for little more than a year. Nevertheless, he had no desire to be thrashed once again on the front pages of

New England's papers. Circumstances beyond his control had forced Kalloch to take early leave of Kansas; now struck him as the perfect time to return and finish his work.

He bid farewell to his congregation on Sunday, May 27, 1860, before again leaving his family in the comfort of more civilized surroundings and departing for Leavenworth. He arrived in a region ravaged by drought. "The Kansas River is lower than ever known, and most of the small streams of the territory are dry," wrote a correspondent for the *New York Times*. Settlers were fleeing the territory by the thousands, placing all they owned in battered wagons in the hope of finding a more hospitable environment. "There is some great social convulsion now being felt in Kansas," the *Times* correspondent reported. "The only thing novel in the meteorological line is yesterday was a cloudy day, and the sun was seen but once—a thing scarcely within our remembrance."

Conditions were detailed in a July 10, 1860, article in Leavenworth's *Daily Times*:

> The heat of yesterday was almost intolerable. It was the remark of every one that they had never experienced anything like it. The wind was dry and burning; and the atmosphere betokened a severe storm or hurricane. The thermometer stood as high as 108°.

The heat was so oppressive four days later, the paper declared the "gates of hell (metaphorically speaking) had been thrown open." Kalloch did not stay long in the sun-baked territory. Concerned by the hardships he witnessed, he returned to the East Coast at year's end to raise funds for the territory's beleaguered settlers. He called upon the charity of his former congregants at the Tremont Temple before heading to New York, where he assumed the pastorate at Laight Street Baptist Church on February 27, 1861. James Pyle, a church member, recalled in later years that Kalloch made quite the impression:

His height was 6 feet, and he had a supple figure, and weighed about 190 pounds. His hands and feet were remarkably small, his head was massive, his hair dark and auburn and curly, his features exceedingly expressive. The women admired Kalloch, ran to him with their stories of trouble, compared notes with one another in regard to what he said to each and then quarreled over what they chose to call the quality of his compliments.

Church leaders were unconcerned with Kalloch's past, believing him to be the victim of vindictive newspaper editors, gossipmongers and powerful business interests who had orchestrated the adultery charges out of Cambridge as a means to discredit Kalloch's character. "He was the foremost preacher in Boston and the most effective and persistent advocate of temperance ever seen, perhaps, in the country," a Laight Street congregant opined. "While he lived and maintained his position he seriously interfered with the liquor traffic. The liquor interest determined to put him down. The quickest way to put a clergyman down is to put a stain, a doubt, upon his reputation."

As he had done at the Tremont Temple, Kalloch drew large and enthusiastic crowds to the Laight Street ministry. "Our church never flourished so well as during Mr. Kalloch's pastorate," Pyle would later recall. "He soon became the best-known pulpit orator in New York, and his church was always too small to accommodate the crowds that flocked to hear him." He preached against the evils of liquor, despite his reported enthusiasm for whiskey, and railed against the moral stain of slavery. His devotion to the abolitionist cause took on an added sense of urgency following the Confederate attack on Fort Sumter in South Carolina on April 12, 1861.

The outbreak of hostilities between the North and South, Kalloch sermonized, was not a war of politics but a "contest between two civilizations; or rather between civilization and barbarism; and its issue bears upon the fate not only of slaves, but of free men; not only of black men, but of white men; not only of America, but the world." He thundered on with passionate eloquence:

The consolidation of a Southern Empire with slavery as its chief cornerstone . . . would be a surrender of all that has been won in the past—would be a relapse into a condition much worse than that from which our fathers emerged through seas of blood. Can anyone doubt the disastrous effects of Southern supremacy? The South is the type and asserter of Oriental Absolutism—the defender of the divine rights of tyrants. We are fighting in the noblest cause in which weapons can be wielded, or armor girded on, or treasure lavished, or willing blood poured out like water.

Churchgoers described Kalloch's oratory as "simply overwhelming" and his arguments as "scholarly," but this did nothing to appease those who viewed the reverend as an abomination to the cloth. Papers continued to harp on Kalloch's past and sought to uncover scandal in his relationships with Laight Street's female congregants. Rumors again began to circulate regarding Kalloch's activities behind closed doors. Congregant and friend James Pyle later theorized the saucy speculation was the result of jealous women in the Laight Street ministry who misconstrued the reverend's ministrations with other women. These were just stories "with scandalous flavors attached," Pyle claimed. No evidence materialized to suggest Kalloch ever behaved improperly.

Kalloch remained at Laight Street for three years before resigning on April 3, 1864. Those who opposed the reverend in later years would accuse him of leaving New York under a dark cloud of drink and carnality. This, however, was not the case and only exemplified the burden of Kalloch's permanently tarnished reputation. "I never saw a fault in his disposition as a clergyman," wrote Pyle. "There are thousands of intelligent people still living in this City who heard him in those exciting days, doing his best for the cause of right and freedom, who will gladly echo what I say."

Memories of the Reverend Isaac Kalloch in Kansas, where he again returned and spent the next eleven years, would not prove to be so kind.

UPON HIS RETURN TO KANSAS, Kalloch busied himself with a number of large-scale enterprises, helping to establish the town of Ottawa and founding several newspapers. Before leaving New York, Kalloch had been appointed by the American Baptist Home Mission Society to be its representative in the West. The society, formed in 1832, offered spiritual encouragement to those settling the frontier. Being appointed its representative granted Kalloch a place on the board of trustees for the germinal Roger Williams University, a Baptist institution of higher learning that had yet to be built. Kalloch's mission in Kansas was to find a suitable location for the school.

Kalloch found an attractive piece of land along the Marais des Cygnes (River of Swans), an area owned by the Ottawa Indians. An agreement was reached between the school's board of trustees and local tribes that called for the native people to sell twenty thousand acres of choice land "in return for the privilege of having children of the tribe, not to exceed thirty in number, clothed, fed and educated each year for thirty years." A percentage of the proceeds from the land sale was earmarked for a permanent fund, interest from which would be applied to educating children from the local tribes. In April 1865, however, with Kalloch serving as the board of trustees' president, it emerged that thousands of dollars had been borrowed from the fund to finance the escalating cost of school construction.

Kalloch, who also served as school treasurer, used the "borrowed" funds to pay off various laborers working on the project before selling 2,800 acres of school land to recoup the costs. Though proceeds from the sale—some $15,000—went unaccounted for, Kalloch used his oratorical prowess to convince the other trustees he had done it all for the betterment of the school, now named Ottawa College. The board accepted Kalloch's story and allowed him to resign on good terms shortly thereafter when he announced that he wished to pursue other business interests. The unfortunate episode would leave a bad taste in the mouths of many, including the editors of the New York Times, who summarized events six years after the fact:

A wealthy, progressive Christian Indian tribe, cajoled by white men,
some or all of whom professed to follow in their actions the precepts
of Christianity, have permitted their entire wealth—school lands,
trust fund, and allotments—to go to endow a pretentious University
for the education of white children, and are dependent on the
charity of individuals or the Government for life itself.

Kalloch had occupied himself with a number of side ventures while
serving on the school's board of trustees. On September 1, 1864, before the
land scandal came to light, he had organized a town company with James
Wind, an Ottawa chief. Like the land the school was being built on, the
acreage for the planned town was located within the Ottawa Indian Reservation, thus providing the town with its name. In June 1865, to lure settlers to
the small establishment on the southern shore of the Marais des Cygnes,
Kalloch published the first issue of the *Western Home Journal*. A weekly newspaper, the publication was four pages in length and featured, in addition to
national news, stories focusing on the home, school and church. It would
prove to be the first of several forays Kalloch made into newspaper publishing.

The town of Ottawa was incorporated in 1866 and voted to become a
city in October of the following year. Kalloch, in the meantime, had added
the occupation of railroad magnate to his growing résumé, incorporating the
Lawrence, Leavenworth and Galveston Railroad on June 5, 1865, as a means
of bringing more commerce and settlers to his burgeoning city on the river-
bank. But as with most Kalloch enterprises, scandal soon followed when it
emerged that local county commissioners had loaned the railroad (meaning
Kalloch) $32,000 to meet certain tax obligations. The loan was not repaid,
prompting conversations among many local residents of public hangings and
other unsavory forms of frontier justice. Kalloch, who keenly interpreted the
public mood, made himself scarce and fled to Missouri until the controversy
blew over.

If the public was quick to forgive Kalloch, John Speer, editor of the

Kansas Tribune, was not. "The infamous life of this besotted priest," he wrote in his paper, "is beginning to be known." Kalloch paid scant attention to Speer's printed attack, for he had a deadline to meet. In securing funding for the railroad, Kalloch had received a $200,000 bond from Franklin County on the stipulation that the first train roll into Ottawa by January 1, 1868. Similar arrangements had been made with neighboring Douglas and Anderson counties. Returning from his self-imposed exile, Kalloch employed cheap Chinese rail workers to lay tracks at a feverish pace across a vast stretch of untamed land, allowing a train to roll into Ottawa with mere hours to spare before the deadline.

ALTHOUGH FAR REMOVED FROM EAST Coast society, Kalloch soon found rumors regarding his past dalliances drifting from town to town across the frontier's prairies like tumbleweed. "I believe one reason why the women worship him is on account of the illimitable capacity of his lachrymal glands," noted one Kansas writer. "There has never existed a man with such a faculty for throwing open the sluice gates of gush." When Kalloch moved to Lawrence in 1869, the *Kansas Tribune* compared him to "The Coming Man," as described in the Book of Job: "Lo now, his strength is in his loins, and his force is in the navel of his belly."

A rumor that soon emerged, suggesting Kalloch had debauched the daughter of a fellow Baptist minister, did nothing to enhance his reputation. The minister in question, Dr. Butler, "was a venerable, grey-haired, old man, respected and beloved by all." One account published several years after the alleged event claimed Butler's daughter, "in the splendor of her youthful beauty, attracted the attention of the Reverend debaucher, Kalloch." He had his way with her in the back room of a Baptist church in Lawrence, thus incurring the apocalyptic wrath of the esteemed Dr. Butler. When confronted by the woman's father, Kalloch supposedly laughed the situation off, telling Butler, "Oh, she's a whore, anyway. You must not blame any man for taking what was laying around loose."

With little concern for its veracity, the press ran with the story. On May 8, 1870, the *Lawrence Tribune* ran an article headlined "Kalloch the Brute":

> If he has any sympathy, let him bestow it upon the poor old Baptist minister whose daughter he seduced. A debased wretch, who baptizes a girl and then seduces her in the vestibule of a sanctuary, is not expected to show generosity to any human being. It has been known for years that this dirty scoundrel involved as good a man as ever lived in Douglas County in difficulties, which broke him in spirit and ruined him. In the Ottawa Indian transaction there was an honest man and a thief, a virtuous man and a prostitute. The honest man travels on foot, the thief rides in a chariot; the virtuous man delivers all his property to his bondsmen, the prostitute conveys his to his wife. The name of that thief, coward and scoundrel is Isaac S. Kalloch.

Galling as such publicity was, it did little to impede Kalloch's professional pursuits. In March 1869, he began publishing the *Daily Republican Journal* and founded the Douglas County Agricultural and Mechanical Association. Two years later, he purchased the Eldridge House, a high-end hotel replete with saloon. His foray into the hospitality business only encouraged more scurrilous rumors. One story that made the rounds alleged that he "never kept a woman in the hotel who didn't come to his room at any hour, day or night, if he sent for her." According to that highly exaggerated account, Kalloch was having drinks with a friend named Charley Garrett one night at the hotel bar when he made the boastful claim:

> By way of proving this, he there and then sent for each woman, one after the other, took them to his room, and staid with them. He sent for seven before he stopped, the majority of them being colored women. "There," he said to Charley, "I have solved the problem of how to run a hotel and a bawdy house at the same time."

Kalloch, as was his usual practice, ignored the abuse lest he draw more attention to it and launched his third newspaper, the *Spirit of Kansas*, in February 1872. He coupled this effort with a run for the state legislature as an Independent despite long denying any interest in public office. The press played up his lecherous side, alleging a ravenous lust for sex and an insatiable thirst for whiskey. So repetitive had such accusations become, they did little to shock the electorate. Kalloch's opponents—one of whom dropped out the day before the election amid rumors that Kalloch had slipped him a handsome sum to concede defeat—were of a lackluster caliber and also did little to threaten his candidacy. In the end, Kalloch, opposed by a sole Democrat, emerged victorious and served as Kansas state representative during the 1873 legislative session.

Whatever good Kalloch accomplished in his new political role was overshadowed by a scandal involving Kansas state senator and friend Samuel C. Pomeroy, who stood accused of bribing another state senator to secure a vote for reelection. The allegations ended Pomeroy's senatorial career and rendered all other issues that legislative session forgettable.

It was just as well, for Kalloch's political career in Kansas did not last long. In September 1873, banking giant Jay Cooke and Company, which helped the U.S. government finance the Civil War and invested heavily in the post-conflict railroad boom, collapsed under the weight of its numerous investments and declared bankruptcy. The ensuing financial panic spread from coast to coast. Investments soured, jobs were lost, and homes were seized. Financial pressures on the home front spurred Kalloch not to seek reelection.

In the depression that followed, Kalloch—now a father of five, his youngest child having been born in early 1872—lost his stately Lawrence manor and nearly all he possessed. His gift for oratory, however, remained immune to the fluctuations of the market and prompted him to hit the lecture circuit for cash. He proved a popular attraction as in his early days and drew enthusiastic crowds wherever he appeared. The elders of the First Baptist Church of Leavenworth took keen interest in Kalloch's popularity and offered him a $3,000-per-year pastoral position in January 1874. The man Kansas papers now referred to as "the Sorrel Stallion" accepted.

The church was an impressive structure with seating for a thousand, but Kalloch's tenure there did not last long. In February 1875, he ventured to San Francisco on the invitation of West Coast Baptist leaders to speak at several city churches. In each case, he drew large crowds. The large audiences prompted the Reverend Edward Hammond, a revivalist of national renown, to suggest San Francisco's two largest Baptist churches come together as one with Kalloch as pastor. Kalloch greeted the idea with much enthusiasm and proposed other Baptist ministries join the effort to create the nation's largest church. He envisioned a temple of grand design with unmatched seating capacity, and was happy when the Baptist hierarchy voiced its approval of the plan, meeting his salary demand of $5,000 per year.

More than satisfied with the agreement, Kalloch returned to Kansas in March to bid farewell to his shocked congregation in Leavenworth. Asked why he was leaving, Kalloch—keeping silent on the financial aspects— replied in grave tones that he felt compelled to "go to San Francisco because there are more wicked people of both sexes in that city than I ever met with in my life, and I feel called by God to convert them."

9

FIRE AND POLITICS

A S THE CLOCK STRUCK SEVEN on Wednesday, July 25, 1877, an evening breeze blew mist in from the water and veiled lantern-lit streets in a spectral gray. Some three hundred people were gathered in a vacant sandlot near the new City Hall on Market Street, where planks had been laid across three trestles to form a makeshift speaker's platform. An appeal in one of the city's morning papers, calling for a "great anti-Coolie mass meeting," had summoned the masses to this sandy lot. Such meetings had become commonplace, earning those in attendance the name "sandlotters." A group of teenage boys lit fires in tar barrels on either side of the stage, attracting more people to the scene.

The meeting, in part, was to voice support for striking railroad workers on the East Coast. Nine days earlier in Martinsburg, West Virginia, Baltimore and Ohio Railroad workers had protested a decrease in their wages—the second such cut that year. Discontent quickly spread to other cities, including Pittsburgh, Pennsylvania, where frustration with meager pay exploded into violent rioting.

The situation was bleak nationwide. The economic panic of 1873 was long-lasting in its repercussions. Unemployment remained a common scourge, as did the slouch-shouldered breadlines. Desperate men in San Francisco gathered each morning before dawn, some slugging it out for a place in line, hoping to be selected for manual labor in Golden Gate Park. Ten hours of backbreaking work would earn the fortunate few one dollar and a corned-beef sandwich.

Reasons for the economic depression were plentiful and complex, but it became a matter of convenience to blame the Chinese. By the mid-1870s, San Francisco was home to roughly fifty thousand Chinese—about seven-eighths of the country's Chinese population. The mines had been tapped of gold and silver, and the final spike had been driven into the Transcontinental Railroad. White laborers frustrated by unemployment lashed out against the Chinese, who posed stiff marketplace competition with their willingness to work for wages others deemed unacceptable. And so the discontents and the curious gathered outside City Hall that Wednesday night in July. Noted a reporter for the *Examiner:*

> The majority bore the ineffaceable stamp that early debauchery and villainy marks as with the brand of Cain, the countenance of the hoodlums who infest this city. Interspersed among the crowd was a sprinkling of decent working men and curiosity-inspired sight-seers.

James F. D'Arcy—organizer of the Workingmen's Party of the United States in Chicago—presided over the meeting, which got under way at 8 PM. Several resolutions were quickly passed; one expressed sympathy for the striking railway workers back East, while another declared, "all railroad property in the disturbed districts should be condemned to public use." Speakers then ascended the stage and bombarded the growing crowd of onlookers with vitriolic rants against the "Celestial" (as the Chinese were often called) presence. A white laborer named N. P. Brock was the first to address the crowd and delivered his poisonous diatribe in a whiskey-induced haze. The question facing the nation, Brock proclaimed with slurred words, was who would be the first to leave the country: the white man or the Chinaman? Right-thinking people had two months to decide, he said, for the Pacific Mail Steamship Company was scheduled to deliver twenty-five thousand more Chinese to San Francisco by the end of October. He suggested blowing any Chinese ship out of the water before it even had a chance to dock. "As a windup," reported the *Chronicle*, "he announced his readiness to instantly lead a forlorn [mob] into Chinatown and burn it down."

"The centre of the meeting was orderly enough, but the many thousands present could not hear or participate in the business transacted on the platform," recalled twenty-three-year-old Jerome Hart, future editor of the weekly *San Francisco Argonaut*. A motley selection of boys and young men on the fringes of the crowd worked its way toward the stage, jeering speakers and routinely pelting them with garbage. When a doctor named Charles W. Moore pushed his way to the front and urged a non-violent resolution to the Chinese issue, a "jocose portion" of the remaining crowd pulled the planks of the stage out from under Moore's feet and knocked him to the ground. "Various agitators," Hart later wrote, "stirred up the crowd."

After the meeting had come to an official end, a crowd of about two hundred young men still loitered in the area. The *Examiner* reporter noted the stragglers seemed "anxious and ready for any villainy at which they could set their busy hands." The tipping of the stage had roused an "appetite for mischief." The crowd now moved as one across the sandlot onto Market Street and down to the corner of Seventh Street. The members—"boys ranging from 12 to 16 years of age, with enough men mixed in with them to guide and give them countenance"—stopped and conversed among themselves. A *Chronicle* scribe stood at a safe distance and recorded the particulars in his notebook:

> The two ringleaders appeared to be a drunken man in a red
> flannel shirt, evidently a Yorkshire man from his dialect, and who

occasionally issued orders in the choices off [sic] thieves' jargon, and
the other was an excellently dressed dapper little fellow, with jockey
cap, who appears to have made out in advance a complete plan of
the night's campaign, as he would walk to and fro through the
crowd and give the exact location of the places to be attacked.

The ragtag collective, with the reporter trailing, moved down the east
side of Seventh and turned onto Howard. When they passed a basement store
"slightly Chinese" in appearance, the younger boys pulled stones from their
pockets and hurled them at the windows. The sound of exploding glass and
raucous cheering prompted neighboring shopkeepers to lower their shutters
and scurry for cover behind their counters.

The gang continued its offensive, stomping down Howard and stopping
outside No. 1051, a washhouse owned by Hong Soon. Urged on by the
drunken Yorkshireman, the gang attacked the premises with stones and clubs.
Windows were shattered and doors were pounded in by heavy feet. "The shiv-
ering glass and crackling timbers," wrote the reporter, "inspired the gang."
Frenzied by violent action, the mob ran to the next block and charged a Chinese laundry at No. 924:

This they stormed, smashing the windows and breaking through the
door, overturned a stove containing a fire. With yells of delight, the
mob hurled a few cobblestones against the house.

E. M. Piercy was the lone officer to respond to the chaos. He set upon the
gang with his locust club, swinging the weapon with much enthusiasm and
dealing several skulls a hard blow before the mob counterattacked with cobblestones pulled from the street. Piercy jumped and ducked to avoid the
improvised cannonade. He returned his club to its sheath and drew his
sidearm with "praiseworthy bravery," threatening to blast a hole in the next
person who dared hurl a rock in his direction.

The sudden flash of iron in Piercy's hand convinced the mob to turn its
destructive attention elsewhere. It fled down the block but stopped long

enough to smash the windows of a washhouse at 707 Howard Street. One ruffian ripped a board from the planked sidewalk and used it as a battering ram to force his way into Yee Wah's washhouse several buildings down. The mob now had an audience:

> During the destruction, crowds of citizens watched the proceedings from Third Street without interfering, as indeed was the case during the whole career of the mob. The band then moved in groups down Howard Street to Second under the lead of a drunken man of gigantic stature, who rent the air with his demoniacal yell . . . Upon reaching Second Street, the mob received reinforcements and now numbered about 250.

The mob cut a destructive swath down Second Street and turned onto Clementina. A seventeen-year-old boy "with a huge collar, a natty coat, jockey cap and jaunty air," urged all onlookers to take foot and fist to the "damned Chinese." The mob grew in size as riotous individuals rushed from their homes and bolstered the ranks. One laundry ransacked by the hoodlums belonged not to a Chinaman, but an Irish woman, who ran from the premises and begged that her business be spared. The crowd, now numbering four hundred people, moved on in search of a better target. Spectators scrambled up on roofs or stood in their doorways and encouraged the hoodlums with rounds of applause.

Swinging planks and throwing stones, the mob charged down First Street before turning back onto Howard. Ning Guin, owner of a laundry shop at No. 565, had done all he could to fortify his business. He shuttered the windows, piled furniture against the door and sought cover in the back when he heard the approaching menace. The hooligans tore up the plank sidewalk in front of the shop and assailed the storefront with wood and stone. One member of the mob, described as a "hoodlum of tender years," scaled the side of the building and kicked down the large sign that stood atop the roof. The sign, advertising Ning Guin's business, splintered in the street below and drew barbaric cheers from the crowd. Some members of the gang, inspired by the euphoric madness, struck matches and decided to burn the place down. Only the pleas of a woman living next door saved Ning Guin's battered shop from a fiery fate.

The crowd made its way back to Howard, turned onto Fourth Street and headed to Minna in search of a new stomping ground. At No. 336, the vandals targeted a Chinese laundry shop. They gripped their clubs and stones and went to work. Recalled one witness:

> After a few blows upon the shutters, the stormers were greeted with a pistol bullet fired through the door by the Celestial within. The ball missed the roughs but hit the church across the way. The hoodlums fled like sheep, tumbling over one another in their haste to get away. The crowd of spectators hissed and yelled, and the hoodlums returned to the assault.

The Chinese man inside the besieged structure fired again. The volley damaged only the shutters drawn across the windows. The crowd on the street cheered the poor man's miserable aim and readied themselves for another attack. It was at that moment a police officer arrived on scene and slapped cuffs on the smartly dressed ringleader. The other chief rabble-rouser—the inebriated Yorkshireman—fled and never returned. The seventeen-year-old boy, who had exhorted his fellow malefactors to stomp all Chinese, assumed command and was promptly hauled off by another cop.

The mob roared its disapproval and threatened physical harm if the officer did not release the teen. Backed by a number of reporters, the policeman drew his gun and arrested several more members of the angry pack. With the newsmen lending a hand, the officer marched his detainees off to the city prison. "This effectively dispersed the mob, which went off in squads to organize gangs and commit other outrages elsewhere," reported the *Examiner*. "This closed the principal raid on the Mongol wash-houses for the evening."

The gang dispersed under a sky that glowed the color of blood.

AT 8 PM, A WATCHMAN guarding the warehouses and lumberyards along the wharf on Beale Street spied a figure crouching between two stacked piles of lumber. Except for the gentle lapping of water against the dock's wooden pylons, all was quiet as the watchman—his security lantern casting a cone of yellow light at his feet—approached the mysterious silhouette. Whoever the intruder was, he appeared to be busying himself with a large stack of wood that adjoined the northwest corner of one of the many warehouses owned by the Lumber Association and Bartlett & Company. The stranger, focused on his task, remained unaware he'd been spotted until the light from the watchman's lantern bathed him in its weak glow.

The intruder, a man with gray hair, leapt to his feet and flashed his heels. The watchman gave chase, jumping to avoid a can of lighted shavings the stranger dropped in his surprise, only abandoning his pursuit when he heard someone scream, "Fire!" He returned quickly to where the chase had begun and found the lumber pile engulfed in flames. The watchman ran to the nearby Pacific Mail Dock and pulled the alarm for Fire Station 59, which was located at the dock.

The fire spread quickly. In the warehouses sat more than a hundred barrels of whale oil, which ruptured and slopped burning oil everywhere. The flaming liquid oozed from the burning warehouses and passed under the many stacks of lumber, sending them up in violent conflagrations. "In one instant, the whole wharf was one intense and living sea of flame," the *Chronicle* reported. "A lurid glare illuminated the southern sky and attracted a large assemblage to the cliffs at the foot of First Street, from which an excellent view of the fire could be had."

It was on this bluff at the end of First Street that the riotous mob assembled after trashing the Chinese washhouses. The hoodlums cheered and hollered at the sight of the flames and made a spectacle of their revelry. Their exultation turned to rage when a woman, leaning from an upstairs window of a nearby house, opened fire on the crowd below. The slugs missed their mark, but riled the vandals into a rock-throwing frenzy. From atop their First Street bluff vantage point, they hurled cobblestones and insults on a crowd that had gathered below to watch the fire. Three police officers, their locust clubs at the ready, approached the mob and ordered them to disperse. The response was immediate. A projectile smashed an officer named Wilson in the side of the head and knocked him out cold. The other officers set upon the crowd with flailing arms and forced a temporary retreat.

Elsewhere, four hundred members of the Vigilance Committee—intent on restoring order—convened at Horticultural Hall under the leadership of General H. A. Cobb. They marched, armed with pick handles, up Fremont Street in the direction of the fire. A number of rioters along the Committee's marching route derided the procession with insults and bodily fluids. One thug pulled a gun, fired into the well-disciplined ranks and sent a man to the cobblestone street with a bullet in his side. A few Committee members split off to drag the injured man to a nearby house and summon a doctor while the others continued on their way.

Once at the fire, the Committee surrounded the burn area to prevent all nonauthorized personnel from entering. This display of order outraged the ruffians on the First Street bluff overhead, where the clash with police continued. "Many of the officers came back with severe contusions on heads and bodies, caused by the volleys of stones," noted one reporter. No one seemed immune to the mob's wrath:

> An engine and hose-cart drove furiously around the corner, and were greeted with a volley of missiles during the passage. The hose-cart ran over a man named Joseph Wentworth, a sail-maker on the ship *Thurland Castle*, who was fatally injured.

Seven police officers, led by Sergeant Harmon, ascended the east side of the First Street bluff and crawled along the edge of the hill to launch a surprise attack. The officers threw themselves at the opposition—by now reinforced by recent arrivals to the growing mob—with admirable ferocity. A news scribe standing below the bluff noted, "The thud of the clubs could be distinctly heard on the plain below as they came down upon the heads of the hoodlums. The crowd melted almost instantaneously in response to the vigorous attack of the officers," retreating halfway down the hill, where a side street passed in front of St. Mary's Hospital. There, the mob readied itself for a final stand. The officers advanced, and the battle was short but savage:

> From one of the houses, volleys from revolvers and showers of stones issued, and in very self-preservation, the officers were compelled to draw and fire in return. About this time, about seventy-five of the Committee charged up the hill in the face of a shower of stones. As they went up the hill, several dropped out of the ranks through having been hit by stones, but the officers above made a vigorous fight, and the combined onslaught of both detachments finally resulted in a total rout of the hoodlums.

A thug named Bailey took a police bullet behind the ear. Another went down when a slug tore through his shoulder. Both survived their wounds. Three policemen were shot—one by his own gun when it fell from his jacket, discharged and put a bullet in his thigh. He was carried to a hospital in critical condition. An officer named Palsons survived a bullet to the head, while another lawman took a round in the leg. At the corner of Spear and Harrison streets, where rioters and police thrashed one another, two ruffians suffered gunshot wounds after shooting it out with officers.

In the following day's *Chronicle*, the paper reported twenty-two men sustained injuries of varying degrees from rocks, clubs and bullets; four were killed that night. The fire at the wharf caused more than $130,000 in damage. "The firemen complained of a lack of fresh water on the wharf," reported the *Examiner*, "and which had to be carried in buckets to feed the engines."

Amid such carnage, one man would find political opportunity.

———————

A MAN NOT AVERSE TO violent action, political agitator Denis Kearney worked San Francisco's poor into a volatile lather that kicked, screamed and beat its way into city politics in the mid-1870s. Born in Ireland in 1847,

Kearney spent his childhood at sea and arrived in San Francisco as a mate on a sailing vessel in 1867. His lack of skill with pen and paper, and his nearly total inability to read, proved to be of little hindrance when he pursued his master's certificate the following year. In 1876, he settled permanently in San Francisco and obtained his American citizenship. He established himself in the draying business, and, through force of personality and a gift for loudmouthed rhetoric, became a leader of the Draymen's and Teamster's Union. In this capacity, he proved to be a dynamic speaker who employed incendiary language to tap into the angst of common workers.

Denis Kearney, the social agitator who capitalized on anti-Chinese sentiment in his bid for political power
[PHOTO COURTESY OF THE CALIFORNIA HISTORY ROOM, CALIFORNIA STATE LIBRARY, SACRAMENTO, CALIFORNIA]

In the wake of the riots, San Francisco's workingmen politicized their discontent by organizing the Workingmen's Trade and Labor Union. The group held its first meeting on August 22, 1877, electing J. G. Day as president and Denis Kearney as secretary. It did not waste time asserting itself on the political landscape. Less than a month after its formation, the union changed its name to the Workingmen's Party of California and began calling for a shorter workday. It demanded city officials be paid the same salary as common laborers, denounced the Republican and Democratic parties and sought the dissolution of major banks to encourage a more equal distribution of wealth. The movement spread to other California cities and marked, in the words of one observer, "the beginning of a movement destined profoundly to affect the government of the State."

In no time the Workingmen's Party was holding regular Sunday meetings.

Kearney loomed large at these gatherings and ranted from the pulpit about his dislike for the Chinese, his hatred for big business and his desire to rout city government. As he made clear in one early speech:

> The Central Pacific Railroad men are thieves, and will soon feel the power of the workingmen. When I have thoroughly organized my party, we will march through the city and compel the thieves to give up their plunder. I will lead you to City Hall, clean out the police force, hang the Prosecuting Attorney, burn every book that has a particle of law in it, and then enact new laws for the workingmen. I will give the Central Pacific just three months to discharge their Chinamen, and if that is not done, Stanford and his crowd will have to take the consequences.

Kearney cut an imposing figure in his drayman's leather apron. Sometimes, while he spoke, he dangled a noosed rope from his hands. "Judge Lynch is the only judge we want!" he roared in his pronounced brogue. He encouraged the party's growing ranks to carry muskets and ammunition. He adopted "The Chinese must go!" as his personal slogan—ignoring the fact he himself was an immigrant—and screamed the phrase at the opening and closing of every speech.

On October 5, 1877, the party met to establish a permanent political organization. Its platform was at once ludicrous and extreme, aiming to expel all Chinese labor from the country, wrestle government from the rich, elect only Workingmen to office and "tax the wealthy so as to make great wealth impossible." The *Chronicle* quoted Kearney:

> We propose to rid the country of cheap Chinese labor as soon as possible, and by all the means in our power, because it tends still more to degrade labor and aggrandize capital . . . The party will then wait upon all those who employ Chinese and ask for their discharge, and it will mark as public enemies those who refuse to comply with their request.

From his Montgomery Street office, Charles de Young viewed Kearney as both a curiosity and a business opportunity. The *Chronicle* and the *Call* were still embroiled in a war for advertising and circulation. The *Call* reigned supreme on the classified advertising front, denying the *Chronicle* and other dailies a valued source of revenue. De Young sought to knock the *Call* from its perch, and saw in Kearney a means to pursue that end. Loring Pickering, too, saw in Kearney a chance to stay on top. Both papers began dispatching reporters to the Sunday gatherings and reprinting the full text of Kearney's incendiary speeches. The competing publishers both hoped to win the loyalty of the working class and bring more readers and advertising dollars to their respective publications.

———

THE MANSIONS OF NOB HILL were palatial in design, built against a backdrop of stunning bay views. Here, on the highest point of California Street, three of the major railroad barons—Leland Stanford, Charles Crocker and Mark Hopkins—resided in cash-drenched luxury. It was just the kind of lifestyle the Workingmen found repulsive: a select few living in opulent monuments to wealth built on the sweat and blood of the underprivileged. Kearney, wanting to take his message directly to the enemy, rallied his followers to a meeting on Nob Hill on the night of October 29. Several thousand people heeded the call.

"California-street Hill is steep and lofty," reported the *Chronicle*, "and enthusiastic indeed must be the workingmen to trudge up its acclivity, to stand in the cutting night wind and listen to the speeches of reformers." They gathered outside Crocker's mansion, where a makeshift platform had been raised for the occasion. Bonfires burned in large lime barrels and gave the proceedings a primal air. Kearney mounted the stage to enthusiastic applause and "thundered forth his philippics against the rich." He trounced from one end of the stage to the other, bellowing in the flickering light of the fires and threatening to hang "railroad magnets, thieving millionaires and scoundrelly officials." His audience cheered when he dared the courts to indict him for inciting violence against the state's business and power elites. If incarcerated, he roared, his legions would "destroy all the rich hell hounds in California."

The speech unnerved city leaders, who feared more riots. Police arrested Kearney on November 3 at a rally on Kearny Street, charged him with attempting to incite a riot and tossed him in the city jail. Rather than intimidate party loyalists, Kearney's incarceration galvanized the movement, which strengthened its ranks with greater numbers. Kearney was quickly acquitted and released. His followers celebrated several days later with a Thanksgiving Day parade in which more than seven thousand Workingmen—toting signs that read, "This is a country for free white labor, not coolie labor" and "Labor shall be King"—marched on City Hall. Speeches threatening fire and destruction to the Chinese and big business were again delivered to a cheering public.

Kearney was now in a position of near-absolute power among the Workingmen. Only days earlier, John Day, tired of Kearney's inflammatory language, had resigned as party president. Where others heard revolutionary ideas in the Irishman's angry rhetoric, Day heard only empty promises. "I'm tired of hearing his nonsensical speeches about what he is going to do if things don't go the way he wants them," Day told one compatriot. He had simply rolled his eyes and shook his head when, at one meeting, Kearney announced, "bullets would replace ballots."

An attempt by Day to ascend the stage at the meeting and speak his point of view did not sit well with the audience. Jeered and derided by Kearney enthusiasts, Day promptly surrendered the presidency and scurried from the meeting.

Kearney was now in charge. He encouraged the militant aspect of the organization, formed military companies within the party and assumed the rank of lieutenant general. Members wore a uniform of black pants, blue shirt and fatigue hat. None of this sat well with the city's politicos, who dabbed sweat from their collective brow and ordered police to haul Kearney behind bars yet again.

Between January 9 and January 16, 1878, Kearney was arrested almost daily on charges of inciting violence when—among other things—he threatened to incinerate the Pacific Mail docks. Each time he posted bail, only to be jailed once again for another vitriolic rant made in public, until finally bail was set so high that he had no choice but to languish in a cell. On January 21, party members gathered for a state convention in San Francisco and formally elected the absent Kearney as their leader. All charges against him were dropped the following day.

The party scored its first political victory two days later when Alameda County voters elected Workingmen candidate J. W. Bones state senator. Political success came quickly to the burgeoning party. Two more victories followed in March when Workingmen loyalists won the mayoral elections in Oakland and Sacramento. April and May saw Workingmen candidates ascend to power in other municipalities throughout the state of California, and Nevada too. The party had become a viable political force in three months, reflecting the discontent of the working masses.

In June, a statewide election was held to choose delegates to draft California's new constitution. There were 152 delegates in total. Some Democrats and Republicans, fearing a Workingmen's majority, came together as a "Non-Partisan" entity. The Workingmen carried San Francisco with 50 delegates. The Non-Partisans won the statewide majority with 85, while the remaining Democrats and Republicans elected eight and nine delegates, respectively.

Some newspapers denounced the Workingmen. The *Daily Record-Union* in Sacramento equated the party to Communists. "All those who are not in favor of running the State," the paper opined, "must decline to endorse the main propositions of the so-called Workingmen's Party of San Francisco." The *Chronicle*, however, stood by the party, declaring under the headline "Injustice to our Workingmen":

> Many of the papers of the country east of the Rocky Mountains
> seem never either able or disposed to properly view the condition of
> things on this coast wherein the laboring men are concerned on the
> one side, and the coolies on the other . . . So far as relates to the
> workingmen of this city, despite incendiary vaporings of blatant

demagogues and public gatherings and the occasional violence of the hoodlum element, there is not a more orderly or peacefully disposed similar class in the whole land. They want work. They are not tramps, and it is but natural and reasonable that they ought to be preferred to coolies, who are simply slaves.

The *Chronicle* set itself apart from its competition by supporting the constitution and the Workingmen, who sought to ensure that the new charter dissolve land monopolies held by the rich, deny jobs for the Chinese, regulate railroads and limit the political influence of corporations. In lending his paper's backing to the cause, de Young saw an "in" to statewide politics. Others simply saw a "mob-inspired monstrosity." Such opinions did nothing to sway de Young from his ultimate course.

In April 1879, the *Daily Record-Union* reported "that 151 newspapers in the state opposed the adoption of the proposed constitution, while only 47 favored it." Many editorial writers feared that limitations placed on railroads and corporations would precipitate the downfall of big business.

The elected delegation, after much hotly contested debate, announced on March 3, 1879, that the document was ready to be put to the people. The vote was set for the first week of May. John P. Young, managing editor of the *Chronicle*, later wrote, "Never was a paper so completely engrossed by one subject as the *Chronicle* was during the sixty-five days between March 3d and May 7th, 1879." One night, a *Chronicle* editor entered de Young's office and presented the publisher with a column headlined "One Hundred and One Reasons Why the New Constitution Should Be Adopted." De Young reviewed the copy, nodded his approval and told the editor to include it in the morning edition. Shortly before midnight, de Young approached the editor's desk and asked on what page the column would run. The editor said he was holding it because of insufficient space.

"It must go," de Young insisted.

"Come and show me where to put it," the editor said, reminding de Young that thirteen columns of space were already devoted to the constitution. Next, wrote the managing editor years later:

They adjourned to the composition room and inspected the forms. It was a hard problem he was called upon to solve, but the solution came promptly. "Take out this, and this, and this," he said, rapidly indicating a number of features on the last page; and the next morning the *Chronicle* appeared minus the bulk of its commercial matter. "They won't miss it," he remarked, "they (the public) are thinking too much about beating us to pay attention to market and stocks."

While the *Chronicle* screamed its support for the new constitution in editorials and columns, San Francisco's weekly *Argonaut* summarized the arguments of de Young's competitors: "There is much in the proposed new Constitution that is both good and new; but that which is good is not new, and that which is new is not good." The voting public, however, disagreed and approved the charter with a ten-thousand-vote majority.

The document became law on July 4, 1879, forbidding corporations from hiring Chinese labor and empowering the state legislature to limit Chinese immigration any way it saw fit. It also came down hard on big business, calling for state regulation of the water and gas industries, establishing a fixed price for railroad travel, and authorizing a commission to monitor the dealings of the major railroads.

Charles de Young relished the thrill of victory. Although San Francisco voters had rejected the constitution, de Young viewed the public's ultimate acceptance of the document as his own doing. His paper, after all, had made the most noise in its support for the law. He now made moves to consolidate what he considered his all-mighty influence, suggesting in his paper the creation of a New Constitution Party with himself as boss. "Charles de Young," notes one account, "did not swerve from a path he saw leading to unchallenged political power." It was quite a change from the young, idealistic publisher who commenced his career by swearing off political agendas and allegiances. De Young revealed his plans in the *Chronicle* a week after the polls closed:

The last election was in no sense a partisan struggle. It was an open and earnest fight for principle—a contest between the advocates of popular rights, on the one hand, and the upholders of the tyranny of monopolies. Republicans, Democrats and Working men were divided . . . Now the question to be solved is, How shall the harmonious co-operation of these voters be secured, in order to put the principles of the new Constitution into active operation?

The answer, de Young said, could be found in a temporary party "in which all the various elements favorable to the Constitution may have fair representation, and thus secure another greater victory than the last . . . It will not interfere with the organization of any existing party."

Seeking political backup, the publisher approached Kearney and the Workingmen to join ranks with the fledgling NCP. It was, de Young considered, a reasonable request in light of the Chronicle's steadfast support. But Kearney, who considered the constitution's passage his own doing, balked at such a notion. In refusing to share the political spotlight with de Young, the Irishman now made his party a target for the Chronicle's considerable firepower.

On Thursday, May 22, under the headline "Kearney's Present Standing," an aggrieved de Young took aim:

It is claimed by Kearney and his admirers that he is a great leader of men—a sort of unlettered MIRABEAU, capable of winning the hearts of the people and creating parties out of nothing. In fact, a greater orator, statesman, reformer by instinct. If the CHRONICLE does not show him up to be the merest humbug, ignoramus, blackguard and pretender, then it will be content to let him stand for all his sycophantic friends think him. KEARNEY never had a thought of his own above that of the common clodhopper.

Three days later, the paper let loose another salvo:

> The treacherous and corrupt blatherskite, KEARNEY, and the miserable dupes he holds under his whip, are telling the people that they carried the new Constitution. It is an impudent falsehood.

Daily, the newspaper slammed Kearney and the Workingmen in poisoned ink. Stories regarding "Kearney's Brutality" and "Kearney's Vulgarity" became commonplace; the paper labeled him a "blackguard" and "blatherskite," and "a stupid bully." The *Chronicle*'s pages were loaded with buckshot, and de Young had an itchy trigger finger.

It would not be long before a certain minister found himself dragged into the line of fire.

10

A WAR OF WORDS

THE METROPOLITAN TEMPLE STOOD ON the east side of Fifth Street between Jessie and Mission, opposite the U. S. Mint. Inside, the Metropolitan rivaled the ecclesiastical glory of Boston's Tremont Temple. A $14,000 pipe organ—a gleaming behemoth of polished brass knobs and rows of shining ivory—dominated the temple's main amphitheater, which sat three thousand people. Musicians played in an orchestra pit situated beneath a massive horseshoe-shaped balcony. A smaller auditorium on the second floor could host an additional thousand congregants. "It was," one witness said, "commodious and handsome." The temple, of course, was the new domain of the Rev. Isaac Kalloch, who, according to one reporter, "always seemed to have a hankering for a newspaper, a woman and an organ."

Kalloch's early days in the city were docile when compared to his previous adventures. He preached at various churches, began publishing a San

The Metropolitan Temple, on the corner of Fifth and Mission, where the Rev. Isaac Kalloch held court, rousing the ire of Charles de Young and the wrath of the *Chronicle*

[PHOTO COURTESY OF THE SAN FRANCISCO HISTORY CENTER, SAN FRANCISCO PUBLIC LIBRARY]

Francisco edition of *Evangel*—a Baptist-themed magazine he first launched in Lawrence—and continued drawing large crowds on the city's lecture circuit. Now weighing a hulking 240 pounds and still maintaining his thick, red brush of beard, Kalloch was known for his imposing physicality. And, although he was far removed from East Coast high society and the Kansas flatlands, faint whispers of something scandalous trailed Kalloch to San Francisco like an unpleasant scent. Occasionally, a reporter would approach the reverend and ask a carefully worded question, seeking to shed light on past events. The reverend would simply smile and shake his head, reminding the eager scribe that a lie—once put in print—cannot be retracted. Interesting advice in a city where newspaper editors were sometimes beaten—or killed— for printing objectionable content.

The bulk of funding for the Metropolitan Temple came courtesy of the deep-pocketed Isaac Lankershim, a real estate mogul turned Baptist deacon in Los Angeles. A thoroughly devout man, Lankershim became an instant admirer of Kalloch's after hearing the "Golden Voice" preach and agreed to sink $250,000 into the reverend's grand vision of the world's largest church. Lankershim, a Bavarian native, knew a good business investment when he saw one. From Lankershim's funds, and those donated by other true believers, Kalloch initially drew a yearly salary of $6,200 in 1876, upon the temple's completion.

Congregants paid ten cents admission in lieu of donations on Sundays to hear Kalloch preach and pontificate on all matters of the day. Kalloch's black manservant, Jim Ransome, sold tickets from a booth in the temple's vestibule. "The house was always well filled," remembered one frequent attendee, "and had quite the air of a theatre." The price of admission, once the temple opened for business, supplemented Kalloch's take-home pay by another $15,000 per annum. Noted San Francisco newspaperman Jerome Hart, who met Kalloch on several occasions:

> The Sunday evening addresses were supposed to be sermons on
> religious topics. These preludes became more and more political as
> Kalloch grew to realize his power. His audiences listened to him
> with bated breath. There was a distinct let-up when the prelude
> ended, and the pulpit orator turned preacher. The audiences then
> lost something of their tenseness.

Amid the chaos of San Francisco's race riots and the violence against railroad strikers back east, Kalloch had plenty to say. He voiced his support for the strikers and distanced himself from other clergy who believed a man worthy of existence could get by solely on bread and water. He did, however, remain largely ambivalent when discussing the Chinese to avoid potential controversy.

The reverend found the Chinese question a confounding one and often seemed indecisive on where he stood. While he openly advocated for the humane treatment of all the races, he also voiced support for preventing additional Chinese from entering the country. In an article that ran in the June 6, 1876, issue of *Evangel*, Kalloch wrote:

The Chinese furnish cheap and efficient labor as house-servants, both in town and country. They do well in our manufactories and our railroads. They fill an important niche in society in their wash-houses and huckstering.

Even in this defense of the Chinese, Kalloch exercised caution, as, opposite the Metropolitan Temple, on the steps of the U.S. Mint, angry crowds routinely gathered to vent their intense dislike for the "Celestial" presence. Kalloch often watched from his office window as the discontents rallied across the street.

He tried to stay on perfectly middle ground, preaching one Sunday, "The Chinamen who are here under treaty stipulation, must be protected from violence at all hazards, and measures taken to discourage any more from coming." But as the anti-Chinese rallies increased in size, and the rhetoric grew more vitriolic in nature, Kalloch became more robust in his arguments against the demonstrations. He watched with a critical eye the rise of Denis Kearney and was sickened by the public calls to violence. He made a strong stand from the pulpit:

These howling declaimers are not laborers. They are incendiaries. They are blatherskites. They are mercenaries. They ought to be suppressed. Their gab cannot be stopped too quickly or too effectually!

Kalloch shed all pretense of diplomacy once rioters trashed the Chinese washhouses. It was time, he bellowed to his congregation on November 18, 1877, to fight violence with violence, for savagery appeared to be the only language many in the city understood:

They are landless refugees from the old world, who neither comprehend nor love our institutions. The refuse of the Paris Commune. Incendiaries from Berlin and Tipperary. European agitators who are

at rest in no country under heaven. The Robespierres of revolution
and riot, and they need to be suppressed. The best argument for
them is the bayonet and Gatling gun.

Nine days later, during another sermon, he told his enthusiastic followers:

Napoleon's advice to quell the mob by loading with grape and firing
low is conceived in the real interest of humanity.

In his church magazine, *Evangel*, Kalloch continued his assault and dismissed the riotous mobs as "anarchists." Kearney and his ilk were reduced to
savage "demagogues."

It was a good time to be an editor. The pages of San Francisco's newspapers were packed with inflammatory words from both Kalloch and Kearney.
The bad publicity, however, did nothing to stem the political ascent of
Kearney and his followers. Following its 1878 gains in state and municipal
politics, the Workingmen's Party grew ever more influential. Threatened,
Republicans and Democrats forged a unified front to thwart the Workingmen's political ascension. It was largely in vain; by July, the traditional
parties had made little headway.

On July 4, 1878, Kalloch—the city's appointed chaplain of the day—
commenced the holiday festivities with a benediction and announced a stunning change of heart. Before a crowd of thousands outside the Metropolitan
Temple, he prayed:

We believe, O Lord, that the foundations of our government were
laid by Thine own hand; that all the steps and stages of our progress
have been under Thy watch and ward . . . We meet together today
to celebrate the anniversary of our national birth, and we pray that
we may be enabled to carry out the divine principles which inspired
our noble sires and others, and we pray that our rules may all be
righteous; that our people may be peaceable; that capital may

respect the rights of labor, and that labor may honor capital; the Chinese must go and good men stay. We believe Thou wilt hear our prayer when we pray what we believe to be right.

The about-face was shocking. Kalloch, a political creature at heart, had taken stock of the landscape and, craving political power as Kearney did, he joined the party he believed would come out on top regardless of its platform. While the crowd roared its approval, the press took a different approach. The *Alta* slammed the reverend for his apparent kowtowing to the Workingmen in an editorial that mourned the loss of a rational voice:

If the success of a prayer is to be measured by the way it "brings down the house," the Fourth of July Committee is to be congratulated on their choice of Chaplain. When the Reverend Mr. Kalloch informed God Almighty that "The Chinese Must Go" the applause showed the gods in the gallery appreciated the sentiment, no matter how it was recognized on higher quarters, and the approving roar which burst forth at the close must have cheered the heart of the Reverend demagogue, as much as it disgusted those among the audience who have any sentiment left.

Kalloch's new political stance brought with it a larger Sunday audience, as he'd likely anticipated. He now extolled the virtues of the working class and the evils of cheap, immigrant labor. The Chinese were a nuisance that no longer deserved the people's pity, Kalloch preached, peppering his sermons with slogans made popular by the Workingmen and whipping the temple's sellout crowds into a frenzy. "This sort of entertainment seemed extremely well adapted to the taste of a certain class who enjoyed hearing 'The Chinese must go,'" recalled one disapproving attendee, "and who reveled in the startling, if not polite, remarks of the Reverend . . . upon the views of the non-conservative classes." Kalloch seemed to forget entirely his past sermons. "I have been a firm, unswerving, uncompromising adherent of the Workingmen's Party since its organization," he told his congregation. "Yes, from before its organization."

Kalloch now backed his newfound stance with action, closing the temple's Chinese Sunday school, becoming editor of the *Open Letter*—the Workingmen's weekly newspaper—and commencing weekly lectures that detailed the Workingmen's noble struggle. The first such speech was titled "The Chinese Must Go." Eight thousand people filled the temple to capacity, while thousands more jostled shoulder-to-shoulder in the street outside. The evening got under way with a rousing rendition of "The Heathen Chinese." As Kalloch took the stage, he led the masses in "Don't Put the Workingmen Down."

Kearney remained skeptical of Kalloch's motives. He thought it strange that a man who initially voiced such stringent opposition to the Workingmen would now turn around and present himself as a party loyalist. The fact that Kalloch's political awakening occurred only after the Workingmen secured hard-gained victories at the state and municipal levels did little to ease Kearney's distrust, but he did not dare voice such concerns in public. The Workingmen had acquired in Kalloch a powerful and influential statesman.

When the party gathered for its San Francisco County convention in June 1879, Kalloch, who had now been an active supporter for a year, was one of five candidates put forward for mayor on the Workingmen's ticket. "Kalloch," noted one newspaper publisher, "saw a great light, like Saul of Tarsus." Kalloch accepted the nomination.

The news disgusted Charles de Young, who considered anyone aligned with Kearney a natural enemy. Rumblings of Kalloch's lascivious past had made their way to the *Chronicle* newsroom, where de Young had previously paid them scant attention. That would no longer be the case. In a column that appeared shortly after the Workingmen announced their ticket, de Young mocked the party's mayoral candidates and speared San Francisco's star preacher with a sharp pen:

> At the head of the list of Communist tyrants stands Kalloch, the
> mock minister, traveling mountebank and carpet-bag demagogue,

who wants to be mayor, not because he is fit but because he knows himself to be unfit for the pulpit, and is probably an atheist and a blasphemer at heart!

It was the opening salvo in a vicious war of words. But industrious reporters and news editors were not the only ones who'd caught the bitter whiff of scandal clinging to Kalloch. Two Workingmen had already approached party leaders and voiced their suspicions. A mass meeting was promptly adjourned at Humboldt Hall on Friday, June 20, 1879, to discuss the allegations. A Workingman named Thomas Terry, originally from Cambridge, Massachusetts, addressed the assembly. "I do this only in the best interests of the party," he said, nervously wringing his hands. "I am satisfied and know that the Democrats tend to make these charges. In 1856 or '57, in my native town of Cambridge, Dr. Kalloch was accused of an infamous crime, and was tried in open court and was acquitted by a jury. In the public mind of Massachusetts, he was not acquitted, and to this day he has not been acquitted."

The crowd murmured uneasily as Terry summarized the episode of the "Lady in Black" and the allegations of sexual misconduct in Boston's Tremont Temple. "Instead of coming forward and denying the charge, he quit the party," Terry concluded. "These are the charges. If Dr. Kalloch can convince you that these are false, I shall vote for and endorse him. I know that the *Chronicle* knows all about him."

Kearney, who presided over the assembly, asked Kalloch to take the stage and present his rebuttal. Wrote one witness to the proceedings:

There was prolonged cheering from the Convention and the packed lobby at this announcement, and as the form of the preacher hove in sight on a chair there were cries of "Take the platform." Kalloch didn't take the platform, but he stepped from the chair to a contiguous table. He said in substance more than even Terry had.

Kalloch said he remained at Tremont Temple for another four years following his trial and left only to pursue other opportunities. He briefly detailed his

Western wanderings and rambled off a long list of subsequent professions—
"New York preacher, a Kansas lawyer, a Western railroad speculator, a fancy
farmer"—at which he had tried his hand. He portrayed himself as a victim, a
martyr to his various causes. "Why have I been abused since my arrival in this
city?" he asked. "Because I had the courage before a company of Christians to
speak kindly toward the Workingmen."

Party members promptly introduced a resolution, declaring, "We have
heard with pleasure the remarks of Dr. Kalloch, our candidate for Mayor, and
his triumphant vindication of the charges made against him. We find nothing
in his record or character that renders him unworthy of our support." The roll
was called and the resolution was adopted with only one voice dissenting.

Though the majority of Workingmen supported Kalloch, they remained
aware many others did not. S. Brambart, who had introduced the resolution,
predicted rough times ahead. "We expect a bitter fight and relentless war to
be made upon him," he said of Kalloch, "because he represented us in our
opposition to the rings, swindles, steals and corruptions of California politics,
and because he is able to lead us with ability and crown our campaign with
success." There were more loud cheers and a chanting of Kalloch's name,
prompting Brambart to raise his voice as he vowed Workingmen would "rally
around him, stand by him, defend him and support him against all enemies
and all assaults from all quarters." The cheers reached a thunderous crescendo
as Kalloch swaggered down the center aisle and exited the hall.

In the street outside, as Kalloch climbed aboard his waiting carriage, a
young man approached from the shadows and introduced himself as an emissary of Charles de Young. The *Chronicle*, the messenger said, had dispatched a
number of reporters back East to expose the various debaucheries dirtying
Kalloch's past. If the reverend persisted in running for mayor, the paper would
have no choice but to publish the more sordid details of Kalloch's life. De
Young, the emissary made clear, "had the ammunition in the pigeon hole of
the *Chronicle*" to destroy Kalloch "both as a politician and a preacher."

Kalloch gave the proposition a moment's thought before uttering his
reply. "Give Mr. de Young my compliments," he said, "and tell him to go to
hell."

———◦———

CHARLES DE YOUNG BRISTLED WITH ANGER when told of Kalloch's rebuke. "If Kalloch doesn't step down and out before the day of election there will be very good reasons for his doing so," he swore. "I know those reasons why he should, and I think he will do it, too."

Throughout July and the early part of August, the *Chronicle* poked and jabbed at Kalloch's character, while de Young waited for his scribes back East to report their findings. Meanwhile, Kalloch rolled with the punches like a prizefighter. He would not surrender his political ambition because of a few libelous comments in a paper he believed would eventually die. On August 17, he fired a warning shot across the *Chronicle*'s bow and threatened to distribute the old *Sun* article that had viciously defamed de Young's mother five years before: "How would the de Youngs like to see the Napthaly *Sun* article republished? We hereby give them fair notice that, if they persist in publishing in the *Chronicle* blackguard articles against the Workingmen's candidate for Mayor, we have secured a copy of that *Sun*."

De Young returned fire on Wednesday, August 20, 1879, with a blistering three-column indictment against Kalloch and the reverend's family. The thirteen-deck headline was massive in size, consuming nearly half a column:

KALLOCH

THE RECORD OF A MISSPENT LIFE.
INFAMOUS CAREER OF THE WORKINGMEN'S CANDIDATE FOR MAYOR.
DRIVEN FORTH FROM BOSTON LIKE AN UNCLEAN LEPER.
HIS TRIAL FOR THE CRIME OF ADULTERY.
THE EVIDENCE THAT FULLY ESTABLISHED HIS GUILT.
TEN OF THE JURORS VOTE FOR CONVICTION.
HIS ESCAPADES WITH ONE OF THE TREMONT TEMPLE CHORISTERS.
THE GIRL AND MOUNTEBANK CAUGHT IN HIS STUDY ROOM.

HIS QUEER ANTICS IN THE STATE OF KANSAS.
EARNING FOR HIM THE SOUBRIQUET OF THE "SORREL STALLION."
HOW HE HAS EVADED THE PAYMENTS OF HIS DEBTS.
NUMEROUS SUITS BROUGHT AGAINST HIM.

The selection of I. S. Kalloch, the notorious pastor of the Metropolitan Baptist Tabernacle as the W.P.C. candidate for the Mayoralty of this city is quite in accord with that of W. F. White for Governor. Notwithstanding his high profession as a Christian minister, a review of his record shows most clearly that he is not only utterly destitute of honor and honesty, but that under the cloak of religion he engages in the most scandalous amours with young girls and married women; that he is as lacking in truth as he is modesty, pompous as a peacock and salacious as a satyr.

Kalloch's ascendancy to the office of mayor, the *Chronicle* cried, would be "a disgrace from which this city could never fully recover." The article continued:

This is the feeling of our best citizens repeatedly expressed of late, but perhaps never more forcibly than in the eloquent address of Prof. H. B. Norton, of the State Normal School, before the California Sunday School Assembly at Monterey, July 2d, when speaking of certain threatening evils "more diabolical and dangerous than Goth or Hun," he called attention to the fact that "one of the most vulgar and beastly of all the alien blackguards that curse America" was assuming to dictate the destiny of this Imperial Commonwealth, and, "worst of all," a professed Christian minister and "doctor of divinity" was bowing down obsequiously before this "modern God of Ekron," in order to win "the notoriety and spoils of office."

The article cut a vicious swath through Kalloch's past deeds and high-lighted every moral lapse of a "wild and rebellious" man. The reverend's behavior, as portrayed in the *Chronicle,* would have shamed Caligula. Kalloch's reputation, the paper argued, was one of "shameless untruthfulness and dishonesty, and the grossest licentiousness," and his amorous pursuits were so lecherous in nature that his eventual public shaming was inevitable. But the incident in Cambridge did nothing to smother Kalloch's "amorous" urgings, the paper reported: Unable to keep his pants up in Boston, he set up shop in Lawrence, Kansas. Noted the *Chronicle:*

> A letter from a prominent and highly respected official of that city informs us that Kalloch's record in Kansas was "ten times worse than it was in Boston, especially with respect to women."

The paper alleged he drank, gambled and pursued almost anything in a skirt. "The Leavenworth *Appeal,* in a recent issue, speaks of his conduct there as exceedingly discreditable," the *Chronicle* reported, "and intimates that no unprotected female of any attractiveness is safe in his vicinity." During his short time in San Francisco, the *Chronicle* article continued, Kalloch's behavior had hardly improved:

> A lady who keeps a lodging-house on Market Street informed a CHRONICLE reporter that Kalloch brought a lady to her house and engaged a room for her, promising to be responsible for the rent. She went away after some weeks without paying, and Kalloch refused to pay as agreed upon until she threatened him with expo-sure, and he then compromised and paid it in part. One bill that there was a suit threatened to collect was for a bed and bed furniture to be placed in one of the rooms of the Metropolitan Temple, as Mr. Kalloch explained when it was purchased, for the accommodation of brethren visiting the city!

Kalloch had not yet been caught defiling young ladies within the confines of his temple, though rumors regarding his sinful behavior were rife. "He has learned caution in such matters," the paper bemoaned, "and some who claim that they could testify to the most damaging facts are unwilling to do so." The article concluded with a final twist of the knife:

> Mr. Kalloch has been in many kinds of business, and he has made a failure of them all. He has managed his own pecuniary affairs in a most extravagant and reckless manner. Is such a man a fit champion of retrenchment and reform? Can such a one be safely entrusted with the city's interests? Let our moral and religious citizens ask themselves if such a candidate is worthy of their support.

Kalloch hardly had time to muster a reply, for the *Chronicle* ran another attack piece the following day. A nine-deck headline summarized the key points:

CORRUPT KALLOCH

FURTHER EVIDENCE OF HIS RASCALITY.
A VERY CURIOUS FORGED CHECK TRANSACTION.
TWO THOUSAND DOLLARS SPENT IN A SINGLE DAY.
HOW IS THAT FOR THE HEAD OF A PARTY ECONOMY?
IKE'S EXPLOITS AS A LEGISLATOR IN KANSAS.
THE PART HE TOOK IN A CELEBRATED BRIBERY CASE.
UNSAVORY "SUBSIDY POMEROY'S" RIGHT HAND MAN.
KALLOCH HIS AGENT AND GO BETWEEN IN PURCHASING VOTES.

Yesterday, the CHRONICLE gave an installment of the record of Isaac S. Kalloch, Sand-lot candidate for Mayor of this great city, showing his gross licentiousness, appalling hypocrisy and financial dishonesty. To-day it supplements that statement by further corroborative evidence of the total unfitness of this wolf in sheep's clothing to fill any position in which wither integrity or morality or honor is a requisite of its occupant.

What followed were nearly two columns of text again harping on Kalloch's adultery trial in Cambridge and accusing him of shady financial dealings. The article reported that, following his trial, Kalloch cashed a check in the amount of $2,000, which he said was from a supporter in Philadelphia to help defray the cost of legal fees. The check was indeed signed by a Dr. Jayne and endorsed by Myers, Claghorn & Co., a supposed Philadelphia company. A day later, the bank discovered that the names on the check were forgeries. When Kalloch received the news, he simply shrugged and said the money had been spent:

> A most fortunate man is Brother Kalloch. He had his lamb, his grog, his trial, and now he pockets $2,000 drawn on a false check and declares that he has spent it—and spent it, too, in twenty-four hours.

The *Chronicle* dismissed any notion that Kalloch was a victim. "It is the more difficult to accept Kalloch's plea of innocence, as the entire record of his life shows him to be shrewd, criminal and corrupt," the *Chronicle* opined.

The article next accused Kalloch of buying votes and bribing officials while serving in the Kansas State legislature, a body that "became a stench in the nostrils of the entire people of the Union." If the previous day's article had thrust a knife in Kalloch, this one gave the handle a good twist:

> Kalloch has a reputation throughout the country, which no man can envy. He is infamous for his lechery as well as notorious for his petty dishonest and wholesale depravity and corruption . . . The choice of a man of such general unsavory reputation as Kalloch to be Mayor of San Francisco would disgrace this city in the eyes of the people of

the entire United States, to whom he is known as an adulterer and a hypocrite.

Kalloch returned fire that same day. He released a statement through the Metropolitan Temple's newsletter and effectively put the de Young brothers on notice:

The attention of all persons who are interested in the subject of vivisection is called to the announcement of the meeting at Metropolitan Temple tomorrow (Friday) evening. Dr. Kalloch, D. S. (De Young Scalper), will there and then give an exhibition of this interesting branch of scientific experiment, which will be highly entertaining and instructive to all who may be so fortunate as to secure admittance to the Temple on that occasion. The nondescript animals, which are to be made the subject of the Doctor's dissecting knife on this occasion are so thoroughly detested by the human family that even the most tender-hearted members of the Society for the Prevention of Cruelty to Animals will not feel called upon to interfere with the operation. No anesthetics will be administered. The operation will commence promptly at 8 o'clock.

The *Chronicle* dismissed Kalloch's saber rattling and served what Charles de Young hoped would be the knockout punch in its Friday, August 22, edition. An eleven-deck headline dismissed Kalloch's career as "A COURSE OF LUST, FRAUD AND HYPOCRISY." In a screaming indictment against Kalloch's moral bankruptcy, the paper stooped low and dragged the reverend's dead father through the mud:

While he was at college, his father became too familiar with some sisters of the flock over which he was established in Rockland. To escape exposure and the indignation and vengeance of the injured husbands, the elder Kalloch settled his affairs, and, without ceremony, severed his connection with the church. He immediately took passage to California, in which State he spent the remainder of his existence, he having died some eight years ago.

The article went on to accuse the younger Kalloch of hating Catholics and publicly denouncing them in Boston as "scum of the earth." It maintained the mayoral candidate was prone to bouts of extreme drunkenness and profanity, and "fit only to associate with beasts and brutes."

The rival *Alta* expressed its disgust and called into question the *Chronicle*'s decency. "A decent man cannot read some of the gross and indecent sentences, even when alone in his private office, without blushing and feeling ashamed of humanity," the paper said. "True or false, the charges are not fit to be published, and no political exigency can justify their publication in a journal supposed to enter some decent family circles."

Kalloch, enraged the *Chronicle* would besmirch his father's name, made no secret of his plan to read the infamous *Sun* article by B. F. Napthaly at Friday night's temple meeting. When word reached de Young, the publisher leapt from his chair and threatened to shoot Kalloch on sight should the reverend make good on his threat.

KALLOCH TOOK THE STAGE TO a warm and rapturous welcome. The temple's upper and lower balconies were filled to capacity, its walls lined with those unable to grab a seat. He spoke for nearly two hours and denounced the *Chronicle*'s assault as "an accumulation of bile and bitterness." He paused frequently to revel in the applause. "All else said by the *Chronicle*, or said by anybody, against me is an unadulterated lie," he boomed from the pulpit. Yes, as a young man, he had been accused of debauching another man's wife, but the charges failed to stick. "I stood my trial like a man," he said. "I beat my accusers and remained four years thereafter the pastor of the same church—the Tremont Temple in Boston." Having set the record straight, he promised to sue the *Chronicle* for libel, and then unleashed a damning rant against the paper and its founding brothers:

It is not necessary tonight—it may be hereafter—to discuss the defiled organ; the bawdy house breeding, the gutter-snipe training of this delectable pair of social pariahs, moral lepers, who vainly struggle for the recognition which decent society denies them, and who, by a persistent and damnable system of blackmailing, have built up a newspaper, which, is a moral volcano—an Aetna in a garden more beautiful that Sicily's, opening its pores like the dark, damp leathery leaves of the swamp to fill the surrounding atmosphere with poison . . .

The *Chronicle* as well as the Chinese must go! If the devil in hell has an organ on earth, it is the *San Francisco Chronicle*. The infamous hybrid whelps of sin and shame, who have become the assassins, ghouls, hyenas of society, may hear the knell of their doom in the ringing bells that proclaim the people's triumph on the third of September. I promised you the other night at Union Hall that if you would elect me, I would make the Chinese go. I promise you now in addition, that if you elect me, I will kill the *San Francisco Chronicle* . . .

A man who has never looked on Niagara has but a faint idea of a cataract. The man who has never looked on the *Chronicle* may be said not to know what it is to lie. The de Youngs approach nearer than any other persons mentioned in history, whether man or devil, to the monstrous model of consummate and unrelieved depravity. In them the qualities, which are the proper objects of hatred, the proper objects of contempt, preserve an exquisite and absolute harmony. There may be as great cowards or as great liars as the de Youngs, but I do not believe it . . . Charles de Young is the wickedest man in the world. He will be without a rival in hell. When I told him to "go to hell," he thought it was profane for a preacher. It might have been, but it was the only locality to which he could be appropriately commended. If he does not go to hell, the institution may as well be abolished—the object of its establishment is frustrated.

The cheering multitudes in attendance leapt to their feet and chanted the reverend's name. Kalloch's vicious verbal eloquence enthralled his supporters but stunned the press, which criticized the diatribe for language "unbecoming a minister of the church." Yet there remained plenty of poison on Kalloch's tongue as he stepped off the stage, left the building and mounted the speaker's platform, where it had been erected outside the temple's main entrance on Fifth Street. Kalloch pulled from his trouser pocket a piece of paper folded over several times. He smoothed the creases and held it out for the many thousands of spectators who had gathered to see. It was the dreaded *Sun* article. Kalloch cleared his throat and read:

> The de Youngs are the bastard progeny of a whore, conceived in
> infamy and nursed in the lap of prostitution.

The vile utterance echoed across the city, and all who heard it knew retaliation would be swift and violent. It was, reported one paper, "fighting language, and all believed that the days of talk and shoot would be revived."

11

THE SPARK OF MANHOOD

THE CALL FOR A RIG was rung through to the office of the United Carriage Company at the Palace Hotel at 8:05 AM on Saturday, August 23, 1879. On duty and waiting for a fare was driver Patrick Smith, who promptly responded to 317 Eddy Street, the home of Charles de Young. When he pulled up in front of the address, Smith found his fare waiting for him in the street with an overcoat draped across one arm, holding two oranges wrapped in paper. The passenger climbed into the covered coupe and ordered Smith to drive to the corner of Mason and Eddy streets. The two men rode in silence, Smith being ignorant as to his passenger's identity.

Smith tugged the reigns at the intersection of Mason and Eddy and dismounted from the box. He opened the carriage door and found his passenger now wearing the overcoat. The man gave Smith a sidelong glance and said he wished to be driven to 961 Mission Street, a branch of the District Telegraph

Company. Arriving at the address, the passenger ordered Smith to go inside and return with a messenger boy. "Smith returned with one, who got into the coupe with de Young," the *Call* reported. "They then drove to Fourteenth and Mission streets, where the coupe stopped, for what purpose Smith declines to say, but states that de Young did not get out, and that the coupe remained there but for a moment."

Smith next drove to the corner of Mission and Nineteenth streets, where de Young ordered the carriage be pulled over on the south side of Mission. The carriage door opened and the young messenger boy jumped out. Smith watched him scurry across the street and knock on the door of 2314 Mission Street, a respectable-looking place and home to the Kalloch family. From where he sat, Smith could see the front door open but could not make out who engaged the boy in conversation. After several minutes, the boy returned to the carriage and leapt in the back with de Young, who ordered Smith to drive to Fifth and Jessie. The coupe came to a stop across the street from the Metropolitan Temple. In the back, de Young pulled the curtains across the carriage windows.

Kalloch emerged from the temple shortly after ten with his servant, Jim Ransome, in tow. Waiting for Kalloch in a buggy on Mission Street was Carl Browne, a Workingman, who for the past three weeks had been helping Kalloch plan his campaign. The two men had business planned that morning. As Kalloch approached the buggy, Ransome expressed concern for the reverend's safety. "I don't like to be in this buggy riding around town, without a gun," he said, "after the speech you gave last night."

Parked several yards away, de Young peered through his carriage curtains and spotted his prey. He pulled the messenger boy to the window. "Do you see that man with the ulster on?" he asked, pointing in Kalloch's direction. "Tell him that a lady wishes to see him."

The boy, dressed in his District Telegraph uniform, approached Kalloch as the reverend climbed into his buggy and told him a woman sitting in a carriage near the temple entrance on Jessie Street desired to meet him. A smiling Kalloch climbed back out of the carriage and walked toward the other coupe, where Smith stood beside his horse, having just draped a blanket over its back.

As Kalloch approached, he removed his hat, as any gentleman would when making the acquaintance of a lady. De Young, who had been lying in wait, pounced the moment Kalloch reached the door. He threw the curtains aside and jammed a Colt revolver through the window. He aimed the pistol low and pulled the trigger. The slug tore through the left side of Kalloch's chest and sent the reverend's considerable bulk reeling backward. De Young leapt from the carriage and fired another shot into Kalloch's left thigh. Kalloch screamed, hobbling toward the temple as blood flowed from the wounds. De Young, still grasping the smoking revolver, turned and yelled at Smith to take him to the old City Hall as chaos erupted around them.

Carl Browne and another witness ran to Kalloch's assistance. The two men helped him into the temple's vestibule and laid him out on the floor. They were joined by G. H. McDowell, who witnessed the shooting while sipping coffee in a saloon opposite the temple. "I asked him where he was shot," McDowell later said. "Kalloch bared his chest and revealed a ghastly wound over his heart." The bullet had entered the body just two inches above the nipple, barely missing the heart.

A doctor was immediately summoned. Recalled McDowell, "When asked if his wife had better be sent for, he replied, 'I don't think it is necessary.' Kalloch, all the while, was perfectly cool, and directed the efforts of the men to relieve his suffering."

Outside, Kalloch's loyal manservant, Ransome, rushed de Young's carriage. He leapt onto the sideboard, thrust his hands through the window and grabbed de Young by his shirt collar. De Young beat the man's wrists and jabbed the gun through the window, sticking the muzzle in Ransome's face and screaming, "I'll shoot you if you touch me!" Ransome stepped back into the crowd now swelling around the coupe.

De Young leaned out of the carriage and waved his revolver in the air. "I'll kill the first one that attempts to put his hands on me," he yelled, as a man stepped forward and grabbed the horse's bridle. The messenger boy, still standing near Kalloch's buggy and unnerved by the morning's proceedings, beat a quick retreat back to the telegraph office. For de Young and his hapless driver, there was no easy escape. "There was intense excitement," reported the *Bulletin*, "and many women became so excited they appeared to be demented." The crowd balanced a fine line between rowdy gathering and full-blown mob.

Walking his beat on Fifth Street between Tehama and Clementina, Police Officer William Fredericks noticed people rushing in a frenzied state of excitement onto Jessie Street. "I ran up as fast as I could," Fredericks said. "When I got there, I was told that Charles de Young had shot Kalloch, and that he was then in a coupe down the street." Fredericks could see the carriage a block away, surrounded by a jeering mass of people. He ran toward the coupe and shoved his way through the crowd. "I got in the coupe," Fredericks said, "and told de Young that he was my prisoner." The officer yelled at Smith to get the carriage moving, but a large group of men and women blocked the hack's progress.

Home in his apartment on the corner of Fifth and Clementina, Special Officer Cornelius Gould heard the commotion. He rushed down the stairs and into the street to investigate. "I saw a crowd on Jessie Street," Gould said. "I saw de Young in a coupe, and also saw Officer Fredericks in the coupe with him."

Gould struggled through the crowd, its mood growing increasingly riotous. "I jumped into the coupe and saw de Young holding a revolver in his hand," Gould said. "I struck his hand and turned the weapon down." The gun fell to the floor. De Young shoved Gould aside and scrambled for the Colt. Gould threw his body at de Young and pinned the publisher against the seat. As the two men tussled, the crowd outside closed ranks around the coupe and began rocking the carriage, its intent clear.

"The coupe was turned over on the side," Gould said. "I fell on top of de Young and the other officer." The three men lay in a bruised and tangled heap. Recalled Fredericks, "De Young got out as quickly as possible, when he was seized by the crowd, thrown to the ground and beaten and kicked. There were cries of 'Kill him!' 'Hang him!' 'Lynch him!'"

Gould and Fredericks scrambled out and fought off de Young's assailants. The officers hauled de Young—bruised, bleeding from the scalp, and his watch chain broken—to his feet and shoved him through the mob. They fought their way with clubs up Fifth Street to the Baldwin Hotel, fending off repeated attacks. "A number of stones were hurled at de Young," Fredericks said, "and a number of them struck him. One of them hit me on the back of the head."

Riding a Market-line car on his way to serve a subpoena, Police Officer E. Stevens saw a crowd rushing Fifth Street from Market to the Baldwin. He rang the bell and disembarked, drawing his club when he saw the flurry of punches being thrown outside the hotel. Stevens joined the fray and found "de Young in the hands of Fredericks and half a dozen men." There were calls for rope and demands for de Young's immediate hanging.

While Gould went in search of a hack, Fredericks flailed his club in all directions to protect de Young and himself. Stevens also beat off de Young's manhandlers just as Gould returned, fighting his way through the crowd with a ride in tow. Fredericks screamed at de Young to move and pushed him into the open-air carriage as the driver snapped the reigns. "The crowd followed down the street," according to one witness, "flinging stones and crying loudly and savagely for de Young's death."

On the corner of Fifth and Jessie, Patrick Smith struggled to upright his overturned coupe. Gould approached and loaned him some muscle. The carriage back on its wheels, Smith mounted the driver's box and hightailed it back to the carriage house. "I know one thing," Smith later told a reporter, "and that is that I don't want anymore such night's work."

FREDERICKS AND DE YOUNG REACHED THE old City Hall on Kearny Street without suffering further physical trauma. They had made the short ride hunkered down on the carriage floor to avoid the missiles being hurled in their direction. The coupe pulled into a courtyard behind the old City Hall and was met by more than a dozen uniformed officers with clubs in hand and pistols on their hips. The officers immediately cordoned off the entrance to

Dunbar Alley, which ran behind the building, and flashed their weaponry to the advancing throng of people who followed in the hack's wake, packing Kearny Street between Clay and Washington. Taking no chances, store-owners barricaded their doors and shuttered their windows.

Inside City Hall, de Young was formally charged with assault with attempt to commit murder. Reported the *Call*:

> When de Young reached the Central Station he was scarcely recog-
> nizable. His face was covered with blood, which had flowed from
> wounds on his head. His clothing was torn, covered with dust and
> blood-stained. He was asked for his revolver. He stated that he
> didn't have it, as it had been taken from him by some of the crowd
> after he had been knocked down on Jessie Street. He was then
> searched and a large bowie-knife was taken from his person.

Disarmed and booked, de Young was escorted to the Central Receiving Hospital. Dr Stivers, the on-duty police surgeon, made note of the would-be assassin's injuries: "a scalp wound on the back part of the head, and a small lacerated wound on the right side, near the temple. His face was swollen from blows which he had received." Stivers cleansed and bandaged the wounds before helping de Young to his cell.

Police Chief Kirkpatrick and Captain Lees dispatched orders for all off-duty officers to report at once. The order "was responded to with alacrity," wrote a reporter for the *Alta*. "The scene in the Court and around the corri-dors was very exciting. Each Captain, Sergeant, Corporal and Private was in full uniform, with belts tightened and ominous clubs and savage looking pistol-bandies peeping out from the folds of their coats."

Outside the old City Hall, people had gathered in such great numbers "that within a block of the prison it was almost impossible to get along on the sidewalks." Officers formed human cordons across Merchant, Kearny and Montgomery streets. Police also roped off Dunbar Alley, which opened onto Merchant at one end and Washington on the other. Only members of the press and those with official business were allowed to enter the premises. Additional officers were sent to protect the *Chronicle*'s newsroom and the printing facilities on Clay Street. Another contingent formed a perimeter around the paper's business office on Montgomery, "where crowds began to assemble with hostile expressions."

News of the shooting reached Denis Kearney by telegram shortly before 11 AM in Napa, where he was scheduled to speak that evening with party loyalists. The telegram informed Kearney "that the people were in a state of wild excitement, and requested he return home immediately to save the city from an impending riot." Reported the *Call*:

> Kearney who was much grieved and horrified by such unexpected news, sent replies to these messages, saying he would postpone his speech in Napa, and arrive in the city in the evening . . . The attempted assassination formed the all-absorbing topic of conversation among the citizens of Napa, who freely expressed their indignation at the cowardly act.

At noon, a dozen Workingmen—led by lawyer and editor Clitus Barbour—appeared in Police Chief Kirkpatrick's office and requested they be sworn in as special deputies. "They wished to satisfy themselves and their friends," reported the *Alta*, "that de Young was in custody and would remain in custody." The chief deputized eleven of the men, pinned silver stars on their lapels and stationed two of them in the hallway outside the jail. The others were placed at various strategic points throughout the building. The chief, along with the district attorney, then took Barbour to de Young's cell, where the newspaperman reclined lazily on his cot. "Mr. de Young," the district attorney said, "I have brought Mr. Barbour here as he wishes to satisfy himself that you are in prison." De Young lifted his head and smiled in greeting. "Yes, I am here," he said, "and will probably remain here for some time to come."

IMMEDIATELY FOLLOWING THE SHOOTING, the party's Committee of the Ward Presidents had scheduled an emergency meeting for 2 PM at the massive sandlot adjacent to the new City Hall. Men hit the streets wearing sandwich boards, urging all Workingmen to attend in support of their fallen comrade. By noon, thousands had gathered in anticipation of the rally. Wrote one witness:

> Many men were perched on adjacent fences. There were a number present in wagons, which were soon improvised as advantageous positions to view the proceedings. The windows of outlying houses were filled with sightseers, and the platform for the speakers literally swarmed with men. The crowd numbered fully five thousand people, among whom were a great many women, whose state of great excitement was evident . . . The men gathered in little knots around the stand, disregarding the driving storm of sand that swept over the waste and cut their faces, engaging in subdued conversation and exchanging particulars of the tragedy.

Numerous party officials addressed the crowd, including T. J. O'Brien of the Twelfth Ward Club, who urged those in attendance to "be calm and watch what you are about." His closing statement, however, undercut his plea for moderation. "We are crying for vengeance," he bellowed, "and we are going to have vengeance." His words were punctuated with cries for de Young's head, as were those of Bible-thumping evangelist and shoemaker William Wellock, an outspoken party member who vowed to destroy the *Chronicle* with his own bare hands.

"If we cannot get satisfaction by fair and lawful means," Wellock bellowed, "the cry will arise right here, from this stand, and I'll lead the van myself, to tear down every vestige of the *Chronicle* office." During the meeting, doctors released the first bulletin on Kalloch's condition. Clitus Barbour, who had just come from the Metropolitan Temple after checking in on de Young, delivered the news:

This great city of San Francisco has received a shock that was
like that the United States received when the news came of the
assassination of Abraham Lincoln. A political murder has been
attempted . . . On the other hand, the murder was not, so far as we
know, consummated. I have just come from the Metropolitan
Temple, and Dr. Kalloch has a chance now for life.

There followed much rowdy cheering, prompting Barbour to raise his
hands and silence the audience before continuing:

They say that the wound is in the breast—the ball must have ranged
downward, probably and may have penetrated the lung, but is not
necessarily fatal. That is what the surgeons tell me. He has a very
powerful constitution and he may live through it and become the
Mayor of San Francisco yet [more mad applause]; and may yet live to
kill the thieves of the City Hall, and make good another proposition
that we propose to add to our motto of "The Chinese must go," by
saying, "The de Youngs must go!"

A thousand voices rose in unison above the wind and whirling sand and
promised death to the de Young brothers. "We're going to hang them!" the
crowd chanted.

The meeting progressed with more fiery words screamed from the
speaker's platform. It concluded with the reading of a resolution drafted that
afternoon by the party's executive committee:

Whereas, the chief manager and proprietor of the San Francisco
Chronicle, not content with attempting to destroy the characters of
reputable men and women, has made a most dastardly and cowardly
attempt at the life of our honored standard-bearer, Dr. Kalloch.

Whereas, the publication of said journal is calculated to disturb the peace and quiet of our city; be it therefore, Resolved, that we, the people of San Francisco, in mass meeting assembled, do hereby demand of the authorities of the city that the publication of the slimy, detestable, assignation sheet, the *Chronicle*, be suppressed.

The resolution passed with a resounding chorus of *yeas*, after which the meeting disbanded. To let the city know they were "ready and able to aid in the preservation of the public peace and welfare," members of the party's Third Ward Club marched up Sacramento and Kearny streets with rifles at the ready. A drummer led the somber procession and beat a steady cadence as the men behind him marched with military precision.

City leaders, made nervous by thoughts of riot, sought outside help. Warships from Mare Island weighed anchor just off San Francisco's wharves. The nation's Secretary of War placed eight companies of the Fourth Artillery, United States Army, at the city's disposal and armed the state militia with fifty thousand cartridges from the Benicia Arsenal.

———

A NUMBER OF "WELL-RESPECTED CITIZENS"—including *Chronicle* Managing Editor John Young and Night Editor John Tummins—stopped by the jail that afternoon to visit de Young. Despite his precarious position and battered physical state, the inmate remained in good spirits and asked to see the proofs for the next day's edition. Kalloch, meanwhile, writhed on a bed in the Metropolitan Temple, coughing up blood and passing in and out of consciousness. A dozen physicians remained in constant attendance. Both slugs remained in Kalloch's body for fear removing them might kill him. "Every possible act is being done to make him comfortable," a doctor told the *Bulletin*. No one could do anything but wait.

———

FROM NAPA, DENIS KEARNEY TELEGRAPHED party headquarters on Market Street and let it be known he would be arriving on the Vallejo ferry at eight that evening. "As the boat did not reach the wharf until 8:10, there was an abundance of time for the leaders to make some suitable preparations to welcome him," reported the *Alta*:

> About fifteen minutes before eight o'clock, four military companies, numbering more than two hundred men, with neat uniforms and bright muskets, with fixed bayonets, marched down Market Street and formed a line just outside the northern gates of the railroad depot. Accompanying them was a large crowd of persons, with here and there a solitary individual with his trusty musket in perfect order. While waiting for the arrival of the boat, the outsiders gathered into small knots of four or six, and in a quiet but determined manner discussed the situation.

When Kearney eventually disembarked from the boat, he was met with a "succession of lusty cheers." The military men immediately fell in formation behind their leader and followed him up Market Street, marching in lines of four. The scene, wrote the *Alta* reporter, was "almost indescribable." Thousands lined the sidewalks and watched the procession—its men grim-faced like soldiers marching off to war—pass by, bringing all horse-drawn traffic to a stop. Spectators at each block joined the militaristic ranks and voiced their enthusiasm with boisterous yells. By the time Kearney arrived at Workingmen's headquarters, more than fifteen thousand people had gathered to greet him. Reported the *Alta*:

> The street was completely blocked by a surging mass of humanity, which kept up a continuous cry. Many of the crowd were armed with clubs, stones and other mob paraphernalia, while others freely exhibited pistols, cartridges, etc., and the wildest threats were indulged in. Kearney arrived at headquarters at 8:40. The mob without became extremely boisterous, shouting, "To the Sand-lots!" "Hang him!" "Bring a rope, Kearney!" "We want Charlie de Young!" "To the City Hall!" and similar exclamations emanated from the exciting crowd.

Kearney waved to his adoring public and disappeared inside the building. He reappeared several minutes later in an upper-floor window and waved again to the cheering masses below. "Friends," he cried, "please retire to the Sand-lot. I will be out in ten minutes." The crowd instantly dissipated under the order of its leader. Where moments prior there had been thousands, there now remained a few stragglers. The massive horde reconvened around the speaker's platform adjacent to the old City Hall and awaited Kearney's arrival. As promised, he arrived within minutes and took the stage to adulation worthy of a conquering hero.

"You will please come to order," Kearney cried:

> I have just returned to the city, and I find the present excitement . . .
> The man who had the courage to support me, tonight lies on his
> death-bed, sent thither by the bullet of the assassin, Charley de
> Young. The vile wretch now lies in prison. Ten days from today will
> be held the election that has caused so much bitterness in our State.
> The eyes of the civilized world are upon us. The abiding people are
> Workingmen. Public opinion demands that de Young be hanged. De
> Young will be hung.

"Hang him tonight!" the people screamed, their faces a ghastly shade of orange in the glow of the tar-barrel fires illuminating the scene. Kearney allowed the crowd a moment to vent its rage then raised his hands for silence. "I want to see Mr. Kalloch," he said. "Mr. Kalloch wants the peace as much as I do, and I know the Workingmen have the capacity for self-government. Are you going to spoil victory? You must use discretion . . . Adjourn in a peaceful manner."

—◦—

MAYOR A. J. BRYANT—FORCED to cut short a stay on his ranch in neighboring Contra Costa County—had returned to the city that evening, afraid Kearney would lead an assault on the *Chronicle* offices or storm the city jail and hang de Young from a lamppost. Although relieved by the surprisingly subdued tenor of Kearney's speech, Bryant ordered local militia to remain at the ready and requested Company B, Second Infantry, to relieve the police department at midnight.

Another man not leaving anything to chance was Michael de Young, who, according to the *Call*, "believed he was safer beneath the aegis of the City Hall than within the precincts of the *Chronicle* office" and turned himself into authorities. By 10 PM, both de Young brothers were in prison.

A reporter for the *Alta*, hoping for a quote, called on Charles de Young and found him "still confined in the iron tank," reclining on a mattress and penning a column for the next day's *Chronicle*. "Beside him," wrote the visitor, "were two reporters, who were also busy writing, and ever and anon he would scan their work and offer a suggestion here or require a change there."

Asked by the *Alta* scribe if he wished to make a statement, de Young politely declined. He said the information circulating thus far was correct, though he denied ever telling the young messenger boy to inform Kalloch a woman wished to see him. The reporter, pointing at de Young's visibly battered head and bloodstained bandages, inquired as to the extent of the injuries. "Well now," de Young said, "I was pretty roughly treated during the few moments that I was among the crowd, having been struck twice in the back of the head, and having a slight cut over my eye. This eye, too, is pretty badly swollen, but I do not anticipate anything serious from my wounds."

In the narrow corridor that ran between the cells, Michael de Young conducted business as usual. He leaned against the bars of an unoccupied cell, "coolly puffing a cigarette" and dictating orders to a number of *Chronicle* staffers who had requisitioned the cramped and unlikely space for a makeshift newsroom. Both brothers, reported the *Alta*, appeared "unconcerned" and "remarkably self-possessed." Michael occasionally "inquired in regard to the feeling of the people outside, the angry murmur of whose voices could be heard now and then, breaking upon the stillness of the cells, and causing the prisoner inside to unconsciously start up."

"It seems," said the *Alta* reporter, turning to Michael de Young, "to be a bad state of affairs."

De Young took a long drag on his cigarette. He hissed the smoke out between clenched teeth and extinguished the butt on the heel of his shoe. "Mr. Kalloch might have known that he could not go on to a public platform and trounce our mother and family without stern and bitter retribution following close upon the heels of the vilification," he said. "There was no law that would reach the matter. He knew that he took his life in his hands when he spoke as he did."

The *Alta* reporter cleared his throat and reminded de Young that Kalloch made his comments only after the *Chronicle* slammed the reverend's father in print.

"That was unpardonable," de Young conceded, "but I will say in justice to my brother and to myself that the statement came as a dispatch from Boston. It arrived at half past one o'clock in the morning. Both my brother and self were away—he at a political conference, and I elsewhere. Even our news editor scarcely read the matter as it came in; but once published, we determined to stand by it without retraction."

It was a startling confession, an acknowledgement that perhaps emotion had clouded news judgment.

"No matter how excited the public is now," de Young continued, "they will take a calmer view of the matter when they come to reflect that my brother simply did what any man would do who had a spark of manhood in him."

AT THE METROPOLITAN TEMPLE, IN a small room off the southeast corner of the vestibule, Kalloch endured his suffering with dignity. "I have done what I could," he told his sobbing wife, "and am resigned to the inevitable." Surgeon Laine and two assistants routinely mopped blood from the still-dripping wounds. Still no attempt had been made to extract the bullets, since such a procedure was likely to achieve what de Young's Colt ammunition had thus far failed to accomplish. At midnight, an effort by doctors Vlack and Barger to remove Kalloch's clothing was abandoned "because of the intense pain occasioned." The doctors administered an opiate to minimize any discomfort and fluffed Kalloch's pillows. "That will do," the patient said before drifting away.

In an adjoining room, Denis Kearney maintained a silent vigil.

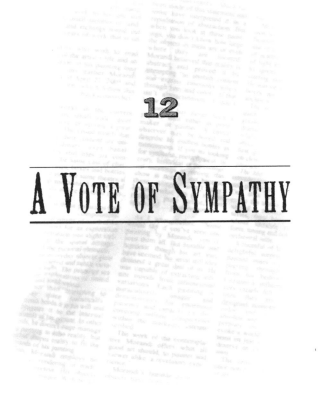

12

A VOTE OF SYMPATHY

THE CHRONICLE'S COMPETITORS WERE QUICK to cast Charles de Young in the role of villain. They characterized him as a vindictive man whose paper "belched forth abuse of a character that nauseated all who read it." Kalloch's comments were "almost justifiable," reported the *Alta*, which blamed the shooting "on the result of sensational journalism and the introduction of personal vituperation and vilification in politics." Taking gun in hand and pulling the trigger, de Young had "brought disgrace not only upon the honorable profession of journalism, but upon the city and the state," the *Alta* cried, and it would take many years for California to shed the shame wrought by de Young:

> This cowardly act has, perhaps, done more injury to the fair fame of
> California than any of the wildest extravagances or lawlessnesses [*sic*]

of her early youth. In these days of our state's early manhood, our citizens had believed that we had at least reached the stage when, if we had not a perfection of a law-and-order system, that at least we were verging upon that point. The cowardly act of yesterday, however, proves that we still have those in our midst whose presence is an element of danger.

Loring Pickering, of the rival *Call*, had spent a good many years nurturing his intense hatred of the de Youngs. In striving to secure the brothers' destruction, Pickering had set for himself a grand ambition that he worked tirelessly to achieve. De Young's recent outburst only served to illustrate the man's lowly nature, as far as Pickering was concerned. Indeed, the *Call* theorized that de Young's method of attack—hiding in a coupe and pretending to be a lady—was "destined to become popular with assassins and go down to rising murderers as quite a secure method of killing as the old way of the bushwhacker or Apache Indian." To bolster its position that de Young and his rag of a newspaper were creations of low caliber, the *Call* ran a column taken from the *Territorial Enterprise* in Virginia City:

> For years, the *Chronicle* has been but a sewer. Its proprietors have from the first delighted in tearing down names more honorable than their own, and in seeking to taint by their slanders homes more pure than the home the de Youngs sprang from. The act of yesterday is but a natural culmination of years of disgrace and shame. The only surprising thing about the matter is that de Young had the hardihood to shoot at even an unarmed man, because, as a rule, cowardice attends cruelty.

Other newspapers across the country weighed in. In the Midwest, the *Chicago Times* had seen fit to render a soft defense on de Young's behalf, calling his actions "a natural if not wholly justifiable response." Likewise, in the East, the Baltimore *Gazette* identified Kalloch as "a curious illustration of the downward tendency of soiled clergyman." In Boston, where Kalloch still carried a tremendous amount of ugly baggage, the papers took the opportunity to again rip the reverend to shreds. "The act which led directly to the attempted assassination would be inexcusable in any man," reported the *Boston Advertiser*, "and was doubly so in a man with a reputation so vulnerable." The *Boston Journal*, the city's leading Republican publication, took it one step further: "Should Kalloch's wounds result fatally, it would be a not unfitting termination." If Kalloch died, opined the New York *Commercial Advertiser*, then Denis Kearney and his Workingmen would reap the benefits. Unfortunately, "de Young is a remarkably poor marksman and Kalloch seems to be the owner of a remarkably fine physique that has not been impaired, despite the dissipation with which he has alternated his ministerial career."

Closer to home, the *Bulletin* in particular maintained a level of objectivity lacking in other publications. Lowly insults and colorful flourishes were noticeably missing from its coverage. The *Chronicle* itself took a unique approach, defending the actions of its founder as opposed to reporting what happened. On page four, under the small-type headline "The Shooting of Kalloch," the paper opined on Sunday, August 24:

We do not propose to comment in detail upon the deplorable event of Saturday morning. The time has not yet come for a calm and candid discussion of the merits of the case. But if there is in this great city one human being in the shape of a man, and pretending to the dignity of manhood, who could tamely have heard the mother that bore him assailed in language too vile to be repeated without offense to modest ears, let that despicable creature throw the first stone at the avenger of the grossest insult that was ever offered to a woman venerable in years and irreproachable in character.

Milton Kalloch, the eldest son of Isaac and now twenty-eight, was not so blasé. He had spent the night at his father's side, fearing each labored breath the stricken man took might be his last. The two were incredibly close.

"There was," remarked one contemporary account, "the strongest affection existing between him and his father." Milton, like Isaac, was a Baptist minister and a man of fiery tongue. Home-schooled as a child, the younger Kalloch eventually studied religion at the University of California and was ordained a Baptist clergyman in 1876. He accepted his first call "from a small society in one of the suburbs of San Francisco" before assuming the pulpit of the First Baptist Church of Oakland. Milton was preaching the good word in Sonoma County when news of the attack upon his father reached him. He immediately returned to San Francisco, traveling by train and ferry, to hold vigil at his father's side.

Isaac's condition had improved little overnight, though doctors remained busy, applying ice to the wounds to combat inflammation. "The bullet has not been probed for fear of rupturing the ligament," the *Alta* reported. "The application of a ligament to a deep-seated artery is impracticable, and the resulting hemorrhage might be fatal to the patient. Kalloch is still suffering intense pain." At nine o'clock Sunday morning, Kalloch's pulse was 120 beats per minute. By noon, it was 115. "Eighty pulsations per minute are made by the normal heart," doctors informed the press. "Thus, it will be seen that there is a steady change for the better, and, considering Kalloch's vigorous constitution, there is some probability that he will recover."

The press, despite the hopeful prognosis put forth by doctors, remained cynical. "From private and reliable sources," wrote one reporter, "it is learned that there is but little hope of Dr. Kalloch's recovering from his wound. It is believed that this fact is well known by the leaders of the W.P.C., and that they have taken every precaution to prevent any possible disturbance which might arise through the angry feelings of an infuriated populace."

The party had in fact invited Milton Kalloch to speak at a rally planned for two-thirty that afternoon, Sunday, August 24. More than ten thousand people crowded the sandlot adjacent to the new City Hall. "Some were hot-headed and in favor of violence," wrote one witness. "The majority was on the side of law and order." Several reporters loitered on the speaker's platform and waited for Denis Kearney to arrive.

Scribes from the *Alta*, *Call* and *Bulletin* scribbled in their notebooks and maintained a safe distance between themselves and a reporter from the *Chronicle*, whose presence had many in the crowd frothing at the mouth. Cries of disgust rippled through the audience and prompted one man to scream, "Throw the *Chronicle* reporter off the stage!" Workingman William Wellock, the shoemaking evangelist, ascended the platform and stood beside the beleaguered newsman. "Workingmen! Workingmen!" he said. "I want you all to understand that we are today living on the American continent and, according to its institutions, we have no right to take exception to a servant of one institution, notwithstanding that the institution and its proprietors are opposed to us."

The crowd's thirst for blood remained unquenched even as the *Chronicle* reporter, having decided no story was worth a beating, scurried from the stage. Wellock moved to the edge of the platform and spoke as if addressing an ill-tempered child. "By God, boys," he bellowed, "you must and shall stop this!" His plea had the desired effect and quelled the demands for violence. Kearney also urged cooler heads to prevail when he took the stage. "A word about reporters," he said. "I want it distinctly understood that reporters are boys working for their bread and butter, and every man that earns his bread by the sweat of his brow should respect them, but not the slimy imps of hell, their employers, whose object is defamation and plunder. I hope that this is the last time I shall hear a voice on this sand-lot raised against reporters."

Kearney went through the expected motions and demanded the party faithful to dispel any thoughts of violence. The Workingmen were at the forefront of a bloodless revolution, Kearney declared, a revolution that would expose the city's "seething, stinking, glittering mass of corruption." The Reverend Isaac Kalloch, a noble soldier fighting for the cause, had been gunned down only because he could not be bought or intimidated.

"I want you and the public at large to understand that it was not for the speech that Dr. Kalloch delivered that this cowardly assassination was attempted," Kearney said, "but in pursuance of a deep-laid scheme and failing fortunes, and the assassin is therefore not entitled to the public sympathy for which he vainly begs in his paper of this morning."

Rubbish it might have been, but it set the tone nicely for Milton's speech, which followed. Remembered one witness:

> Mr. Kalloch was received with immense cheering. He reorganized his greeting as a mark of respect and gratitude to the man who was lying upon his bed, perhaps at the point of death, and all for the sake of the Workingman.

Milton opened his mouth and channeled his father. "I expect to see the corpse of that bastard brute," he said of de Young, "and to see my father tread on his grave. I appeal to you all, if the law does not follow its course, and if Charley de Young does not die by the law, to help me kill him!"

CHARLES DE YOUNG RESTED ON HIS jail cell cot and read the day's papers. He found the *Call*'s coverage particularly galling, riled as he was by Loring Pickering's apparent enthusiasm for the words "murderer" and "assassin." De Young tossed the paper aside and took in his drab, gray surroundings. Proofs of pages and raw copy from reporters littered the stone floor. The ghostly sounds of disembodied voices from the angry crowds outside had haunted his cell all through the night. By morning, the mob surrounding the jail had thinned and left few potential targets for the Gatling guns that covered the jail's front and rear entrances. Now, in the early morning, save for the sound of water dripping from somewhere and the occasional slam of an unseen door, the cell remained silent.

De Young stretched, his back cracking like a symphony of broken walnuts. He imagined Pickering in more comfortable surroundings, perhaps stomping about the *Call*'s newsroom and urging his scribes to compose articles with de Young's ultimate public shaming in mind. The *Chronicle* would set the record straight, de Young vowed to himself, and, in the process, remind Pickering of the skeletons he kept in his own closet.

THE CHRONICLE, MONDAY, August 25, 1879:

A PURELY PERSONAL MATTER DISTORTED TO MALIGNANT ENDS

Attempts are being made by malicious and interested parties to impart a political complexion to the affair of last Saturday morning . . . The encounter did not arise out of politics; it had no political significance and was purely personal in its origins and character. In the course pursued by Charles de Young, he acted in his individual capacity as a man[,] the female members of whose family had been the object of an unutterably vile attack in the public streets and in the presence of a multitude: as a private citizen, not as the member of a party or the proprietor of a newspaper.

The column slammed Sunday's edition of the *Call* for praising Kalloch's "filthy speech" as a "model of invective." The *Chronicle* noted that the praise seemed somewhat questionable as, on Saturday, the *Call* had refused to print portions of Kalloch's address because "it was so vile and obscene in its language that the females who were listening to it from their windows suddenly drew in their heads in haste and confusion." The attack continued:

The same paper, with malignant and unblushing mendacity, declares that Kalloch was attacked for defending the cause of the Workingmen, when the real cause of the attack is known by every soul in San Francisco to have had nothing to do with any political controversy or antagonism.

As it had the day before, the *Chronicle* appealed to all men who loved their mothers:

We put it to any brave and honorable man in this community, who has a mother or the memory of one, and who loves, respects and reveres her, if such language as that used by Kalloch in the hearing of thousands does not provoke personal chastisement to the death. It would be infinitely worse than death to bear such an insult put upon one's mother, and no man has a right to give it without being prepared for the worst consequences. The man who would not resent it is meaner than a dog.

That same morning, a Police Court judge—whose level of affection for his mother remains unknown—ordered de Young to remain behind bars in lieu of bail.

———————

TWO DAYS LATER, ON MONDAY afternoon, news came from the doctors at the Metropolitan Temple that Kalloch was alert and "recognized his friends." The patient, although in considerable pain, had hardly uttered a complaint. "His fortitude," reported the admiring *Alta*, "is remarkable."

———————

ON TUESDAY, AUGUST 26, THE *Chronicle* published a retaliatory scoop: Loring Pickering had once taken gun in hand to settle a grievance. Under the headline "An Indiscreet Accuser," the paper declared, "Mr. Pickering is scarcely the person to parade a virtuous indignation and holy horror over a street encounter." It seemed that while working as a newspaper editor in Missouri some years before, Pickering had tried to kill Gen. Frank P. Blair—a Union soldier and congressman—over some perceived slight. The general had sent Pickering a letter, challenging him to a duel on "the field of honor." Pickering, doubting his aim and penchant for survival, discarded the invite and sought to settle matters in a less formal manner. The altercation took place, according to the *Chronicle*, on "a dark and rainy night, in an unlighted street, and the first notice Blair had of his danger was the sound of a pistol-bullet whizzing past his head."

Hearing the shot, Blair spun around to face his would-be assailant. His gun, unfortunately, was not so easy to reach beneath a buttoned-up box coat. Blair's difficulties afforded Pickering the chance to squeeze off two more shots, the flames from his gun revealing his position in the rain and shadows. Blair managed to free his sidearm and took aim through the downpour, but Pickering had already "slunk ignominiously away."

The authorities wasted no time apprehending Pickering and slapping him with a charge of "assault with intent to kill." The Grand Jury indicted, but Blair refused to see the matter through and asked that all charges be dropped. It was only "Blair's forbearance and reluctance to prosecute," wrote the *Chronicle*, that "kept the cowardly assailant out of the penitentiary." The article concluded:

> A man who has received mortal offense at the hands of another, an offense so awful that law can offer no possible reparation or atone-ment for it, may be excused for shooting down his assailant in broad daylight, in the presence of his abettors, and without affording him a chance for his life. But it was not so in the case of Pickering . . . These are facts which out [*sic*], it would seem, to abate somewhat the fervor and vehemence of Loring Pickering's indignant eloquence in commenting upon recent occurrences.

The article was the work of Michael de Young, who maintained his tem-porary residence at the old City Hall in the interest of self-preservation. From these new headquarters, in the days following the shooting, his pen had spilled much ink in defense of his brother's actions. In publishing the sordid details of Kalloch's past, the *Chronicle* had done nothing wrong, he argued. "It was not a pleasant work," he said, "but it was a duty, as honest and fearless journalists, that we owed the public, and we never shrink from such a duty."

Pickering did not share Michael's noble point of view and shot back in his paper the following day. "Charles de Young and his brother Mike still remain in the 'tank' at the City Prison, cheerful, safe and growing fat," the *Call* reported. "The face of Charles has about recovered its usual color, and he now looks none the worse for the battering he received at the hands of the indignant populace." Pickering branded Michael de Young "a wild and unmanageable demon," and, under the heading "The Valiant Mike," portrayed him as a man soft in the spine. On Tuesday, Pickering wrote, de Young, imprisoned for protection and not punishment like his brother, stepped outside the city jail to enjoy a brief respite from its musty confines. He ventured beyond the range of the Gatling gun "with a reckless daring" and strolled onto Merchant Street. He eyed the buildings on either side of the thoroughfare to ensure no sharpshooters lay in wait to drop him on sight and crossed the street "with an easy bravado." He entered a carpet store and began chatting up the shopkeeper when someone bellowed, "There's de Young!" A crowd quickly assembled:

> They ran to see him—so great is the public curiosity to look upon this anatomical specimen. Mike heard the footfalls! The raging mob was swooping down upon him! With a wild snort, he sprang about five feet into the air, shot across the street, cleared Dunbar alley with one tremendous leap, and bounding over one of the Gatling guns in his way, disappeared into the jail as though he had been fired from a [cannon].

The "valorous Mike" swept past the guards in a blur of flailing arms and flapping coattails. He scurried back to his quarters and sought solace in his voluntary confinement. "His vermillion countenance," Pickering wrote, "had turned white, with a streak of yellow around the gills . . . Several officers smiled, and Mike remained in jail the rest of the day."

———— ❦ ————

IN THIS SHOW OF JOURNALISTIC one-upmanship, where dramatic flair and exaggerated detail overpowered objectivity, the residents of San Francisco were in no short supply of entertaining reading. B. F. Napthaly, former arch nemesis of the de Young family clan, was one such reader, surveying the headlines and scouring the articles. He had heard the fond recollections of vigilante justice and muttered accusations of police and judicial favoritism that came from the saloons and card dens, the flophouses and diners. Along with the rest of San Francisco, Napthaly wondered why de Young had not yet been indicted on charges of attempted murder. If Kalloch died, the indictment could always be amended, Napthaly figured.

When Napthaly opened the Monday edition of the *Bulletin*, he found a report that all but accused the police department of knowing about de Young's desperate plan in advance. The paper questioned the department's uncannily timely response and focused much of its attention on Chief of Detectives Lees. It seemed several individuals claimed to have seen Lees, dressed in plain clothes, hanging around the Metropolitan Temple just moments before de Young pumped Kalloch full of lead.

"The appearance of police officers so soon after the shooting, in the usually quiet vicinity of the Temple, is also commented upon," the *Bulletin* stated. "Many openly express the opinion that more than de Young knew of his purpose to kill Kalloch." No sooner had the article appeared in print, than Captain Lees was summoned before the Board of Police Commissioners to detail his whereabouts that Saturday morning. The fact that, five years earlier, Lees had helped de Young raid the offices of the *Sun* and smash that paper's printing presses in response to Napthaly's article only gave weight to the rumors.

An indignant Lees appeared before the board of inquiry late Monday night and said he "desired to resent the imputation" put forth in the *Bulletin*. Lees told the board he reached his office at the normal time of nine-thirty on Saturday morning and was reading an account of Kalloch's speech in the paper when news of the shooting reached him by telephone. Lees had then dispatched several officers to the scene:

> It was an hour of the day when the officers were scarce about the
> Hall. Lees went into the Police Court and ordered several officers,

who were waiting as witnesses, to go to the Metropolitan Temple . . . several officers were collected from the guardroom below. Those officers who were first dispatched met the carriage containing de Young and officers coming down Kearny Street, and drove into Dunbar alley just as Lees with a squad was leaving the station to proceed to the scene of the shooting. De Young was covered with blood from head to foot. Lees ordered him to be locked up.

As de Young was led into the jail, he turned to Lees and asked that officers be sent to the *Chronicle* building to guard against vandals. These were the cold, hard facts, the chief of detectives insisted.

Lees demanded the officers he ordered to the scene Saturday morning come before the board and testify. "The Board consenting," reported the *Alta*, "a large number of police were admitted . . . and corroborated the statement of Lees as to his arrival time at the office, and the action taken on the news of the shooting coming in." All seemed to be on the level. Major Hammond, the board president, considered the matter closed.

For Napthaly, the matter remained wide open. His past had come back to haunt him, as he had himself been blamed for the recent bloodshed. In fact, at the very moment of the shooting, Napthaly—still a working journalist—had been interviewing a deputy at the sheriff's office. When news of the shooting reached the sheriff, things turned ugly for Napthaly. "There were present a number of well-known and reliable gentlemen," noted one news report. "They reproached him with being the cause of all the trouble." Napthaly mounted a vigorous defense on his own behalf, cursing the day he defamed de Young's mother in print. The article penned for the *Sun*, he insisted, had been nothing but a cheap means to rile a man with whom he once held a personal grudge.

He had actually sworn as much the year before in an affidavit he hoped would set the official record straight:

I was editor and proprietor of the daily newspaper known as *The Daily Sun*, which was published in said city and county in the year 1874, and as such editor I composed, wrote and published the annexed article reflecting on Charles and M. H. de Young and their mother and sisters. What induced me to do so was simply this: They had made a severe personal attack on me in their paper, which highly enraged and incensed me, and, while in the heat of passion, I sat down and thought over how I would be most likely to deeply wound and disgrace them in the community. The idea struck me that to attack their mother and sisters would be the most terrible punishment I could give them for the injury they had to done to me. Following out this idea on the spur of the moment, I sat down and concocted, out of whole cloth, the annexed article. As far as relates to the mother and sisters of the said De Youngs, there is not one word of truth in that portion of the article, as far as I know, or have any belief or information, and I did not believe it myself at the time I published it, but drew on my imagination, spurred on by anger and resentment.

Now, the venomous words he had long regretted had reentered the public consciousness. The vile words Kalloch spoke outside the Metropolitan Temple had come from Napthaly's pen, prompting the former *Sun* editor to now suffer a crisis of conscience. Hoping to alleviate this emotional burden, he went to the city jail and sought an audience with the de Youngs. A guard escorted Napthaly to Charles's cell, where he found the brothers planning the next day's *Chronicle*. They bid Napthaly a friendly welcome and asked what brought the young man to such a dire place. Napthaly leaned against the bars and confessed Kalloch had summoned him several days before the shooting and asked for a copy of the *Sun* article.

Napthaly said he had refused Kalloch's request and then was issued a second summons from the reverend's inner sanctum several days later. Against his better judgment, Napthaly heeded the call and found Kalloch sitting behind his desk in a jovial mood. He invited Napthaly to take a seat and asked once more for a copy of the offending story. When Napthaly again refused, Kalloch brushed the rebuttal aside and "exultingly announced that he had one."

Napthaly winced. The last thing he wanted was a starring role in another public dispute. He urged Kalloch to disregard the article, explaining the piece had been written with malicious intent. "Kalloch declared that he did not care whether it was true or false," Napthaly now told the de Youngs, "he would use it and more of the same sort, too." Napthaly warned Kalloch that if he read the piece in public, he would likely suffer a violent death—a sentiment echoed by Kalloch's loyal manservant, also in on the meeting. But their admonitions were in vain; the reverend was determined.

The details of Napthaly's story appeared in the *Chronicle* on the morning of Wednesday, August 27. "Kalloch's Act Premeditated for a Week," declared the headline. The article that followed charged Kalloch with cowardice:

> Kalloch did not, under the circumstances, deserve the treatment of a man. He had placed himself outside the pale of any privilege of self-protection. A man, who, in the presence of eight or ten thousand persons, attacks another man through that most sensitive avenue to his feelings—his mother—when he applies the vilest epithets known to the English language; when he forgets his calling, his audience, common decency, the most sacred properties of life, the precepts of the religion he pretends to inculcate, what can he expect?

In shooting Kalloch, the *Chronicle* argued, de Young had displayed the true essence of bravado:

> If there was no danger to Mr. de Young from Kalloch, there was abundance of peril from persons in the vicinity, and especially from workingmen, who are never absent from the neighborhood of the Temple. Though Mr. de Young had a loaded pistol, he never attempted to use it on those who were attacking him . . . It is not easy to see wherein lies the cowardice of one who perils in an affair of this kind his own life, his own liberty, his own chances of being

misunderstood, and held as one dishonored for the sake of the mother who bore him.

———◆———

FAR FROM THE CONFINES OF de Young's cell where the brothers engineered efforts to lift their name unsullied from the gutter, Kalloch continued his amazing recovery. By Wednesday, four days after the shooting, the doctors declared Kalloch to be in stable condition. A natural color had returned to his features and the fear of hemorrhaging had subsided—albeit slightly. He remained bedridden for fear that any sudden movement might burst an artery. The exact location of the bullets in his chest and thigh remained unknown. At 11:30 AM, Dr. Lane released a statement: "After careful examination, the physicians attending Dr. Kalloch agree in pronouncing his condition highly favorable, and better than at any time since he was wounded." Three days later, the reverend agreed to receive a reporter from the *Bulletin* for the purpose of an exclusive interview.

The reporter entered the room and found Kalloch, propped in place and reclining on his cot with inflatable rubber pillows behind his back. The reverend greeted the reporter with a hearty "Good morning" and "a warm pressure of the hand" before settling back and sharing his thoughts on recent events. "I had no suspicion of an attack when I went to the coupe," he said. "I believed that de Young, after the unmerciful abuse he had heaped upon my dead father through his newspaper, would not go further, but I am convinced now that there was a political plot to assassinate me, and that others than de Young were accessories before the fact. De Young knew that I would be elected if I lived, and believed that the only way to prevent my election was to kill me."

A physician lingering in the corner stepped forward and urged the reporter to change the line of questioning. Discussing the attempted assassination and the possible motives behind it would cause the patient to become overly excited, he warned. Kalloch waved his head in a gesture of dismissal. "Before the election I will say something to the voters of San Francisco," he said, casting a glance in the doctor's direction, "if the physicians do not object."

The physicians did object. Kalloch issued no other statements from the Metropolitan Temple prior to the election. The *Chronicle*, however, had a few words of its own. Kalloch's survival was a contingency Charles de Young had not considered, nor had he contemplated the political consequences of his actions. Public sympathy ran strong for Kalloch, a man shot for defending the name of his deceased father (never mind that he was attacked for calling another man's mother a whore). Written off for dead only days earlier, Kalloch had rallied with sheer will and a constitution doctors likened to that of a "grizzly bear." Such characteristics, said the man on the street, were just what the city needed in a mayor. Most of the city's papers still opposed the Workingmen and their "Communist" agenda. Pickering in the *Call* and *Bulletin* now proved the exception. "You have with unexpected magnanimity agreed to deter any lawlessness and insurrectionary action until after the election," he wrote to the Workingmen's Party, "and therefore we endorse you as worthy of being elected."

De Young's reporters kept him abreast of the public sentiment. The brothers sought to undo any feelings of pity the denizens of San Francisco harbored for their fallen candidate. "If Kalloch was not a suitable candidate a week ago," the *Chronicle* argued, "there is no logical reason for regarding him as more suitable now." The *Alta* also urged voters to think with rational minds and not sympathetic hearts when casting their ballots. In an editorial dated Friday, August 29, and headlined "LEAD AS A QUALIFICATION," the paper reminded voters that being shot did not automatically qualify one for public office:

> If a murderous attack were sufficient to prove that the victim was previously fit for high public trust, or would confer all the qualifications, then it might be a good plan to pen up the Kearneyite candidates on the Municipal ticket in a row, and hire the practiced pistol of the Jessie-street "affray" to plug every fellow with a bullet. As it is

now, most of them are qualified for nothing save defeat, which we
hope and expect will be their share in next Wednesday's lottery.

The public went to the polls on Wednesday, September 3. The day
remained quiet throughout, free of drama and the melodramatic theatrics the
Workingmen had honed to an art. Five days would pass before the final
results were announced, but early returns showed Kalloch faring well, with
support from both his party and a smattering of Republicans. "We hear that
some Republicans have said that they will not vote the Republican ticket
because the *Chronicle* has published it in its columns," the *Alta* reported.
"That, surely, would be 'running it into the ground.'"

The final results came as no surprise when they were announced on the
morning of September 8. "The crack of de Young's pistol from behind the curtains of a coupe," wrote Henry George, "fired Dr. Kalloch into the Mayoralty." Kalloch received 20,069 votes against 19,550 ballots cast for
Republican candidate B. P. Flint. "When the result of the election was
declared," noted one newspaper editor, "Kalloch speedily recovered."

Public support for the Workingmen did not stop with Kalloch's election.
The party had claimed the mayor's office and those of eight other high-
powered officials, including sheriff, district attorney and treasurer. Two
snatched seats on the Board of Supervisors and nine donned robes and joined
the ranks of San Francisco's Supreme Court judges. The Workingmen now
held sway over the largest American city in the West. The governor's office
had gone to Republican George C. Perkins, though that did nothing to sooth
Charles de Young's angst.

Loring Pickering could not resist gloating. "Not a candidate that the
Chronicle supported," he wrote in the *Call*, "has been elected."

13

FINAL EDITION

MAYOR-ELECT ISAAC KALLOCH TOOK THE oath of office on December 2, 1879, having only recently emerged from his forced seclusion in the Metropolitan Temple. The swearing-in ceremony was a late-night affair held in the chamber of the Board of Supervisors. Anyone who thought Kalloch's journey to the brink of death had blunted the man's sharp tongue was quickly proved wrong when he stepped to the podium and delivered his inaugural address. In addition to promising the people an honest government, he viciously maligned a certain newspaper. "There must be something radically wrong, and needing good toning up, in the moral status of a community," he said, "many of whom advertise in, support, and get their mental pabulum from a newspaper built up on the wreck of hearts and homes, and edited by an assassin."

The de Young–Kalloch fray may have left a bad taste in the mouths of

The Rev. Isaac S. Kalloch, the fifteenth mayor of San Francisco, whose two-year term was wrought with conflict and personal drama. His life before City Hall wasn't that peaceful, either.
[PHOTO COURTESY OF THE SAN FRANCISCO HISTORY CENTER, SAN FRANCISCO PUBLIC LIBRARY]

many people, but it did little to impede the *Chronicle's* continuing evolution. On September 29, the paper moved from its offices on Clay into a "pretentious building at Kearny and Bush streets." A massive five-story affair, it was the first building in California designed for the sole purpose of operating a newspaper. It proved to be more than just a fine piece of modern architecture; it served as a proud monument to the *Chronicle's* success and a reminder to San Francisco's 234,000 residents that the de Young brothers had no plans to go anywhere.

The de Youngs proclaimed the paper's new digs to be "the most elegant office on the coast." The newsroom on the fifth floor was large and spacious, a far cry from the paper's former cramped and dingy quarters on Montgomery Street more than a decade ago. The basement boasted the latest in printing technology, and the brothers were more than happy to invite the public—and rival journalists—in for a look. Crowds filed past the two gleaming web presses that September day and voiced their astonishment when told that each machine churned out 33,000 copies of the *Chronicle* an hour.

Six arc lamps affixed on sculpted iron posts bathed the building's exterior in light after sunset, creating quite a spectacle. Charles de Young—a strong proponent for the use of electricity over gas—had experimented with this new form of illumination the year before, when he returned from the Paris Exposition with a primitive electric generator and several Jablochkoff candles. He had placed the candles, early arc lamps that ran on an alternate

Chronicle Building, N. E. Corner Bush and Kearny Streets, 1884

The *San Francisco Chronicle* building, on the corner of Bush and Kearny streets. It was here that founding editor Charles de Young fell to an assassin's bullet.
[PHOTO COURTESY OF THE SAN FRANCISCO HISTORY CENTER, SAN FRANCISCO PUBLIC LIBRARY]

current, in the newsroom and outside the *Chronicle*'s business office near the corner of Montgomery and Commercial. "It was the first attempt in the United States to utilize electricity for lighting purposes," wrote Managing Editor John Young:

It was not a great success, the candles sputtering, the current created being defectively supplied, but it was a newspaper triumph of the first magnitude, and caused more talk in San Francisco than any of the previous feats of the *Chronicle*, affording one of the earliest illustrations of "the journalism that does things."

With the *Chronicle* now housed in its modernized headquarters, the latest technology at its disposal and boasting the "LARGEST CIRCULATION," the de Youngs stood ready to launch a new offensive against San Francisco's mayor.

———◦———

KALLOCH ALLOWED HIS WIFE TO examine his wounds three weeks after the inauguration. The flesh where the two bullets had entered his body remained red and tender, but appeared to be healing. After fresh bandages had been applied to the chest wound, Kalloch let his wife dress the bullet hole in his thigh. Applying the clean bandage, Caroline saw on her husband's thigh something that looked not unlike a raised bruise. Kalloch cautiously jabbed the discolored area with his finger and felt something hard and round just beneath the skin. It was, he told his wife, the bullet. She sterilized a knife, pierced the skin and retrieved the bloody slug. The following day, Kalloch spotted a similar bruise in his armpit, the final resting place for the bullet that had pierced his chest. Removal of the slug was left to professional surgeons, as the ball had positioned itself near a major artery. The operation required Kalloch to stay in bed for several days, but he was now permanently out of harm's way as he immersed himself in his new role.

Mayor Kalloch's office in the new City Hall was a palatial space of rich woods and dark leather. Its tranquil décor belied Kalloch's combative reign. Open hostilities between the newly elected mayor and the Board of Supervisors erupted almost immediately after Kalloch took office. Ten of the twelve supervisors were Republicans who cared little for Kalloch or his party and sought to undermine him at every turn. There were attempts to limit his term to a single year instead of the normal two and trumped-up charges of corruption and embezzlement. They accused Kalloch of spending a $150 monthly stipend afforded to all mayors for charity donations on himself, despite the fact he had not yet received any such allowance. Kalloch fought back, striking down proposed municipal ordinances favored by the board, which only served to increase the animosity on both sides.

In February, Kalloch sought political capital in an old issue: the Chinese. Skyrocketing unemployment prompted thousands to march daily in the streets and demand that Chinese labor be permanently banished from the city's workshops and factories. Kalloch wasted no time in trying to manipulate the situation to his advantage. He put together a committee, under the auspices of the Board of Health, to investigate the quality of life in China-town. The result was a sixteen-page pamphlet published in mid-March titled "CHINATOWN DELCARED A NUISANCE!" The three-by-five inch publication detailed the filthy conditions in the Chinese quarter and blamed wealthy Republicans, who owned vast landholdings in the district, for creating a public health hazard:

> The first impression created by visiting the portion of the city called "Chinatown" is that of unnatural crowding created by there being a vastly larger number of people in a contracted territory than can possibly exist without detriment to their own health and endangering the health of the city.

The report described human waste being discarded in cardboard boxes that were dumped in the streets, and an overall environment of "smoke and stench and rottenness." It detailed cramped and squalid living quarters that allowed the unencumbered spread of disease, and where multiple men and women "huddled together in beastly promiscuousness." The report stated such unsanitary environs threatened to overrun San Francisco with "leprosy, lupus and syphilis"—diseases, which, according to the Board of Health, were "inherent in the Chinese race" and would likely result "in the deterioration of our healthy American race."

It was obvious who shouldered the blame. The Board of Supervisors, the pamphlet argued, had turned a blind eye to the disgusting state of Chinatown. "These vile politicians of the Republican Party," the document declared, "care not for the lives of citizens." Celestial labor and the filth in Chinatown were the primary factors contributing to "the destruction of life, the ruin of families . . . all by the willful and diabolical disregard of our vanity laws by this infamous race."

Kalloch offered a preview of the pamphlet's contents with a speech outside the Metropolitan Temple on February 22, 1880, just prior to its publication. Before a crowd of thousands, he detailed the numerous allegations leveled against him by the Board of Supervisors during his short time in office, blasted the Chinese and worked Republican state boss Frank Pixley—editor of the influential *Argonaut*—and Charles de Young into the vitriolic mix:

> If it becomes apparent there is no hope for American labor only by
> its degradation to Chinese prices, Chinese customs and Chinese
> living—then there will be trouble; then there will be conflagrations;
> then there will be bloodshed—and when that day comes, the de
> Youngs and Pixleys—all murderers and all slanderers—will want to
> take out good accident insurance policies.

Kalloch said he realized the city papers would distort his words and portray him as a man threatening "slaughter and fire," but what right did the press have to pass moral judgment on anyone?

> How stands Charles de Young as a keeper of the peace? He has one
> by one assaulted in the most indecent and aggravating manner every
> man put forth by the Workingmen to advocate their cause, and
> when you had united on me as your standard bearer we had every
> reasonable assurance of a peaceable victory. He jeopardized the
> lives, the peace, and the prosperity of the city by a cowardly and
> infamous attempt to assassinate me, and when I had no strength to

say anything else I whispered to the sand lot, "Keep the peace," and
God bless your noble hearts, you kept it.

Kalloch dismissed the *Chronicle* as a "blackmailing paper" and warned
de Young not to take gun in hand again. Any further attempts at assassination, Kalloch said, would result in "a retribution whose horrors it may not be
wise to anticipate." The diatribe elicited cries of approval down Mission
Street, but was propaganda that made little impact. Unemployment rates
remained high, and Kalloch and the Board of Supervisors continued fighting.

CHARLES DE YOUNG, MEANWHILE, had fled the city.

When it became clear in October Kalloch would survive his wounds,
de Young posted bail. Paying a $15,000 bond to breathe free air after putting
two bullets in a mayoral candidate struck many as overly lenient. De Young,
wise to the mood on the streets, was eager to avoid another public thrashing.
Rumors of a planned lynching and other ghastly acts of vengeance had made
the rounds, prompting de Young to consider his options. The police could
only afford him so much protection, and his daily routines and place of residence were well known. Anyone could snatch him off the street or gun him
down from a passing carriage. One can assume the fate of James King of
William was never far removed from his thoughts.

It quickly became apparent the only option available to him was a self-
imposed exile, banishment to some place far beyond the reach of a vigilante's
noose. So, after overseeing the *Chronicle*'s relocation into its new quarters,
de Young packed his bags and disappeared for four months. Michael de Young
claimed his brother had ventured east to scout paper manufacturers. There
were reports he'd gone south of the border to Mexico. Others believed he had
packed a trunk full of whiskey and was simply camping on an island in San
Francisco Bay until the controversy blew over.

Kalloch entertained a different theory entirely.

"Mr. de Young is at the present time apparently a gentleman of leisure,
instead of a candidate for San Quentin, traveling through the country to see

if I did something when I was a boy to justify him in shooting me," the mayor told supporters, steadfast in his belief that de Young was on a fact-finding mission, dirtying his fingernails and digging through the mayor's past in search of more scandal and depravity. "A portion of the San Francisco public gathers eagerly around his moral slaughter-house every morning to see if they can smell the grateful perfumes of fresh human sacrifice."

In February, confident that angry public sentiment had blown over, de Young returned to San Francisco and his duties at the *Chronicle*. He met with his defense attorneys and learned a tentative trial date had been set for May 3. While de Young's legal team wrangled with the courts to postpone the trial, life assumed its tumultuous routine. Kalloch clashed with the Board of Supervisors, vetoed ordinances and verbally beat his opponents. The *Chronicle* mercilessly thrashed the mayor and his decisions with unwavering regularity. Things continued on this bruised and battered course until the week of April 19, 1880, when a certain pamphlet began appearing on city streets. Its title was lengthy:

> Only Full Report Of The Trial Of Rev. I. S. Kalloch, On Charge of
> Adultery—A Full History Of The Affair—Doings Of The Church—
> Kalloch's Pulpit Experience—Arrest—Arraignment, Trial, And
> Result, With Accurate Portrait Of Kalloch, And The Beautiful Lady
> In Black, And The "Lecture Room" Of the Lechmere—Boston,
> Ederhen & Co., 1857.

The "report" was an illustrated transcription of Kalloch's adultery trial more than two decades before. "It is ever a painful task to record, in a public print," noted the introduction, "the departure from the path of rectitude of one who has formed a connection with the church." Painful as it might have been, it made for an entertaining read:

> When we are called upon to record the commission of a heinous
> crime by one who occupies the high, and most responsible relations
> of a pastor, how does the heart ache and rebel against an exposé of

the facts, and seek to cover the guilt with the cloak of charity, reflecting that even a pastor is only a man, subject to the same impulses, the same passions as his people, and that even shepherds, while watching their flocks, may engage in alluring pastimes, and the weak ones of their charge become their dangerous and insidious enemy.

On the afternoon of Thursday, April 22, John Young, the *Chronicle*'s managing editor, entered Charles de Young's office and dropped the pamphlet on his desk. De Young flipped through its pages, stopping to read the occasional passage before leaning back in his chair with an exasperated sigh. The party responsible for its appearance in San Francisco remained a mystery, though many harbored a sneaking suspicion a certain newspaper mogul was to blame.

De Young pushed the pamphlet across the desk toward his managing editor and shook his head. He claimed to know nothing about its origins. Much to his chagrin, the *Chronicle* had been inundated with requests from curious readers eager to get their hands on any available copies. He rubbed his brow in a contemplative gesture and pondered the rogue publication. Surely, the prosecution would use it against him in his upcoming trial. He shook his head and wondered how many had been printed.

———◦———

THE POST OFFICE HAD CIRCULATED thousands of copies. The raunchy literature dominated conversation in the city's saloons and card rooms. Kalloch's alleged moral transgressions had been well known in the city, but the sordid details were left to the imagination. Not anymore.

The mayor's office remained surprisingly silent on the matter, as did Milton Kalloch, who, like his father, had done little to conceal his hatred for the de Youngs and their paper. Since his father's shooting, Milton had been serving as assistant pastor at the Metropolitan Temple. His speech the previous August in which he vowed to kill Charles de Young had made him a well-known figure about town. His sermons had capitalized on that popularity, ensuring the temple's pews remained filled when he assumed the pulpit.

But unlike his father's rhetorical barrage, Milton's preaching was more subdued and did not rely so heavily upon theatrics and thunderous oratory. Where some might have considered Milton dour and lacking in personality, others simply viewed him as a serious young man. A Republican who cared little for the fanaticism of the Workingmen's Party, Milton nevertheless worked as a clerk in his father's mayoral administration for $250 a month. He took the job begrudgingly, as he sought to make a name for himself free of his father's influence.

Milton's silence on the matter didn't mean the pamphlet hadn't riled him up. He was incensed by the rumors that accompanied the pamphlet's West Coast debut. One, favored by the mayor, suggested de Young had spent his time back east putting together a detailed history of Kalloch's past sins "to offer in evidence as justification at his trial." If such details came out under oath, they would be given much greater credence than if they merely appeared in some vindictive newspaper column. De Young, the rumors continued, had gone so far as to bring a mystery woman from Kalloch's past to San Francisco—all expenses paid—to testify at his trial.

Milton cared little for the rumors' veracity. He had tired of de Young's antics and the *Chronicle*'s tireless assault on the Kalloch name. He hoped to confront de Young and voice his low opinion of the man; perhaps supplement the verbal beating with a well-placed boot. So, the same day the pamphlet appeared, Milton staked out the de Young house on Eddy Street, leaning nonchalantly against a lamppost opposite the residence, his gaze fixed on de Young's front door. But he had little patience for the hunt. After waiting no more than several minutes outside de Young's home, he turned up his collar in a belated attempt at disguise and scurried away. No sooner had he wandered off than de Young appeared from the opposite direction and entered the house.

The following day, Friday, April 23, Milton sat brooding at his desk in City Hall and sorted the afternoon mail. A copy of the offending pamphlet lay among the envelopes addressed to the mayor. He saw no return address but felt confident only one man possessed the audacity to send such material. Milton's temper simmered then rose to a high boil as he ran his eyes over the offending copy. He kept news of the delivery to himself, tossing the pamphlet into a wastebasket beneath his desk and setting a match to it. As the paper curled up in flames and turned to ash, Milton unlocked the second drawer on the desk's right-hand side and withdrew a loaded pistol. He slipped the gun into his pocket and watched a thin wisp of black smoke reach slowly for the ceiling.

The burden of his father's celebrity and the expectations it placed upon him weighed heavily on Milton. The Kalloch–de Young feud only intensified the strain. Solace on past occasions had been found in a bottle, as Milton had inherited his father's taste for liquor. "His associations for the past few months," reported the *New York Times* in April 1880, "have been as such to encourage undue indulgence to a marked degree." He never drank himself blind, but downed enough to soften the edge. This night was no different, as, upon leaving City Hall, he made his way to several saloons, where his poison of choice was whiskey. He sat hunched at the bar and made no attempt at conversation. The reassuring weight of the firearm at his hip was all the company he needed. After drinking his fill, he resumed the previous day's stakeout at de Young's house.

Shortly before 7 PM, a *Chronicle* reporter—having finished his day's work—left the newsroom and sauntered up Market to the Baldwin Hotel, where he turned onto Eddy. The reporter crossed Jones Street to the south side of Eddy, his mind set on a drink, when he saw Milton Kalloch, dressed in a yellowish-brown ulster and black slouch hat, standing in front of the de Young home. "His hat was drawn over his eyes," the reporter noted, "his left hand was in his coat pocket, while his right hand was rubbing his nose."

The reporter coughed loudly to attract Milton's attention. Milton started walking and made an obvious attempt to avoid eye contact. The reporter, "thinking it rather extraordinary that I. M. Kalloch should parade in front of Mr. de Young's residence," stopped and watched Milton's retreating figure. "He never looked back once," the reporter said, adding the man appeared "particularly sullen."

Milton had only just missed his quarry. Damon Nichols—a de Young

The key players in one of the most outrageous episodes of San Francisco history
[IMAGE COURTESY OF THE CALIFORNIA HISTORY ROOM, CALIFORNIA STATE LIBRARY, SACRAMENTO, CALIFORNIA]

neighbor, who lived on the southwest corner of Jones and Eddy—saw Milton walk past the publisher's house at 6:20 PM. Milton kept walking, unaware Charles de Young was no more than a few minutes behind him, heading home for his nightly dinner with Mother. As Milton disappeared in the direction of Van Ness Avenue, de Young walked up from Market and entered his home.

Dr. H. H. Thrall, a dentist, lived at 118 Geary Street with his wife and daughter. While Milton was busy spying on the de Young residence less than a mile away, Mrs. Thrall gazed out the living room window and saw a well-dressed man approach the house opposite at No. 115, where "a colored family lived upstairs." Mrs. Thrall recognized the man as the mayor and watched him ascend the exterior staircase. She had kept the house under steady surveillance since Wednesday night, when she first saw two "large and well-dressed men" enter the premises. Mrs. Thrall had called her husband to the window. "I'm positive one of them is Mayor Kalloch," she said. The doctor, peering through the gloom of evening, concurred. "I do not know I. S. Kalloch personally," he recalled. "I have seen him but once, but from the pictures and descriptions I have read and seen I was at once convinced that one of the men was Mayor Kalloch." Dr. Thrall assumed the other man was Kalloch's eldest son, Milton.

Now, on this Friday night, the mayor had returned. Mrs. Thrall continued spying from the window. Several minutes past seven, she saw a young man in a tan overcoat and black hat approach the opposite house. He climbed the stairs and disappeared inside, only to emerge about twenty minutes later and walk toward Market Street.

At about the same time, Charles de Young left his house after dinner and returned to work. He entered the *Chronicle* business office at 8 PM and engaged two customers—Edward Spear, an auctioneer, and E. B. Read—in conversation. Lost in social pleasantries, he failed to see the face peering through the large window that looked onto Kearny Street.

Outside, Milton cupped his hands against the glass and eyed de Young. He dropped one hand into his coat pocket and fingered the Smith and Wesson's grip.

Inside, the *Chronicle*'s assistant subscription clerk and collector, William Dreypolcher, conversed with customer and friend Charles Potter. "We were standing at the lower end of the counter," Dreypolcher said. "I heard the door open and shut very quick, and glanced up and saw Kalloch just inside the door . . . When I looked up and I saw Kalloch, he had a pistol in his hand."

Without saying a word, Milton raised the pistol and fired. The bullet scorched the air above de Young's head and sliced through a nearby door. The publisher leapt behind Read, then dashed for the far end of the room. Milton lunged forward, thrust his gun arm over Read's right shoulder and squeezed off another round. The muzzle blast singed Read's whiskers and blackened his cheek. The bullet ricocheted off a wall and shattered a glass door that opened onto a hallway on the Bush Street side of the building. Milton pushed Read aside and fired again. The slug buried itself in a window frame. It was enough to send Potter scrambling over the business counter and crawling behind a safe for cover. De Young followed suit and ran behind the counter, where he crouched low and fumbled frantically for his own sidearm.

From where he stood, Dreypolcher could see his boss was having trouble. "His overcoat was in the way," Dreypolcher said, "and he was trying to get his pistol out of his pocket." As de Young fought with his clothing, Milton ran forward to finish him off. He leaned across the counter, stuck the gun in de Young's face and pulled the trigger. The bullet ripped through de Young's mouth and sent him reeling backward. De Young scrambled to his feet with surprising vitality, still struggling to draw his Colt as blood flowed from the grizzly facial wound. He freed his weapon with one last desperate tug and staggered toward the large cashier's desk to his right. Milton fired again and missed. The bullet vaporized the frosted window in the door to Michael de Young's office.

From his position, Potter witnessed de Young's final stand. "Charles de Young was so weak, that he could not raise his pistol or use it," he said. "He dropped it on the desk. Then I saw him sinking."

De Young fell backward and into the arms of his half brother, Elias, who had emerged from his office seconds before to investigate the commotion. "Charley," Elias cried, "are you shot?" De Young did not respond. "I laid him down on the floor," Elias later recalled. "He did not say a word. He could not speak. The blood was pouring from his mouth." Milton, too, remained silent, and ran from the building. "Catch him," Dreypolcher cried as Milton fled out the door, but no one moved.

POLICE OFFICER PECKINPAH HEARD THE first crack of a pistol while standing on the southwest corner of Bush and Kearny streets. A second shot drew his attention to the *Chronicle* building, where—through a window—he saw an armed individual in the paper's business office. Peckinpah ran across the street toward the building and heard three more shots fired in rapid succession. Officer Edward Ward, passing the *Chronicle* on a Kearny streetcar, also heard the gunfire and jumped off to investigate. He and Peckinpah converged on the *Chronicle* just as the gunman came running out with the smoking pistol still in his right hand.

Both officers leapt upon Milton and wrestled the gun from his grasp with little effort. The weapon was still warm to the touch. Ward opened the cylinder, saw all five chambers had been emptied and passed the gun to Peckinpah. Officer William Walsh, who missed the action, arrived on scene just in time to help Peckinpah haul the suspect to the city jail.

Word of de Young's shooting spread with the speed of an urgent news flash. Within minutes, wrote one *Chronicle* reporter, "a tremendous throng had gathered outside the office on Bush and Kearny streets." A dozen officers led by Captain Lees quickly arrived on scene and surrounded the building. Inside, Charles de Young had lost consciousness.

A dentist, Dr. F. H. Dennis, had been the first doctor to respond. "I was seated in my office and was startled by the report of a pistol shot followed by two, three or four," he later told a reporter. "I ran to the front window looking out on Kearny Street and saw a crowd gathering at the front entrance of the *Chronicle*, and observed smoke in the office." Dennis ran across the street and entered the building, where he found a man he recognized as de Young reclining in the arms of another. "I discovered that he was in *articulo mortis*," Dennis said, using the medical term for point of death. "I laid him in a horizontal position, examined his pulse and found it small and rapid." Dennis could do little to help the patient. An initial examination of the wound suggested the bullet had entered the mouth, lacerated the palate and angled upward.

Ten minutes later, Charles de Young—in the blunt words of one of his own reporters—"was a corpse." An officer was dispatched to the de Young family residence and broke the horrible news to Michael, who rushed to the *Chronicle* office. Noted a reporter for the *Call*:

> M. H. de Young, the brother of the deceased, arrived on the scene
> about half-past eight o'clock, gazed at the livid and blood-stained form
> of his brother, and, half fainting, was carried upstairs to the private
> office of his brother, where he lay in a state of complete prostration.

Friends of the de Young family were permitted to enter the building and stay with Michael, who lay sprawled across his brother's desk in a state of inconsolable grief. "The workings of his face muscles and the spasmodic action of his jaw," said one witness, "betokened intense emotion."

Many staffers in the *Chronicle* newsroom were ignorant as to what had transpired several floors beneath them, despite the commotion in the street below. Questions posed by a *Call* reporter, who managed to infiltrate the editorial offices, were met with quizzical gazes and a few coarse words. "They heard the discharges," the reporter wrote, "but thought that the noise was merely that caused by moving some heavy machinery in the basement."

The grim reality hit home at quarter to nine when Coroner Dorr arrived, inspected de Young's mortal remains and immediately called for a coffin and wagon. "A few minutes after 9 PM, a cry was heard that brought the reality of de Young's death home to every one of the vast crowd that pushed and surged around the *Chronicle* building," reported the *Call*. "The ominous cry, 'Here comes the hearse to take away the corpse,' sent a chill to the hearts of all present." The vehicle's driver backed the wagon up to the building's entrance on Bush Street. Two coroner deputies removed a black pine box from the wagon's flat bed and disappeared inside the *Chronicle*. The *Call* reporter described the scene with dramatic flair:

> In the short interval before the bearers came out with the corpse, all
> was hushed and still, not a sound was uttered by one of the many
> thousands who lined the streets. The time was very short, but it

seemed almost an age, before the coffin again came to sight, and it was almost a sigh of relief that greeted the dull sound of the grating boards as the coffin was placed in the wagon.

———•———

MILTON SAID NOTHING UPON HIS arrest. At the city jail, he gave his name, was charged with assault to commit murder—the fatal result of his action was not yet known to the station keeper or arresting officers—and placed in cell 4 down in the tank. Milton betrayed no signs of emotion. He sat cross-legged on the small cot and wore on his face "an expression of countenance indicating the utmost coolness." He maintained the appearance of a man with no worries, even when a *Chronicle* reporter approached the bars with notebook in hand.

"You shot Charles de Young this evening?" the reporter said.

"I did," Milton replied with a casual nod.

"What was the cause of your action?"

"I have nothing to say," Milton said.

"I would like to get any statement you desire to make," the reporter pressed on, pursuing his exclusive.

"I have no statement whatever, sir. Nothing to say," Milton said. "I have informed you that I did the shooting, and you must get along with that."

The reporter thanked Milton for his time and ran off to file his story. Several minutes passed before the heavy clang of the tank's iron door signaled the arrival of Sheriff Desmond. He unlocked the bars and entered the cell with an outstretched hand. Milton stood and shook the hand in warm welcome. "I guess you'll have to sit down there, sir," Milton said, pointing to the cot. Desmond nodded and took a seat. Milton pulled a chair over from the corner of the cell and sat opposite his inquisitor.

"Well, Milton," Desmond said, "has anyone been to see your father?"

"I don't know," Milton shrugged, "but I suppose he has heard of this before now. Still, you can go out or send word by telephone. There is a telephone office a block from the house, and one of the boys can carry the message to the house."

Someone outside the cell cleared his throat. Milton looked up to see a young man with a notebook and pen at the ready—a reporter from the *Call*.

"I don't want to see any reporters right now," Milton said.

"I suppose then that you don't wish to make any statement at the present," the reporter ventured.

"No, sir."

The reporter passed his card through the bars and left without a quote. The sheriff, needing to notify the Kalloch family, also got up to leave. But first, he pulled two cigars from his shirt pocket and offered one to Milton, who accepted, bit off the cigar's end and leaned forward for a light. Desmond struck a match against the cell's stone wall, applied the flame and left Milton reclining on the cot, enjoying his smoke like a man without a care.

<hr />

THE DEAD-WAGON BEARING CHARLES DE YOUNG'S body pulled away from the *Chronicle*. A dozen officers, clubs in hand, marched alongside the wagon to deter any violent demonstration. Several Workingmen's clubs had by now heard of what transpired and rushed to the scene in large numbers. They made no effort to conceal their jubilation.

"A boisterous, ruffianly mob drew in from all quarters of the city, cheering and hooting in exultancy," reported the *Alta*. "The mob made louder the cheers and hoots, and at every step launched foul oaths at the man who had been murdered by the son of their reverend leader." A man standing in the doorway of a Kearny Street saloon found the apparent glee of two Workingmen so repugnant, he set upon them with swinging fists. One managed to escape, but the other was not so fortunate and suffered a vicious beating.

Thousands lined the procession route. At the intersection of Market, Dupont and O'Farrell streets, near the morgue, police officers formed a human cordon to prevent riotous spectators from overturning the cart. Another contingent of club-wielding officers surged ahead of the wagon and, "using all their force and determination," shoved and beat aside a number of Workingmen hooligans who blocked the morgue's side entrance on Bagley Place. His path clear, the hack driver steered the wagon into Bagley and pulled alongside the morgue's side door. Two morgue attendants carried the coffin inside and removed the lid. A *Call* reporter, allowed in with the coffin, recorded the scene:

> The few who had been admitted caught sight of the body wrapped in a blood-stained sheet. The body was lifted out of the coffin and placed on a cooling board, which was subsequently laid on stretchers. The sheet was then pulled aside, and then the face of the dead man was still hid from view by a cambric handkerchief, which was also stained with gore. When this was taken off, the face was unrecognizable by reason of being covered with clotted blood.

An attendant dipped a sponge into a wooden bucket of water and gently wiped away the grotesque crust, revealing powder burns on the right side of de Young's face around the mouth and chin. "There was," wrote the reporter, "a look of pain on the features of the deceased." The attendants stripped the corpse of its clothing and examined the body for additional wounds. None were found. Coroner Dorr stepped forward and gently rolled the head to one side, causing a thick rivulet of blood to dribble from the corner of de Young's mouth. The deceased's mustache hid the fatal bullet wound.

Standing at the coroner's side, the *Call* reporter asked Dorr if the body had been searched before it was placed in the casket and brought to the morgue. "A bowie knife was found on the deceased, and I am informed that he had a revolver, but it was not on him," Dorr said. "I was told that he drew it and attempted to fire, but did not have strength, and the weapon fell by his side." An officer was assigned to guard the body overnight, while others stood sentry at the morgue's entrances. "Until a later hour a crowd kept gathered in the vicinities of the morgue and the *Chronicle* office," reported the *Alta*, "but though a will to begin a reign of fiendish brutality undoubtedly existed, that fiendishness was held in check by its very cowardice."

14

BAD BUSINESS

THE EXCESSIVE AMOUNT OF BLOOD the night before had made it all but impossible to determine the true extent of the damage done, but the autopsy—performed early on the morning of Saturday, April 24—revealed the bullet's path. The slug had blown away de Young's two front teeth, ripped its way along the left side of the mouth and come to rest in the inner jugular vein. Such a wound, Dorr proclaimed, would take no more than fifteen minutes to kill a man. "The external bleeding from the wound was profuse and over a half gallon of blood was found in the stomach," the coroner noted. "The orifice made by the fatal wound is a very small one, making scarcely any disfigurement of the features."

While the coroner and his assistants examined de Young's remains, Milton Kalloch made his appearance in the city's Police Court. "He was cool, self-possessed and careless in demeanor," reported the *Chronicle*. "His father accompanied him and sat beside him in the dock." Neither man reacted when the prosecution announced its intent to amend the charge to murder.

Prominent defense attorney Henry E. Highton requested the hearing be postponed until Thursday afternoon. He gave no reason for the desired delay, but the prosecution—convinced its case was ironclad—had no objection. Reporters clamored for a comment as sheriff deputies led Milton back to his cell. Isaac, more subdued than normal, informed the ravenous horde of journalists that counsel had advised his son to keep quiet. Milton returned to the stone-and-steel environ of the city prison. Kalloch returned to his Mission Street mansion, now guarded by a contingent of heavily armed Workingmen.

Reporting the assassination that Saturday morning, the *Chronicle*'s rivals struggled to balance their righteous indignation with an underlying attitude that de Young had received what he deserved. "SHOCKING TRAGEDY," screamed the headline in the *Call*:

> This community has suffered enough in reputation and in material interests to inspire thoughtful men with a determination to put an end to the era of violence. Each individual in the community should ask himself, to what extent his voice or influence has encouraged the lawless acts we have so often been called upon to report . . . If lawlessness prevails in a community, it is because the individuals composing that community tolerate such a condition of society.

The *Alta*, while more forthright in its condemnation of the killing, did not hesitate to point out that the *Chronicle*'s founder "had commenced hostilities":

> The killing of Charles de Young was a vulgar assassination, and is a dark blot on San Francisco's record. The dead man was far from blameless, but he, on whose account the crime was committed, was not irreproachable in reputation, or reticent in speech, and had little excuse to have slander against him avenged by the bullet . . . It

is not necessary for us to repeat the history of the quarrel between
the de Youngs and the Kallochs. Some of its disgraceful incidents are
sufficiently notorious.

The *Bulletin* blamed the bloodshed on reckless journalism and questionable politics. The de Young–Kalloch vendetta, the paper argued, had "cast a
hateful shadow upon the business, morals and prospects of the city." De
Young had all but guaranteed his own violent end at the hands of a Kalloch.
"No rival Corsicans," the paper declared, "ever pursued one another with
more envenomed hate." The *Bulletin* article also suggested de Young had vio-
lated the tenets of his trade: "There is a line in journalism which cannot be
overstepped without provoking retaliation. It is, in a large sense, the dead
line. The public acts of public persons are just subjects of public criticism. But
even that latitude is not justified if personal malice is a leading motive."
Indeed, said the *Bulletin*, de Young had sacrificed news judgment for personal
animosity and vitriolic one-upmanship.

The *Chronicle* detailed the shooting in a surprisingly objective manner,
forgoing dramatics and hyperbole. It saved the sugary language for its ode to
the fallen publisher. In his chosen profession, the paper gushed, de Young
stood without equal. His "Napoleonic" genius, impeccable judgment
and "sublime" courage and energy were the qualities of great generals and
statesmen. He sought to destroy all evil and those who practiced corruption
and rascality:

And when once he made up his mind to attack an evil or evil-doer,
no threats or persuasions, from foes or friends, could swerve him
from his purpose. His taking off right in the intellectual and physical
prime of his manhood will be felt as a public calamity throughout
the city, State and coast. By those who best knew his soul, and have
followed the course of his noble life, from boyhood to death, the loss
will be most keenly appreciated and mourned. Brave heart, true
friend, trusty public servant, hail and farewell!

A longtime joke in the *Chronicle* newsroom had been a human skull with a bullet hole in the forehead perched on a shelf. Above the skull, someone had pinned a sign that read, "The man who demanded a retraction." Staffers now removed the morbid prop and buried it in a drawer.

A day after the shooting, a still-grieving Michael released a statement to the press. "The *Chronicle* will be conducted in the same course as before," he said, "though it must, of course, lose the individuality of Charles de Young." *Chronicle* reporters, meanwhile, scurried about town and worked their sources, uncovering what they believed to be "strong evidence of a deep-laid plot."

One reporter learned of the strange happenings in the house opposite the Thrall residence on Geary Street. Dr. Thrall's wife had told the reporter that moments after the shooting, someone in the house opposite extinguished all the lights. Several men were then seen entering the residence and appeared "to be excited over something." That was all she had to report, so the reporter wrapped up the interview and strolled past the house in question, where he spotted "I. S. Kalloch's colored man" standing on the outside stairs. Intrigued, the reporter staked out the residence from a spot across the street for the better part of an hour. The plot thickened when the city auditor and former sheriff—both active members of the Workingmen's Party—arrived at the home and were met by Kalloch's servant.

Another *Chronicle* reporter tracked down Charles Van Auden, a cabbie who had parked his hack on the corner of Pine and Kearny streets just minutes before Milton entered the *Chronicle* office and opened fire. "It was about eight o'clock at night," he said. "As I stood by my cab door, two men approached me coming from Pine Street." One of the men, sporting dark whiskers and black hair, asked if Auden had a fare. When Auden answered he did not, the man ordered the cabbie to be ready to ride at a moment's notice. "I took the blanket off my horse," Auden said. "As I was folding it, I saw the two men, as I supposed, go into the Wine House near Bush Street, next door to the *Chronicle*. I supposed they were going to take a drink. Immediately after they disappeared from my view, I heard two shots fired. The next thing I saw was young Kalloch in [the] charge of two policemen rushing towards the City Prison." The *Chronicle* theorized Milton had employed two associates to arrange a quick getaway. "The *Chronicle* assumes that these movements, taken in conjunction with sundry minor circumstances, indicate that the killing of Charles de Young was the result of a deliberate conspiracy between Mayor Kalloch and his son," reported the *New York Times*.

The *Chronicle* informed Captain Lees of its findings, and he dispatched detectives Jones and Coffey to investigate. They questioned Auden but failed to locate the individual the cabbie referred to as "the dark man." They had better luck at the Geary Street house, where Jim Ransome, Kalloch's manservant, opened the door. "I want to tell you that we are detective officers," said Coffey, flashing his badge. "We know about this thing and want you to give us the true business without any lying. We know whether you are lying or not."

Ransome led the two men into a cramped room furnished only with a bed and bureau. He walked with a cane that did little to ease his limp. The detectives grilled Ransome for an hour. Ransome said he suffered from rheumatism and was being nursed back to health at the house; the people seen coming and going were friends and acquaintances checking on his well-being. He'd been a servant to the Kalloch family for seventeen years, and Milton and the mayor routinely dropped by to keep him company. The story checked out when Ransome's physician, Dr. George E. Davis, confirmed everything.

The *Chronicle*'s conspiracy theories had fallen flat, so it seemed Milton had operated alone. Rumors flew that Michael de Young would soon take gun in hand and exact a bloody revenge.

───◦───

ON THE MORNING OF SUNDAY, April 25, thousands gathered outside the de Young family residence on Eddy Street. A number of uniformed officers lined the sidewalk to keep the crowds away from the house. The body, received by the family the previous afternoon, lay in state in the front parlor. The luxurious casket was made of polished walnut with satin lining, gleaming silver handles and matching trim. On the lid, a silver plate declared, "Charles De Young, Died April 23, 1880, Aged 36 Years." Floral tributes covered the coffin's top and surrounded the casket on more than a dozen display stands. "Among the most prominent pieces was a large pillow of small white blossoms, with tube-roses and camellias interspersed, and a border of maiden's hair, fern and cypress leaves," wrote one attendee. "The inscription, which in dark blue violets was arranged across the pillow, was 'DIED FOR HIS MOTHER.'" A gilded frame surrounding a black piece of silk embroidered with flowers hung from a nearby wall. A piece of ribbon stretched across its center read, "To Charles, from Mother, 1880."

Amelia de Young, in shock since receiving the news, remained bedridden. Family members, initially unable to come right out and deliver the devastating news, told her Charles had been shot and rushed to a hotel. They prepared her for the worst later that Friday night and said his condition had deteriorated. Nothing, however, could blunt the awful blow of his passing when she was told just hours before the wake. Some feared the shock would kill her. A doctor prescribed opiates and forbid her from attending her son's funeral. "It was," reported the *Alta*, "the saddest phase of all the tragedy."

Shortly before eleven, the coffin was opened to allow those waiting outside to bid the deceased farewell:

> The top part of the lid was removed, revealing the features of the
> dead through the glass case that covered them. The lineaments of
> the familiar face wore a natural repose, although somewhat swollen
> and greatly marked with powder grains, in consequence of the conti-
> guity of the murderous weapon to the face when the fatal shot was
> delivered.

The mourners entered the house through two large double doors that opened onto the parlor. They filed past the coffin in silence, their heads bowed, casting mournful glances and dabbing wet eyes. Many came as a show of respect, others simply out of morbid curiosity. Members of the Yerba Buena Lodge, No. 15, Independent Order of Odd Fellows—of which de Young had been a member—arrived shortly before one, dressed in full Order regalia and bade their final farewells. One elderly woman entered the home with a simple arrangement of flowers clasped in her bony hands. A gentleman standing nearby offered to place them on the casket for her.

"I want to put them there myself if I may," she said. "I picked them myself because I loved him."

"Did you know him?" the man asked.

"No," she replied, "but I heard what he did for his mother, and I love him, and I'm sorry, so sorry."

The procession continued for two hours, winding through the grand doors, past the coffin and through an adjoining drawing room. Ushers then led them down the home's front steps and into the street. "Many were unable to pay this last tribute to the deceased," reported the *Chronicle*, "as it became necessary to close the door in order that the funeral services might begin before all could be admitted who desired." Crowds continued to gather outside and push toward the house. "Many assembled in the street were women," reported the *Alta*. "They were the most persistent in attempting to effect an intrusion . . . though they stated they did not know any member of the family, and had never seen the murdered man."

Inside, friends and family crowded the parlor and surrounded the casket for a simple service. A picture of Charles de Young, framed in black crepe, hung above the coffin, while the room and windows were draped in black cloth. At the head of the casket stood the Rabbi Elkan Cohn, of the Congregation Emanu-El, who delivered a brief eulogy that explored the root cause of all that had transpired:

> What more than distinguished his name, what even his enemies
> cannot help admitting—aye, what in the eyes of God, before whose
> tribunal of justice he is now standing, will, as we sincerely hope,
> atone for many shortcomings and errors to which all frail human
> nature is liable to succumb, that was his filial love, veneration and
> devotion to his old mother. To love, to cherish and to respect her
> was as natural to him as to breathe. She was the object of his heart's
> dearest and holiest affections; she was the idol of his worship; she
> was the center of his feelings, thoughts and actions. I doubt whether

he ever claimed to be governed in life by strict religious principles, but we all know that the sacred commandment of God, "Honor they father and mother," glowed in his heart like a burning fire in the depths of a volcano . . . But woe to him, who, by a malicious viola-tion, either provoked and aroused, shook his volcanic nature and caused this sacred fire to break forth in furious eruptions. Alas, my friends, that flame which animated his manhood with the most sacred feelings of filial love, at last consumed his own life. He fell a victim to the highest duty and virtue of life.

The coffin's lid was closed and securely fastened before seventeen pall-bearers carried it to a waiting hearse outside. Members of the Yerba Buena Lodge, marching two-by-two, took position at the head of the funeral proces-sion. Behind them, a hundred and fifty employees of the *Chronicle*—clerks, typesetters, carriers, editors and reporters—fell in line. Friends of Charles de Young were next, followed by Rabbi Cohn's carriage and the hearse draped in black ribbon. The de Young family and more friends brought up the rear in a long line of carriages adorned in black crape.

Police struggled to part the crowds and clear the procession's way to the Odd Fellows' Cemetery. "When it started, the crowd followed for several blocks," recalled one witness. "Then, as if seized with an impulse not to let the ceremony be finished without them, they went in flocks to the nearest car lines, en route for the cemetery. The cars were crowded to an extraordinary extent, men and women risking life and limb in their scramble to get aboard."

The mournful toll of the bell in the Odd Fellow chapel echoed across the cemetery shortly before three and signaled the procession's pending arrival. A large crowd, benefiting from public transport, beat the funeral cortege to its final destination and surrounded the receiving vault. So dense was the gath-ering of spectators, only Rabbi Cohn's carriage and the hearse managed to gain entry to the cemetery. De Young's family and friends were forced to quit their rides at the front gates and enter on foot. The pallbearers dragged the coffin from the hearse and set it gently in an open space before the vault. Weeping family members bowed their heads for the final rights. Rabbi Cohn

The following to Photos an 1/x... The funeral of Charles de Young. in front of residence

Crowds gather outside the de Young residence on Eddy Street to watch Charles de Young's funeral procession. His casket is being carried in the wagon to the right.
[PHOTO COURTESY OF THE CALIFORNIA HISTORY ROOM, CALIFORNIA STATE LIBRARY, SACRAMENTO, CALIFORNIA]

read a Hebrew text before uttering the final words: "Earth to earth, ashes to ashes, dust to dust." The pallbearers lifted the coffin and placed it inside the vault, where it would remain until a permanent plot could be found. Members of the de Young clan lingered momentarily to whisper their last goodbyes.

For all the eulogies and final farewells, the most poignant words that day appeared far away in the *New York Sun* under the headline "FOLLY FROM BEGINNING TO END":

> It was folly for De Young to print in his paper any scurrilous abuse of
> a private individual. It was folly for the Rev. I. S. Kalloch to pro-
> claim an infamous falsehood about the De Young family. It was folly
> for De Young to shoot Kalloch. It was folly for Kalloch's son to shoot
> and kill De Young. De Young has died as the fool dieth. Young
> Kalloch may be executed for his crime. He may be only imprisoned,

or on some ground he may be set free. In any event, he bears for life the hand of a murderer. From beginning to end, it is all very foolish and a bad business.

———————

ON MONDAY, FOLLOWING HIS WEEKLY meeting with the Board of Supervisors, Isaac told a reporter at City Hall he had no intention of escalating the conflict between his family and the de Youngs. Milton, in a jailhouse letter, had urged his father to no longer stoke the fire of angry rivalry. "You don't need any advice, I know, but there is an impression on my mind, stronger perhaps than any other, that the recent events have so cleared away the rubbish that nothing ought to be said in public about the colors of past events," Milton wrote. "It looks to me as if the record would now be made anew. If the *Alta* and *Chronicle* folks reply, there will be a measure of excuse for continuing the old war. It will take two parties to continue the agitation for the benefit of these papers. Our appeal on everything is to the people."

With his arch-nemesis now consigned to the afterlife, Kalloch said he bore the de Young clan no ill will. "In that grave," he told a reporter, "I bury my revenge."

———————

CORONER DORR CONVENED AN INQUEST on the afternoon of Thursday, April 27, at his O'Farrell Street office. More than a dozen witnesses sat before an eight-man jury and testified that Milton Kalloch had fired the first shot on that fateful evening and continued firing while de Young struggled to draw his gun.

One man, however, told a different story. A dapper gentleman with an English accent, John Hobson Clemetshaw said he was in the *Chronicle* office at the time of the shooting. (The fact other witnesses could not recall seeing him near the scene hardly mattered.) Clemetshaw told the jury he left his home after dinner on the night in question and stopped by a nearby tobacconist on Market. He made a purchase and strolled to the paper's office on Bush Street. "I stayed when I got to the *Chronicle*, at the first window on the

Bush Street side, from Kearny," Clemetshaw said. Rolling a cigarette, he took a moment to read the news boards on the building's exterior. "I saw something about Kearney and *habeas corpus* and being out of jail, or something. I looked around toward the *Chronicle* door and saw I. M. Kalloch inside of the office. I thought to myself, 'What is he doing there?' as he should be the last to go in there from what I had heard of the differences between the de Youngs and the Kallochs."

Clemetshaw sauntered back to the window on Bush Street, through which he saw Kalloch with his back to the wall. Facing Kalloch was a man "with dark side whiskers and no chin beard," later identified by Clemetshaw as Charles de Young. Without provocation, Clemetshaw said, de Young pulled a pistol from the waistband of his trousers and shot at Kalloch. The mayor's son flinched but held his position, drawing a revolver from his right coat pocket and returning fire.

"When Kalloch fired that shot, there were two men standing around Kalloch," Clemetshaw said. "The men all made a rush. One passed between Kalloch and me, and all seemed to be making for the door to get out of the range of shots. The dark-whiskered man went toward the rear of the office, and Kalloch stood facing him. They were in the middle of the corridor leading to the rear. Both arms were extended, each holding a pistol leveled at each other. The muzzle of each pistol was not more than twelve or fifteen inches from each man's face."

With his nose pressed against the glass of the Bush Street window, Clemetshaw saw Kalloch fire another round. The dark-whiskered man staggered backward behind the office counter. "I saw the central line of fire from Kalloch's pistol, and it went directly toward the dark-whiskered man's face," Clemetshaw said. "I saw blood trickling down his chin." The wounded man remained on his feet and stumbled toward the large cashier's desk, where he finally collapsed—but not before Kalloch let loose another round.

"Kalloch fired five shots and the dark-complexioned man one," Clemetshaw said. "My attention was then directed to Kalloch, who made a break for the door. I rushed to the door for the endeavor to intercept him but saw he had the pistol in his hand. As he came out, Kalloch said, 'Gentleman, let me out of this.' He seemed very much frightened, agitated and scared." Officer Peckinpah arrived on the scene and slapped chains on Kalloch's wrists before Clemetshaw had a chance to play hero.

"I went to the Sheriff's office to tell about this because I thought that was the proper place to go and lodge information," Clemetshaw testified, explaining that he identified himself to a sheriff's deputy as Alex Watson because "Clemetshaw" was too hard a name to pronounce. He eventually decided to use his real name only to advance the cause of justice.

No one seemed to buy the Englishman's tale. Why Clemetshaw would choose to fabricate such facts remains a mystery, but the reporters covering the inquest smelled a story. Their curiosity regarding Clemetshaw's testimony was piqued when the coroner produced de Young's Colt revolver. "Mr. de Young's pistol was, for the first time since the shooting, taken apart," wrote a reporter for the *Alta*, "and every one of the six chambers found loaded with uniform cartridges." De Young had not fired a single shot.

After brief deliberation, the jury delivered its findings:

> We find that the deceased, Charles de Young, aged 36 years, came to his death on the 23d day April, 1880, at the *Chronicle* building, on the northeast corner of Bush and Kearny streets, in this city and county, from hemorrhage from bullet wound to the left internal jugular vein, inflicted by one Isaac M. Kalloch, on the above mentioned date, and we charge the said Isaac M. Kalloch with the crime of murder.

Milton was bundled from the coroner's office in chains and returned to his cell. Reporters rushed from the building to file their stories and begin digging into Clemetshaw's back story. The *Chronicle* soon discovered the Englishman's Mormon past and his expulsion from the Church of Latter Day Saints for being a man of dubious character. "His reputation here is of the worst character," wrote a reporter from Salt Lake City, "having been accused of burglary, theft and other crimes, and any number of good and reliable businessmen of this city will testify under oath as to his bad character generally."

The previous summer, Clemetshaw had cracked a safe in the offices of the Provo Manufacturing Company and absconded with a considerable amount of cash. Police subsequently arrested him for an unrelated crime—one the paper determined to be "less serious in nature"—and charged him accordingly. Clemetshaw jumped bail and skipped town, owing considerable money to his landlord, "to persons whom he made purchases on trust, to others from whom he borrowed money on time, and some, it is alleged, he has swindled outright." He told his various creditors his uncle in Europe had died and left him a large inheritance, but, naturally, they received not a single cent owed them. The next anyone in Utah heard of John Hobson Clemetshaw was a wire story detailing his testimony before the San Francisco coroner in the matter of Charles de Young's murder.

"Can this be the John H. Clemetshaw, the trunk-maker who left this city under a rather dark cloud a few months ago?" asked the *Salt Lake City Herald*. "The fact that the San Francisco Clemetshaw appears to be unreliable and of questionable morals, and the Salt Lake Clemetshaw was ditto, ditto, would seem to indicate that the two are one." On the evening of Wednesday, April 28, Detective Dan Coffey knocked on Clemetshaw's door at 507 Mission Street with an arrest warrant in hand. Clemetshaw, having just sat down to supper, finished his meal at Coffey's polite urging. The Englishman slurped down a bowl of soup and drank a cup of tea in the officer's disquieting presence. Once Clemetshaw had consumed his supper, Coffey informed him he was under arrest for perjury. "The announcement fell on him like a thunder clap," reported the *Chronicle*, "and, flushing a deep red to the roots of his sparsely settled hair, Clemetshaw laconically replied, 'All right.'"

He was eventually tried and sentenced to five years in San Quentin for "illegal lying." His reasons for fabricating details regarding the murder of Charles de Young remain unknown. One can only assume he enjoyed the publicity.

⸺◦⸺

ON THURSDAY, APRIL 29, MILTON Kalloch was set to appear before Judge Rix in San Francisco Police Court on the charge of murder. An hour before the two o'clock hearing, eager reporters scuffled with curious spectators for seats in the public gallery. The scramble for chairs became so chaotic, attorneys and witnesses were unable to enter the courtroom for fear of injury. "The police," noted a *Call* reporter, "after some difficulty removed from the Court-room all that were standing and a number of persons within the railing which separates the attorneys from the spectators."

A bailiff brought Kalloch up from the jail and sat him at the defense table. Dressed in the same suit he wore the night of the shooting, he appeared most confident, smiling and nodding at those in attendance, though detention in the underground cell had left him looking rather pale.

The mayor and Michael de Young were noticeably absent.

Defense attorney H. H. Highton waived the right to preliminary examination. The prosecution, led by District Attorney Blaney, called to the stand those who had witnessed the shooting. The testimony was no different from that presented at the coroner's inquest and reported in the papers. The defense asked not a single question and called no rebuttal witnesses. Rix ordered the shackled Kalloch held without bail and placed him in the custody of the sheriff, who whisked him away to the county jail on Broadway.

Hours later, the prisoner released a statement to the media. "I have not a word to say about the facts or merits of my case," Milton said. "I wish to be tried in the ordinary way. Fair play—especially toward a man charged with murder—is supposed to be a characteristic of American communities; but I expect no fair play on or before my trial if the fast men and corrupt detectives who surround the *Chronicle* office and assume to run this city can prevent it." He went on to suggest the arrest of Clemetshaw was an intimidation tactic. Although he refused to comment on the veracity of the Englishman's testimony, Milton made no qualms about weaving a conspiracy theory. "I do not know the man . . . but I do declare that he had no motif [sic], so far as I can see, to conceal or pervert the truth. It looks to me as if his arrest is intended by the *Chronicle* and the detectives to warn citizens of San Francisco that they must not testify to any facts that would even point toward my exculpation."

That same day, the *Chronicle* reprinted a column from the *New York World*. It implied the mayor had encouraged John Hobson Clemetshaw to commit perjury:

The people will naturally suspect that Kalloch suborned the evident perjury, which was committed at the inquest upon the body of Mr. de Young. It seems perfectly plain that the perjurer had obtained permission to view the body before the inquest in order to fabricate a story that would be consistent with the known facts of the murder . . . The man was hired to tell the story and the most natural supposition is that he was hired by Kalloch. Kalloch had a warm personal interest in getting perjury committed in favor of his son, and Kalloch is not commonly supposed to be too good to concoct or procure perjury, for a motive much weaker than to save the life of his son.

The facts were highly questionable, as there was no hard evidence to back such a claim. An exasperated Kalloch slapped Michael de Young with a libel suit the following day. Perhaps to the relief of San Francisco's citizenry, guns on both sides of the dispute remained holstered.

15

IMPEACHMENT AND TRIAL

ISAAC KALLOCH HAD ALWAYS THOUGHT his problems would be solved if he were rid of his rival, but life remained a tumult of chaos and conflict. His son faced possible execution if convicted, and the Board of Supervisors continued to make his political life miserable. Rumors swirled that depression had taken its toll and forced the mayor to seek tranquility in the depths of a bourbon bottle. The supervisors—ever eager to push Kalloch out of office—capitalized on the moment. The board launched an investigation into Kalloch's behavior as mayor, eventually deciding he had used "incendiary language" to incite violence, pocketed free streetcar passes and doled out political favors to his Sandlot cronies.

On May 3, 1880, at its weekly meeting, the board presented Kalloch with its long list of accusations. Isaac listened as the charges—contained in Resolution No. 14,589—were read into the public record. Among the charges listed were "counseling the vicious and turbulent" and "pandering to the unruly and evil-disposed." "The report on the conduct of Mayor Kalloch in his relations to the Kearneyite mob, submitted to the Board of Supervisors, has the double merit of being an extremely lively public document, and of expressing the sentiments of a large number of the most intelligent citizens in San Francisco," reported the *Alta*. Kalloch seemed not even to care when the board's two Workingmen voted with their ten Republican colleagues to indict. Isaac simply banged his gavel and adjourned the meeting.

The case went before a five-judge tribunal on Monday, May 24. Following three days of testimony, Kalloch was acquitted; the judges decided his alleged transgressions had occurred before his election to public office. "If he received free railroad passes and corruption money," the panel ruled, "it was as a private individual, not as Mayor."

Case dismissed.

———⊙———

ON ANOTHER LEGAL FRONT, KALLOCH'S libel suit against the *Chronicle* went to court on Wednesday, May 26. "The precincts of the Police Court were crowded to their utmost capacities," noted one observer. "The Mayor was present accompanied by half a dozen select retainers, who appeared to act as a body guard . . . He kept his eyes open most of the time, holding consultations and conversations with counsel and companions." John Shimmons, a longtime Kansas resident and a former Kalloch acquaintance, testified for the defense.

"State what his general reputation for truth, honesty and integrity was among the people who knew Kalloch," the *Chronicle*'s lawyer asked Shimmons, referring to the plaintiff's years in Ottawa and Lawrence.

"It was bad," the witness replied.

Kalloch's attorney objected when the defense asked Shimmons to elaborate. The mayor's behavior in Kansas had no bearing on the allegations set forth in the offending editorial, he argued. The judge agreed and decided to postpone the proceedings until June 4 in order to grant both sides time to prepare their arguments and track down additional witnesses. Before court could resume, however, Kalloch dropped the case. He was tired of courtrooms. "The truth is," reported the *Chronicle,* "that the comments of the *World,* which have so excited the ire of the father of the murderer[,] are mild and tame when compared with the scathing denunciations, which other impartial and conservative journals have poured forth."

One publication that sought to highlight Kalloch's past sins was neither conservative nor impartial. It appeared on city streets within two weeks of Charles de Young's murder. Entitled "A Faint Idea of a Terrible Life! The Rev. I. S. Kalloch (Mayor of San Francisco)," the pamphlet detailed Kalloch's alleged debaucheries from his time at college to the present day in language that would have made the Marquis de Sade blush. "For sale wholesale by J. K. Cooper, bookseller, 746 Market Street," noted the pamphlet's cover, "and retail by all Newsdealers who are not Bulldosed."

The front-page illustration was a cartoonish rendering of Kalloch, complete with a pouty lower lip, puppy-dog eyes cast skyward and his hands clasped in desperate prayer. Half the publication's 123 pages revisited the infamous adultery trial, while the rest highlighted other instances of Kalloch's insatiable sexual hunger. The publication made no attempt to mince words and explained its purpose in a blunt introduction:

> The Rev. I. S. Kalloch is, in an exceptional sense, PUBLIC PROP-
> ERTY . . . If he is a bad man, the public have a right to know it. If, in
> every relation of life, he has proven himself a scoundrel, the fact
> cannot be too widely made known, even though it be proclaimed
> from the house-tops. If his name, fame and reputation, are widely
> known to be disgraceful, then the sooner the whole city is made
> acquainted with all the facts, the better. If he has been a corrupter of
> Courts, a giver and taker of bribes, a dangerous politician, a perjurer,
> a man whose frauds have been gigantic, and in number beyond
> belief, a religious mountebank and hypocrite, a fellow drunken with
> whiskey and lust, a life-long seducer of virtue, and now and always a
> lecherous beast, then, surely, in view of his present position towards
> this city, its government, its politics, its society and its religion, he

who knows the facts, is in the strict line of duty when he makes them known.

Sordid tales of carnality were just the beginning. The pamphlet also alleged Kalloch traveled the country, spreading his seed along with the gospel. In the wake of his departure from each town he visited, the leaflet proclaimed, women wept and parents hung their heads in shame. And still he craved more:

> When under the influence of liquor, Kalloch used to tell his friends
> what he considered would be an earthly paradise. He said, "I would
> have, if I were rich, ten or fifteen girls, nice and plump; I would then
> strip myself, and, with these naked girls around me, I would enjoy all
> the delights of a Turkish harem." Then he would go on and describe
> the most extravagant scenes of licentiousness, with which his
> prurient imagination seems to teem. There is nothing in Hume's
> descriptions of Roman debauches, which could compare with the
> acts, which this depraved wretch wishes he could participate in. A
> mind so rotten, a heart so sallow, a conscience so blunted, or a taste
> so depraved was surely never before heard of.

According to the pamphlet, while in Kansas, Kalloch and some friends had visited Chicago for a "roaring good time." There they consumed vast amounts of whiskey in various saloons and engaged with more than a few women in various dens of ill repute. In one brothel, Kalloch supposedly approached the madam and asked, "How much for the whole house for the night?" The madam smiled and told him that, for the bargain price of $150, every girl in the place would be more than happy to plumb the depths of his sexual imagination. Kalloch pulled out his billfold and paid the fee. The madam counted the cash and told Kalloch to go and wait in the parlor.

He made himself comfortable on one of the chintz settees and smoked a cigar as the girls sauntered in one by one. They stood before him, a luxurious line of perfumed flesh, silk and curves, allowing him to inspect their ranks like a drill sergeant inspecting his cadets. Satisfied with what he saw, Kalloch locked the parlor door and pocketed the key. "In a nude condition," the pamphlet said, "they had what Kalloch called a circus." From there, things became downright raunchy:

> As a part of the entertainment, Kalloch marched the girls around
> the room on their hands, he holding them by their feet,
> wheelbarrow fashion. But we must draw the veil—what followed is
> unutterable. Nothing like it has probably ever appeared in print.
> The description of the bacchanalian orgies in profane times, by the
> world's greatest satirist, Juvenal, comes nearer to it than anything of
> which we have any knowledge.

The debauchery continued in San Francisco, the pamphlet concluded. "He is now, as he ever has been, a gross, sensual libertine," it said. "He is a drunken, foul-mouthed visitor at houses of ill-fame, and has been so during the time he has been Mayor of this city. A receiver of bribes in office, a violator of his oath, an incendiary demagogue, and a dangerous chief-magistrate."

The fifty-cent pamphlet sold 5,000 copies within hours of its publication, prompting a second printing. It was an instant bestseller.

The man behind the stunning piece of literature was a rogue newspaper editor named William McCann Neilson. Some wondered whether the de Young family had financed the publication, but Neilson brushed aside such speculation. "I did it without the knowledge of any individual," he proudly proclaimed. "My own family did not know what I was engaged in. No human being, so far as I know, ever saw any part of this pamphlet, except the printers, until after publication. It was submitted to nobody, and it was paid for by myself. I alone am responsible for it." Neilson said he considered it his civic duty to present to the citizens of San Francisco the "facts" of Kalloch's past. "It was the right and duty of any gentleman," he said, "to offer them to the people."

Police arrested Neilson and charged him with libel days after the pamphlet's publication. The plaintiff was not Kalloch, but a supposed supporter of the mayor named Alexander Kydd, who claimed to be outraged by the allegations put to paper by Neilson's pen. The case went to court on Thursday, June 3.

Although represented by legal counsel, an unrepentant Neilson delivered his own opening argument before the judge, claiming "a gentleman from Kansas" had provided the pamphlet's source material. "I propose to prove, as this pamphlet alleges by undeniable and overwhelming evidence, that this man, the mayor of this city, has led a life of treason against the labor of man, the virtue of women, the integrity of public life and the sanctity of the laws under which we live," Neilson said. He prattled on, referring to Kalloch as a whoremonger and demagogue: "I expect by testimony to prove that, and, by way of commencement, I propose to call Rev. I. S. Kalloch as a witness, which I do now."

The mayor was noticeably absent—and not just from the courtroom.

The police judge asked Neilson's attorney, George W. Tyler, whether Kalloch had been subpoenaed. Tyler said several subpoenas had been issued over the past week, but none had found their way into Kalloch's hands. It seemed the mayor had vanished; not even the police knew of his whereabouts. A detective had been dispatched at noon the day before to serve Kalloch court papers at the Palace Hotel, his Mission Street residence and his office at City Hall—all to no avail. The judge ordered the police to continue their search for the city's missing leader.

The following day, Friday, June 4, attorney Davis Louderback made an appearance on Kalloch's behalf. "It was a very easy matter to find the Mayor if desired by the defense," he said, "as he has been in the city all of the time, upon the streets and attending to his business." Approaching the bench, Louderback said the mayor wished the case to be dropped. "This proceeding was set on foot," he said, "for the purpose of aiding in the circulation and sale of a vile, obscene and infamous publication." Never, in his years of service to the legal system, had Louderback seen a court issue a libel warrant solely on the complaint of someone who had not actually been libeled. The plaintiff did not represent the interests of the mayor, Louderback proclaimed, but was working in collusion with Neilson as part of an intricate publicity stunt.

An incredulous George Tyler then addressed the court for the defense, saying if the mayor could be located so easily, "there must be something wrong in the police department." The judge agreed that Kalloch was clearly avoiding court and ordered the case forward.

The Case of the Disappearing Mayor generated a considerable amount of interest from the press. "A pretty spectacle is that of the Mayor of San Francisco dodging a policeman who wants to bring him into court to testify that he is an adulterer, a liar, a swindler, a thief, a Turk in sentiment, an accepter of bribes, and the biggest scalawag generally that ever disgraced a public office or a church," noted the *Exchange*, a financial paper. When the case resumed Saturday morning, the *Chronicle* reported, "The three days' street hunt by the police for the mayor came to an end. Kalloch was in court, an officer having found him late Friday night." The paper did not state where Kalloch had been hiding.

The mayor spoke only through his attorney, who read a lengthy affidavit outlining the mayor's position on the case and his desire to see it thrown out of court. "I am a citizen of the United States, over the age of 45 years, descended from respectable American stock," the affidavit began. It continued, detailing his religious background, his troubled time in New England and his various adventures in Kansas. "I took a leading part, which ought to shame those who are virulently pursuing me in San Francisco, and, as minister, lecturer and railroad superintendent, and incumbent of public office in that State, I became well known to the people. I was often discussed by the newspapers and was praised and abused to a degree only equaled in my recent experience."

In the document, Kalloch said he considered legal action when he heard Neilson was preparing the pamphlet, but ultimately ignored the publication when he learned the "gist" of its accusations. The libel suit brought by Kydd—who Kalloch claimed was neither a supporter nor a member of the Metropolitan Temple—was merely designed to publicize Neilson's efforts. Kalloch acknowledged his past would likely be dragged out for all to see in the coming months even without the pamphlet. "On the trial of my son for the alleged killing of Charles de Young," he wrote, "I shall be examined as a witness—if living—and my whole life, private and public, be thrown open to the fullest judicial scrutiny and investigation."

After reading the affidavit, Kalloch's attorney asked the case be dismissed. "It was not commenced at the instigation or with the approval or consent of the party libeled; and because on the face of the affidavit, it appeared to be collusive," he argued. The court agreed and tossed out the case, reprimanding Neilson for his shameless self-promotion.

———————

JURY SELECTION IN THE TRIAL of Milton Kalloch got under way on Monday, January 24, 1881. The sensational nature of the crime and its presence in headlines for so many weeks meant the vast majority of potential jurors already harbored strong opinions about the case. Many saw nothing wrong in what Milton had done and viewed de Young as the true villain, a miserable rapscallion who smeared reputations to increase his circulation. To others, the Kalloch name—tainted as it was with unfathomable depravity—implied guilt. Lawyers on both sides spent four weeks wading through a jury pool of thousands before seating the final panelist, marble cutter Thomas Farrell, on Saturday, February 19. Spectators crowded Judge Temple's courtroom in Department 11 for the commencement of trial later that afternoon.

"At two o'clock," reported the *Call*, "the information charging the defendant with the killing of Chas. De Young was read to the jury. During the time occupied by the reading, a profound silence reigned, interrupted only by the clamors of those outside endeavoring to obtain admission."

Assistant District Attorney D. J. Murphy delivered his opening argument in a short, half-hour address. He summarized the sequence of events that fateful day as everyone knew it via the newspapers. "If these facts are made out, then we think that the law, not only of our state, but of the entire civilized community, pronounces that it is murder," he said. "We shall offer evidence, and prove, that the defendant's act was premeditated, and that before the act was done, the defendant was lying in wait for his victim; and, further, that at various points, where he well knew the deceased to be in the habit of passing, the defendant was also there."

Milton Kalloch, neatly turned out in a suit, sat beside his attorney as the prosecution tied the hangman's rope.

The people's case seemed a simple affair, armed as they were with eyewitnesses and motive. The trial began with testimony from the physicians who rushed to Charles de Young's aid and the coroner who performed the autopsy. There was little the defense could do with the witnesses on cross-examination. Next, E. B. Read, his face no longer marred by powder burns from Milton's pistol, testified no one but the defendant fired a shot during the fatal confrontation. Again, the testimony offered little for the defense to bend in their favor.

Some comic relief was had on Monday, February 21, when Gustavus Spear—witness to the killing—took the stand for the prosecution. Asked by Murphy where he was when the shooting began, Spear replied he was running for the door. "I expected more shots to be fired and supposed Mr. de Young was about to shoot," he said. "I knew that Mr. de Young had been in several shooting scrapes, and expected him to do some shooting then."

In total, half a dozen witnesses testified to having seen the defendant gun down Charles de Young. Defense attorney Highton could hardly dispute such facts, but hoped instead to manipulate the jury's sympathy. Paramount to Highton's strategy was the portrayal of Charles de Young as a man obsessed with Kalloch's destruction—a man whose desire to trigger his opponent's downfall transcended "the line of decent journalism." He delivered his opening argument on Tuesday, March 1, 1881, the twenty-seventh day of trial.

"Charles de Young had been indicted for an assault with intent to murder Dr. Kalloch. There had been proceedings in that case in the Supreme Court of this State, which had occupied some nine sittings in that Court. Mr. de Young had gone east for the purpose of bringing together such evidence as would destroy Dr. Kalloch, and with him his entire family, a circumstance which provoked this young man's sensitive nature and haunted his mind," Highton said, pointing to his client. "Through the long watches of the night, sepulchral shapes were ever present in the tortured faces of this young man's mother, wife and sisters. It is well for this community, it is well for this civilization, it is well for this nation, indeed, if out of this terrible tragedy, which we are investigating here, shall grow a sentiment that will eradicate from the hearts of men that love of morbid scandal that is the foundation of libel and homicide—moral and physical destruction."

Highton called to the stand Caroline Kalloch, who testified her son "was always of a very nervous temperament." She explained how in August 1879, the actions of Charles de Young had forced Milton to leave his wife and pastoral position in Sonora to attend to his gravely wounded father.

"After his arrival, he remained at the Temple for about three weeks, as nearly as I can recollect. The condition of his father during that time was very critical from his wounds," Caroline testified in a soft voice. "When my son arrived from Sonora, he was very much excited and weary. The circumstance of leaving his family, the long journey and want of sleep had overcome him very much. And that, in connection with finding his father in such a low condition, made him almost wild for a little while. He was very attached to his father . . . There was a public meeting of the Sandlot, and he was invited to go there and make a speech. I advised him to tell them that if they valued his father's life, not to have anything said by anyone to aggravate his case. His condition was so much excited that I feared he might act unwisely. I could see his excitement in his face. He was more uneven than before."

The normally warm and attentive Milton became brooding and solitary, his mother said. "He would take the papers and look them over, and then remain silent for a long time. He would soon close the conversation and go into another room." Despite the change in Milton's demeanor, Caroline never imagined her son would take up arms against his father's adversary.

Finished with the diminutive Caroline, Highton called Mayor Isaac Kalloch to the stand.

"Did you ever meet Charles de Young?" Highton asked.

"I have," Kalloch replied.

"Met him personally?"

As Kalloch answered, "I have, sir," Assistant District Attorney Murphy leapt from his chair like a jack-in-the-box. "We object," he cried. "I don't see any relevancy."

The objection overruled, Kalloch continued with his answer. "It was the day before my nomination for mayor by the Workingmen's Party here . . . At this interview, Mr. de Young said that I should not run for Mayor of San Francisco. 'If you do,' he said, 'I will ruin you and your family. I will drive you out of this state and from your business. I will make the name Kalloch so odious that no man or woman will ever dare wear it in California again.'" Kalloch turned to the judge. "My son was specifically mentioned, your Honor. He said he had my record from the beginning, and that of another young preacher of the family. He referred to others who had got in his way and that of his family." The witness now swung his gaze toward the jury. "Mr. de Young said, thumping his desk, that he even had the detective police force under his control and that of his paper."

"Your Honor," said a clearly flustered Murphy, "I move to have this answer stricken out."

"Now, I wish to object to this continual interruption of the witness by these objections," Highton shot back. "He is never allowed to conclude his answer."

The judge seemed amused. "I think that is entirely permissible under the circumstances," he said, overruling the prosecution's objection.

Highton continued, "Now, Dr. Kalloch, in view of the ruling of the Court, was there any other language made use of by the deceased that imported personal danger to you or your son?"

"It was all threatening," Kalloch replied. "He said, 'I will make it hotter than Hell for you.'"

"Did you have any further communications with Charles de Young, personally, after that interview?"

"I believe I never spoke to him after that interview—at least not to my recollection," Kalloch said, as he retrieved two small objects from an inside jacket pocket. "There were several attempts to make interviews."

"Did you have any interview with Mr. de Young on the 23rd day of August, 1879?" Highton asked.

"I can say I did," Kalloch said with a smirk, rattling the two objects in his right hand.

"And where did that interview take place?"

"Jessie Street, near Fifth; near the Jessie Street entrance to the Metropolitan Temple."

"Whereabouts were you, and where was Mr. de Young?" Highton asked.

"Well, now," interjected Murphy at the prosecution table. "I don't know what this refers to, although I have, of course, a very prompt suspicion of what it tends to. If he intends to involve the trouble between Dr. Kalloch and the deceased, I shall object as immaterial."

The judge dismissed Murphy's concerns and told Kalloch to proceed.

"I stood on the sidewalk at the Jessie Street door in front of the coupe. He was in the coupe, as I have reason to believe. The instant I stepped to the coupe, I was shot in the left breast and, on turning, in the back." Again, he jangled the objects in his cupped palm. "The two bullets entering my body, I now have in my hand—if you would like to have them."

"You produced the bullets that were taken from your body after the 23rd of August?"

"Yes, sir," replied Kalloch. He clicked the bullets like castanets.

"I wish to offer these bullets in evidence to the jury."

The judge overruled Murphy's objection before the prosecutor could even get the word out of his mouth. The mayor handed the bullets to the jury foreman, and the jurors passed them among themselves, muttering and nodding. The prosecution could do nothing but sit and watch the hangman's noose slowly unwind.

On cross-examination, Assistant District Attorney Campbell sought to shift attention away from de Young and refocus on the defendant. "Do you know of any threats of personal violence being made against your son directly, in your presence?" the prosecutor asked.

"As well I know almost anything," Kalloch answered, "yes."

"Well, what threat of that kind was made in your presence?"

"I don't mean to say that Charles de Young made any direct threat in my presence. Our lives were constantly threatened."

"By Charles de Young?"

"Well, I didn't mean by Charles de Young himself," Kalloch said. "If you had included him in person, I would have answered differently."

"I will ask you again," said Campbell, agitation clearly evident in his voice. "Did you ever hear Charles de Young threaten your son with personal violence?"

"Charles de Young?"

"Yes, Charles de Young?"

"In my presence?"

"Yes," Campbell shot back. "Have you ever heard Charles de Young make a direct threat of personal violence against your son?"

"No," Kalloch conceded. "I haven't."

———✦———

WHEN MILTON TOOK THE STAND on Saturday, March 12, he told the crowded courtroom he began carrying a pistol after the attempted assassination of his father. "I had an idea that the attack made upon my father would be followed up by more if opportunity offered," he said. "I carried it to protect myself."

Easing into his testimony, Milton said he never meant to hurt anyone.

"When I left the office of the mayor, I had no more intention of shooting Charles de Young than I did of shooting myself," Milton testified. "I did intend to see him, but if he had met me in the same spirit that I went to see him, he would have been living today as far as any act of mine is concerned. These attacks had made every member of my family very unhappy. My mother's health had been well-nigh broken down by the care of my father during his sickness and attacks during that time. On her account, I was extremely anxious that there should be no more hostility. While Mr. de Young was in the East, I was in almost daily receipt of letters that conveyed to me the intelligence that he was interesting himself to ruin our family. I believed that my father's health was failing under the strain. Mother and I knew he was failing, although I said nothing about it. Often, as early as six o'clock in the evening, he would go to bed in complete exhaustion. I also knew that if any new attack was made, it would result in his death."

Milton looked at the jury. "While it would be untrue for me to say that I had any friendly feelings for the man who shot my father, I can truly say that

I cherished no intention of violence. When I received the pamphlet, I supposed it to be the result of Mr. de Young's labors in the East, and knew that if it was put into circulation it would bring about an act of retaliation from Father, to be followed by fatal results. I determined then that if I could, I would see Mr. de Young and, if possible, say something that would result in withholding the publication from circulation, or, if already circulated, to cause him to withdraw it from circulation. My object was as peaceful as one could be to another—I had no other object in seeing him."

Highton leaned against the jury box and asked Milton to explain what happened.

"When I arrived at the *Chronicle* office on the corner of Bush and Kearny streets, Charles de Young saw me as soon as I entered the door," Milton said. "He was nearly facing me, and the instant he saw me, he drew a pistol. If I had not exercised the utmost speed, he would have killed me in my tracks. His appearance was malignant and, knowing what I did of his attack upon my father, I didn't hesitate very long. As to what happened after that, I am not competent to tell you. I can recollect nothing about it."

Highton approached the witness stand. "I wish you to state clearly and distinctly the precise object you had in going into the *Chronicle* office that evening."

"I had no thoroughly defined idea of what I should say to Mr. de Young," Milton said. "I desired to say something to him to influence him, if I could, to withdraw from circulation, or not to circulate the pamphlet. That a word from me might tend to stop the circulation, I thought might be possible. Were I to neglect this, I would be remiss in my duty. I desired to do everything in my power to end the trouble."

When it was his turn for cross-examination, Prosecutor Campbell forced Milton to admit to loitering around de Young's house and the *Chronicle* office prior to pulling the trigger. "When you went into the office," Campbell next asked, "what was the first thing that happened?"

"The taking of an attitude on his part," Milton replied, "looking threatening and drawing a pistol."

"Did you see where he got the pistol from?"

"I couldn't tell what pocket he got it from."

"Where was your hand?" Campbell asked.

"Getting into my pocket," said Milton.

"Did you see him shoot at you?"

"I wouldn't say that he did."

"Do you remember shooting at him?"

"I don't know that I do."

"Were you very much frightened?" Campbell inquired.

"I don't know that it should be called fright," Milton said. "My whole organism was centered in a desire to protect myself by shooting him."

Campbell strolled to the prosecution table and picked up a copy of the *Chronicle*. "Did you see anything in the *Chronicle* from the time of the shooting of your father that indicated on the part of Charles de Young any intention to do personal violence to you or to your family?"

"I have never said that," Milton replied. "I think they were threatening."

"Did you not know that your father, after he was shot by Charles de Young, in public speeches made attacks upon Mr. de Young, who did not resent such attacks in his paper?"

"No, sir," Milton said. "I do not."

Campbell had no further questions.

———◆———

WAS IT MURDER, OR JUSTIFIABLE homicide? The jury faced this question when it commenced deliberations on Wednesday, March 23, 1881. Reporters jostled for space in an overcrowded courtroom; everyone seemingly anxious to play spectator to judicial history. As the deliberations dragged on, those hoping to witness the reading of the verdict grew despondent and surrendered their staked-out seats in the courtroom. Recalled jury foreman Alfred Earle:

> After the first ballot, which stood eight to four in Kalloch's favor,
> one of the jurors went over, making it nine to three. There the jury
> hung. We deliberated until half past twelve, or somewhere about

there, but there being no prospect of a verdict, one by one we made ourselves as comfortable as circumstances would permit and camped on the field. After breakfast . . . we got to work again, and passed around the hat again and again. Lunch time came around and found the opposing forces in the field. It was a matter of surprise when we passed around the hat again about four o'clock, just by way of fishing for what we could catch . . . when the whole strips of paper [were] read.

At quarter to four on Friday, March 25, after a day and a night of deliberation, the jury announced it had reached a verdict. Only the officers of the court, Milton and his father, and the attorneys for both sides were present in the courtroom. Outside, large crowds had gathered and were clamoring to get in. "The street beneath was fairly black with impatient humanity," wrote one reporter.

Milton stood as the jury entered the courtroom and filed into the box. He maintained a composed and dignified front, though his features were pale. During the jury roll call, excited members of the public shouldered their way into the courtroom and quickly filled the seats.

"Gentlemen of the Jury, have you agreed upon a verdict?" the judge asked.

Rising from his seat, foreman Earle said, "We have."

"What is your verdict?"

Earle stepped from the jury box and handed the judge a sealed envelope. Judge Temple studied the envelope's contents without expression before handing them to the court clerk. "The verdict should be entitled The People of the State of California against I. M. Kalloch," Temple said. "I shall direct the clerk to entitle the verdict."

The clerk rose from his chair. "Gentlemen of the jury," he intoned, "listen to your verdict as it stands recorded. 'We, the jury in the case of the People of the State of California against I. M. Kalloch, do find . . .'"

Milton nervously wrung his hands.

" . . . the defendant not guilty."

It seemed that, in considering the history between the Kallochs and de Youngs, the jury had decided Milton's actions were those of a man temporarily pushed to the edge. The spectators in the public gallery surged forward in a frantic bid to congratulate the young man. "We will arrest everyone of you for contempt. Sit down!" the bailiff roared over the celebratory screams and cries of hysterics that could be heard from the street below as news of the verdict quickly spread.

The crowds gathered along Washington and Montgomery streets rushed toward the courthouse. Rowdy celebrants charged past squads of officers who flailed their batons in a fruitless effort to keep the masses at bay. They charged up the courthouse steps and surrounded the building, laying siege to all entrances in the hopes of catching a glimpse of the acquitted.

Thunderous applause greeted Milton when he emerged from a side entrance with his attorneys and a protective throng of sheriff deputies. He waved and smiled and was hurried down the courtroom steps by his armed entourage. Sheriff Desmond forced his way onto Montgomery Avenue and commandeered an abandoned hack parked nearby. He and Milton scrambled on board and, with a snap of the reigns, the hack began pushing its way through the boisterous celebrants and past the carriage's rightful owner, who had stopped to investigate the cause of the commotion. But Milton's supporters would not let him escape so easily. A jovial mob surrounded the carriage and unhitched the horses to a chorus of cheers and laughter. Picking up the harness and carriage tongue, they pulled the carriage themselves toward Montgomery Street, then made its way toward Market. Recalled one witness:

> At the intersection of Bush and Montgomery streets, those having hold of the rope to which the hack was attached, looked up Bush Street, and were in the act of turning toward and changing their course to the *Chronicle* building, but were dissuaded from doing so by those on the box, not abandoning their intention, however, till they had lustily responded to a call for three groans for the *Chronicle*.

Women leaned out windows, waving handkerchiefs and blowing kisses, as the jubilant procession marched past in a celebratory frenzy. Cries and cheers followed in its wake, echoing down Market Street and New Montgomery. "The excitement manifested," reported the *Call*, "beggars description." At Fifth Street, residents ran from their homes and joined the parade. They streamed past the Mint and the Metropolitan Temple and cheered the Kalloch name as they went. The procession turned onto Mission Street and made its way toward the Kalloch home. Isaac had already shared news of Milton's acquittal with the family, having rushed from the courtroom upon hearing the verdict. Now, he stood in front of the house, Milton's wife by his side, and prepared to welcome his son home. As the procession approached, Milton's wife excitedly called to Caroline inside the house, "Here he is, mother!"

The mayor hurried to the sidewalk and met the carriage. He took his son in a warm embrace and walked him up the front garden with an arm slung around his shoulders. The crowd chanted Milton's name as father and son disappeared inside the house. Several minutes later, both Kallochs appeared again on the front steps to hearty applause. "I have no inclination to talk," Milton said, "but would much rather leave it to you. I just want to thank you for the kind, warm-hearted sympathy you have expressed for myself and family in this great trouble. I hope to live among you long enough to show how deeply I appreciate your kindness, and thank you heartily, and to tell you what good honest people those of San Francisco are."

The two men retreated back inside the house. In the street, the jovial mob gave three loud groans for the *Chronicle* before chanting the Kalloch name.

———————

AT FORTY-NINE DAYS, THE TRIAL of Isaac Milton Kalloch was—up to that point—the longest in California criminal history. Two hundred and eight witnesses had testified, generating thousands of pages of transcript. Many more were generated by the reaction of San Francisco's newspapers to the surprising verdict.

The *Daily Alta California* accepted the jury's decision "for good or ill," though it scolded Milton for allowing the raucous citizenry to pull his carriage through the streets as though he were some conquering general. "In a cooler moment, he never would have permitted himself to be drawn through the streets by an excited and shouting crowd of adherents—to be made, as it were, a hero," it wrote. "This scene was a discreditable one, and, in the history of this whole miserable business, must be put alongside of that, which shows another crowd hooting the wagon which bore away the body of a dead man." It continued:

> Let us hope that our city has now seen and heard the last of a series
> of incidents that have marked one of the most disgraceful and
> troublous epochs in her exciting history. May she never again be so
> swayed and torn by angry passions and demagogical turbulence . . .
> Out of all the clamor and disorder no good has come to the commu-
> nity or to individuals. The sown wind produced only the whirlwind.
> Let us put all the sorrowful and unpleasant past resolutely out of
> sight, and direct our eyes toward better things in the future.

The *Call* laid partial blame for the verdict on the actions of Charles de Young. Had he not tried to kill Milton Kalloch's father, the paper theorized, the jury would have perhaps doomed the young man to a harsher fate. If any-thing, though, the *Call* recognized the verdict as a blow against reckless jour-nalism. "It would not be possible for people to form an opinion as to the justification of the accused without giving some consideration to the princi-ples of action which had formed the basis on which the particular act rested," opined the paper. "The verdict of the people which condemns one acquits the other. The methods and character of journalism which have caused so much scandal in this city were condemned when Isaac M. Kalloch was acquitted."

Only the *Chronicle* voiced its outright disgust in a tersely worded editorial slamming the judicial proceedings. The jury's decision, the paper cried, had rendered the California legal system a cheap joke:

"NOT GUILTY"

The verdict of the jury in the Kalloch case, acquitting the defendant, must have profoundly surprised the respectable and law-abiding element of the community. At no time was there any doubt that CHARLES DE YOUNG had been shot down in cold blood in his office, almost in public sight . . . If a man can be shot down in cold blood, in the presence of unimpeachable witnesses, and the jails and gutters be scoured for men who will perjure themselves to clear the murderer, and to deny the testimony of those who undoubtedly saw the crime—if this can be done, what safety is there for human life . . .

We cannot help speaking of the matter with some feeling, but it must come home ultimately to the people . . . With this we dismiss the matter, convinced the judgment of the civilized world will be that this extraordinary verdict is a blot upon the fair fame of California.

In its issue dated April 24, 1880, the *Stock Exchange* wrote in epitaph, "Charles de Young's good qualities may be truly said to have been of the head; he had few of the heart." Whatever his shortcomings, Charles de Young had thrived and left his mark in a field where so many others perished in anonymity. He built his paper through sheer determination and a sharp understanding of what people wanted. And yet he fell victim to an increasing lust for power. "Had de Young here paused, satisfied with his laurels, his paper would have existed unchecked in its career of prosperity, and he would be alive as we now write," stated the *Stock Exchange*. "But he became dazzled at the successes he had achieved."

EPILOGUE

ISAAC KALLOCH SPENT TWO YEARS as mayor, making a mortal political enemy out of nearly everyone who crossed his path. He resigned in July 1883 after his party refused to endorse him for a second term, and moved to the Washington Territory, where he became a farmer. Occasionally, he ventured out on the lecture circuit and spoke to crowds of diminishing size. Every now and then he returned to San Francisco, though his visits went unnoticed by the media. On one such trip, he lectured at the Union Hall, his topic of conversation being "The Use and Abuse of the Pistol." Hardly anyone showed up. Realizing his golden voice was a thing of the past, he returned to the Pacific Northwest to live out the remainder of his days. His end came on December 9, 1887, in Seattle, where the once dynamic man fell victim to a fatal stroke.

Charles de Young's final resting place
[COURTESY OF THE AUTHOR]

Milton Kalloch successfully put the de Young debacle behind him and went on to become a successful litigator. He practiced law in San Francisco until his death in 1930.

In November 1884, Michael nearly suffered the same fate as his brother after publishing an article accusing sugar magnate Claus Spreckels of stealing from shareholders. Like Milton Kalloch, Claus's enraged son, Adolph, armed himself and stormed the *Chronicle* building, firing two shots at Michael and hitting him in the left arm. Michael survived and Adolph went to trial on charges of attempted murder. A jury found him not guilty.

In addition to helming the paper that began its life as a theater and gossip sheet, Michael de Young left an indelible mark on the San Francisco landscape, building the West's first skyscraper in 1890 where Market, Geary and Kearny streets converge. The new *Chronicle* headquarters dominated the city skyline until the 1906 earthquake and fire. In 1924, the paper moved into its current location on the corner of Fifth and Mission. (Catty-corner to the *Chronicle* is the Hotel Pickwick, former site of the Reverend Isaac Kalloch's Metropolitan Temple.) Michael de Young died in 1925, leaving his daughter the newspaper and the people of San Francisco the M. H. de Young Museum in Golden Gate Park.

The *Chronicle* remains Northern California's largest newspaper, with a daily circulation of more than three hundred thousand readers. For more than a century, as San Francisco papers came and went, the *Chronicle* and *Examiner* waged a fierce battle for supremacy—but even that competition has gone the way of the *Alta*, *Call* and *Bulletin*. The Hearst Corporation sold the *Examiner*—owned by William Randolph Hearst since 1887—in March 2000 as part of a complex, $660-million deal to purchase the *Chronicle*, which up to then was run by descendants of Michael de Young. Today the *Examiner* is published in tabloid size as a free daily, a shadow of its former self.

Bay Area journalism today is not as colorful as it once was. A near monopoly of newspaper ownership in the nine-county region has diminished almost all local competition. Denver-based MediaNews Group holds dominance over the market, surrounding the *San Francisco Chronicle* with nine metropolitan dailies—including the *Oakland Tribune* and *San Jose Mercury News*—and a host of smaller publications. MediaNews "clusters" its coverage, sending one reporter from a single newspaper to cover an event for multiple papers in the chain. Editorials are also shared among newspapers, providing readers with cookie-cutter coverage and points of view. While arguments of economy can be made in favor of clustering—it allows newspapers to share printing and advertising, thus ensuring the survival of otherwise financially weak operations—critics lament the demise of journalistic diversity and unique voices. With the single ownership of multiple dailies, all sharing resources and articles in a single region, there is less competition to present multiple facets of every story.

Charles de Young's final resting place is in Cypress Lawn Memorial Park. Above his grave, Michael raised a life-sized statue of his brother. With a feather quill in his right hand, the figure gazes out across a serene landscape of rolling hills, not too far removed from San Francisco, but seemingly worlds away from the hectic metropolis in which his legacy lives on.

ACKNOWLEDGMENTS

I WOULD VERY MUCH LIKE to thank the following for their help and support in the writing of this book. On the research front, I'm grateful for the assistance provided by the photo archives staff at the California State Library in Sacramento, the San Francisco History Center at the main branch of the San Francisco Public Library and the folks at the Bancroft Library at U.C. Berkeley. Thanks to Dr. Gray Brechin, author of *Imperial San Francisco*, for his research advice; and Jonathan Elkus, great-great-grandson of Amelia de Young, for his knowledge of the Kalloch–de Young feud.

My agent, Ed Knappman, has always worked hard on my behalf—something for which I am extremely grateful. Thanks to Philip Turner and Iris Blasi at Sterling Publishing for their enthusiasm and for helping me see this book come to fruition. William Mays, editor and proprietor of the *National Police Gazette* archives, needs to be acknowledged for his kind offers of assistance. For producing a wonderful-looking book and doing their utmost to ensure clean copy, project editor Hannah Reich, designer Richard Oriolo and copyeditor Isaiah Wilner are all due immense thanks. I am truly grateful for the work they did.

On the personal side of things, many thanks go out to Simon Blint (for the accommodations), Danny Hoffman, Ryan Sawyer, Brian Reiser, Jeanine Benca, Debbie Brooks, Lee Morrell, Keith Bennetts (for the mediocre Sean Connery impersonation) and his wife, Jamie. The memory of Mike Brooks was very much present during the writing of this book. My family, as always, have been incredibly supportive; they've always believed. Thanks to Tony, Phil and Mike for the ever-present music.

These acknowledgments would not be complete if I didn't mention Katie Censky, my partner in life and crime, who—with love and patience—continues to put up with me.

BIBLIOGRAPHY

NEWSPAPERS FROM THE TIME IN question proved to be the primary
source of information for *War of Words*. The colorful editorials, advertisements
and news coverage paint vibrant pictures of a wild time in history. The papers consulted for the writing of the book were the *San Francisco Chronicle* and its main rivals:
the *Daily Evening Bulletin*, the *Morning Call*, the *Daily Alta California*, and the *San Francisco Examiner*.

The punctuation in many of the newspaper excerpts I've included might seem
somewhat quirky. Commas and capitalization, for example, are sometimes different
from modern English usage in the United States. For the sake of authenticity, I have
kept the grammar as it appears in the source material.

NEWS ARTICLES SPECIFICALLY QUOTED AND REFERRED TO IN THE TEXT ARE AS FOLLOWS:

"Salutatory," *Daily Evening Bulletin*, October 8, 1855.

(Untitled), *Daily Evening Bulletin*, Saturday, October 13, 1855.

"Mr. A. A. Selover," *Daily Evening Bulletin*, Thursday, December 6, 1855.

"From the Sacramento Correspondence," *Daily Evening Bulletin*, Wednesday, May 14, 1856.

"Attempted Assassination of James King of William," *Daily Evening Bulletin*, Thursday,
     May 15, 1856.

"The Felon and Assassin Casey," *Daily Evening Bulletin*, Thursday, May 15, 1856.

"An Attempt to Assassinate James of Wm. by J. P. Casey," *Daily Alta California*,
     Thursday, May 15, 1856.

"The Public Feeling," *Daily Evening Bulletin*, Thursday, May 15, 1856.

"The General Feeling," *Daily Evening Bulletin*, Friday, May 16, 1856.

"Rescue of the Prisoner Casey and Cora, Without Resistance," *Daily Alta California*,
     Monday, May 19, 1856.

"Death of Mr. King," *Daily Evening Bulletin*, Tuesday, May 20, 1856.

"San Francisco in Mourning," *Daily Evening Bulletin*, Wednesday, May 21, 1856.

"The Death of Mr. King," *Daily Evening Bulletin*, Wednesday, May 21, 1856.

"The Funeral of James King of Wm.," *Daily Evening Bulletin*, Friday, May 23, 1856.

"Yesterday," *Daily Evening Bulletin*, Friday, May 23, 1856.

"The Execution of James P. Casey and Charles Cora," *Daily Evening Bulletin*, Friday, May 23, 1856.

"Our Circulation—Acknowledgement to the Public," *Daily Evening Bulletin*, Friday, May 23, 1856.

"Trial of Mr. Rev. Kalloch for Adultery," *New York Times*, Friday, April 3, 1857.

New York Tribune dispatch in the *Republican Compiler*, Monday, April 20, 1857.

"From Kansas: Reality of the Drought . . .," *New York Times*, Monday, September 3, 1860.

"Sermon of Rev. I. S. Kalloch," *New York Times*, Friday, May 1, 1863.

"Ourselves," *Daily Dramatic Chronicle*, Monday, January 16, 1865.

"Sad Accident," *Daily Dramatic Chronicle*, Monday, January 16, 1865.

"Pretty Girls," *Daily Dramatic Chronicle*, Monday, January 16, 1865.

"Bigoted," *Daily Dramatic Chronicle*, Tuesday, January 24, 1865.

"Astonishing," *Daily Dramatic Chronicle*, Monday, February 20, 1865.

"Death of the President," *Daily Dramatic Chronicle*, Saturday, April 15, 1865.

"The Effect in San Francisco," *Daily Alta California*, Sunday, April 16, 1865.

"Irregular Justice," *Daily Dramatic Chronicle*, Monday, April 17, 1865.

"Human Nature," *Daily Dramatic Chronicle*, Monday, April 17, 1865.

"An Expression of Anger—A Word of Caution" *Daily Evening Bulletin*, Monday, April 17, 1865.

"Our Second Volume," *Daily Dramatic Chronicle*, Monday, July 17, 1865.

"Disgusted," *Daily Dramatic Chronicle*, Friday, January 12, 1866.

"Look on this Picture!" *Daily Dramatic Chronicle*, Monday, January 22, 1866.

"Word Coining," *Daily Dramatic Chronicle*, Thursday, January 25, 1866.

"Trap Slop Hopper," *Daily Dramatic Chronicle*, Saturday, January 27, 1866.

"Teachers Taught," *Daily Dramatic Chronicle*, Wednesday, February 7, 1866.

"Compelled to Enlarge," *Daily Dramatic Chronicle*, Saturday, March 16, 1867.

"The Chronicle Past, Present and Future," *Daily Dramatic Chronicle*, Tuesday, September 1, 1868.

"EXTRA: EARTHQUAKE," *Daily Dramatic Chronicle*, Wednesday, October 21, 1868.

"Earthquake Over the Bay," *Daily Dramatic Chronicle*, Thursday, October 22, 1868.

"Destruction of Property in Various Parts of the City," *San Francisco Morning Call*, Thursday, October 22, 1868.

"The Course of True Love," *Daily Dramatic Chronicle*, Sunday, October 17, 1869.

"Scandalous Publications," *Daily Examiner*, Monday, April 10, 1871.

"Gagging the Press," *San Francisco Chronicle*, Tuesday, May 9, 1871.

"An Indian Swindle," *New York Times*, Wednesday, May 24, 1871.

"The Zealous Hop," *San Francisco Chronicle*, Sunday, July 2, 1871.

"An Outraged Citizen," *Daily Alta Californian*, Tuesday, July 4, 1871.

"Partial Justice," *San Francisco Examiner*, Wednesday, July 5, 1871.

"A Disgraceful Attack," *Daily Morning Call*, Saturday, December 2, 1871.

"Attempted Assassination of One of the Proprietors of the *Chronicle*," *San Francisco Chronicle*, Saturday, December 2, 1871.

"Attempted Assassination," *San Francisco Chronicle*, Saturday, December 2, 1871.

"A Bad Example," *Daily Evening Bulletin*, Saturday, December 2, 1871.

"Yesterday's Furore," *Daily Alta California*, Sunday, February 1, 1874.

"The Sequel," *Daily Alta California*, Tuesday, February 3, 1874.

"An Atrocious Libel," *San Francisco Chronicle*, Tuesday, February 3, 1874.

"Still in Jail," *Daily Alta California*, Thursday, February 5, 1874.

"Threats to Kill," *Daily Alta California*, Thursday, February 5, 1874.

"The Ball Opened," *Daily Alta California*, Sunday, February 8, 1874.

"A Slanderer's Fears," *San Francisco Chronicle*, Tuesday, February 10, 1874.

"Birds of a Feather," *San Francisco Chronicle*, Thursday, February 12, 1874.

"Two Unclean Birds," *San Francisco Chronicle*, Friday, February 13, 1874.

"Those Foul Birds," *San Francisco Chronicle*, Saturday, February 14, 1874.

"In Vindication," *San Francisco Chronicle*, Tuesday, June 17, 1874.

"Fighting Editors," *New York Times*," Saturday, June 28, 1874.

"A Destructive Fire," *San Francisco Chronicle*, Thursday, July 26, 1877.

"The Hoodlum's Work," *San Francisco Examiner*, Thursday, July 26, 1877.

"The Anti-Coolie Meeting," *San Francisco Chronicle*, Thursday, July 26, 1877.

"Raid on the Wash-Houses," *San Francisco Chronicle*, Thursday, July 26, 1877.

"The Killed and Wounded," *San Francisco Chronicle*, Thursday, July 26, 1877.

"The Workingmen," *San Francisco Chronicle*, Saturday, October 6, 1877.

"Injustice to Our Workingmen," *San Francisco Chronicle*, Monday, October 8, 1877.

"On Nob Hill," *San Francisco Chronicle*, Tuesday, October 30, 1877.

"The Incendiary Agitators," *Evening Bulletin*, Monday, November 5, 1877.

"The New Constitution Party," *San Francisco Chronicle*, Tuesday, May 13, 1879.

"The Reasons for It," *San Francisco Chronicle*, Sunday, May 25, 1879.

"Kearney's Brutality," *San Francisco Chronicle*, Wednesday, June 4, 1879.

"Kearney's Vulgarity," *San Francisco Chronicle*, Saturday, June 7, 1879.

"Kalloch's Record," *San Francisco Chronicle*, Saturday, June 21, 1879.

"Kalloch . . . ," *San Francisco Chronicle*, Wednesday, August 20, 1879.

"Corrupt Kalloch," *San Francisco Chronicle*, Thursday, August 21, 1879.

"Kalloch's Career," *San Francisco Chronicle*, Friday, August 22, 1879.

"Indecent Publications," *Daily Alta California*, Friday, August 22, 1879.

"Rev. I. S. Kalloch," *Daily Evening Bulletin*, Saturday, August 23, 1879.

"Kalloch Shot," *Daily Evening Bulletin*, Saturday, August 23, 1879.

"The Shooting of Kalloch," *San Francisco Chronicle*, Sunday, August 24, 1879.

"Dastardly: A Terrible Termination of a Political Fight," *Daily Alta California*, Sunday, August 24, 1879.

"Atrocious!" *San Francisco Morning Call*, Sunday, August 24, 1879.

"The Sand-Lots," *Daily Alta California*, Monday, August 25, 1879.

"A Purely Personal Matter Distorted to Malignant Ends," *San Francisco Chronicle*, Monday, August 25, 1879.

"A Fair Statement of the Case," *San Francisco Chronicle*, Monday, August 25, 1879.

"A Warm Friend of Kalloch," *New York Times*, Monday, August 25, 1879.

"The Necessity of the Hour," *San Francisco Chronicle*, Tuesday, August 26, 1879.

"An Indiscreet Accuser," *San Francisco Chronicle*, Tuesday, August 26, 1879.

"The Attempted Murder," *Daily Alta California*, Tuesday, August 26, 1879.

"Kalloch's Career in Boston," *New York Times*, Wednesday, August 27, 1879.

"De Young's Deed," *San Francisco Morning Call*, Wednesday, August 27, 1879.

"A Statement," *San Francisco Chronicle*, Wednesday, August 27, 1879.

"Dr. Kalloch: His Condition Unchanged," *Daily Alta California*, Wednesday, August 27, 1879.

"More 'BULLETIN' Lies," *San Francisco Chronicle*, Thursday, August 28, 1879.

"Lead as a Qualification," *Daily Alta California*, Friday, August 29, 1879.

"Dr. Kalloch: An Interview with Him," *Daily Alta California*, Sunday, August 31, 1879.

"Kalloch on the Workingmen," *San Francisco Chronicle*, Tuesday, September 2, 1879.

"A Weak Reason," *Daily Alta California*, Wednesday, September 3, 1879.

"A Journalist Jackal," *San Francisco Chronicle*, Monday, September 8, 1879.

"Ottawa's Founder Had Checkered Past," *Williamsburg (KS) Review*, September 4, 1879.

"The Chronicle," *San Francisco Chronicle*, Monday, September 29, 1879.

"Kalloch's Attempt to Intimidate," *San Francisco Chronicle*, Saturday, April 1, 1880.

"Murder of Charles de Young," *San Francisco Chronicle*, Saturday, April 24, 1880.

"Shooting of Charles De Young," *San Francisco Morning Call*, Saturday, April 24, 1880.

"Assassinated," *San Francisco Chronicle*, Saturday, April 24, 1880.

"Last Night's Tragedy," *Daily Evening Bulletin*, Saturday, April 24, 1880.

"Murder of Charles de Young," *San Francisco Chronicle*, Saturday, April 24, 1880.

"More Blood," *San Francisco Examiner*, Saturday, April 24, 1880.

"Shot Down," *Daily Alta California*, Saturday, April 24, 1880.

"The Murdered Editor," *New York Times*, Sunday April 25, 1880.

"The De Young Tragedy," *Daily Alta California*, Sunday, April 25, 1880.

"The Assassination," *San Francisco Chronicle*, Sunday, April 25, 1880.

"The Last Rites," *San Francisco Chronicle*, Monday, April 26, 1880.

"Buried," *Daily Alta California*, Monday, April 26, 1880.

"Eastern Sentiment," *Daily Alta California*, Monday, April 26, 1880.

"The Murder of De Young," *New York Times*, Monday, April 26, 1880.

"De Young's Death," *Daily Evening Bulletin*, Wednesday, April 28, 1880.

"A Verdict of Murder," *Daily Alta California*, Wednesday, April 28, 1880.

"A Stupid Piece of Perjury," *San Francisco Chronicle*, Thursday, April 29, 1880.

"John H. Clemetshaw," *San Francisco Chronicle*, Friday, April 30, 1880.

"Held to Answer," *Morning Call*, Friday, April 30, 1880.

"Kalloch's Impeachment," *Daily Alta California*, Tuesday, May 4, 1880.

"Mayor Kalloch," *Daily Alta California*, Tuesday, May 4, 1880.

"A Bad Reputation," *San Francisco Chronicle*, Thursday, May 27, 1880.

"Bad Man, Good Mayor," *San Francisco Chronicle*, Friday, May 28, 1880.

"Arrest of W. M. Neilson," *San Francisco Chronicle*, Thursday, June 3, 1880.

"Neilson's Witness," *San Francisco Chronicle*, Friday, June 4, 1880.

"Please Don't!" *San Francisco Chronicle*, Saturday, June 5, 1880.

"Begging Off," *San Francisco Chronicle*, Sunday, June 6, 1880.

"The Last Juror," *Daily Morning Call*, Sunday, February 20, 1881.

"The Kalloch Trial," *Daily Morning Call*, Tuesday, February 22, 1881.

"The Kalloch Trial," *Daily Morning Call*, Wednesday, March 2, 1881.

"The Kalloch Trial," *Daily Morning Call*, Friday, March 4, 1881.

"The Kalloch Trial," *Daily Morning Call*, Saturday, March 5, 1881.

"The Kalloch Trial," *Daily Morning Call*, Saturday, March 12, 1881.

"The Kalloch Trial," *Daily Morning Call*, Sunday, March 13, 1881.

"Kalloch's Trial," *Daily Morning Call*, Tuesday, March 15, 1881.

"Kalloch's Trial Ended," *Daily Morning Call*, Friday, March 25, 1881.

"The Kalloch Case," *San Francisco Chronicle*, Friday, March 25, 1881.

"Kalloch's Acquittal," *Daily Alta California*, Friday, March 25, 1881.

"Acquitted," *Daily Morning Call*, Friday, March 25, 1881.

"Not Guilty," *San Francisco Chronicle*, Friday, March 25, 1881.

Isaac S. Kalloch obituary, *New York Times*, December 12, 1887.

Caroline Kalloch obituary, *Seattle Post-Intelligencer*, March 16, 1909.

"First Municipal Elections Held in San Francisco," *San Francisco Chronicle*, Sunday, November 3, 1912.

"Chronicle Sold to Hearst," *San Francisco Chronicle*, Saturday, August 7, 1999.

"Examiner Sold," *San Francisco Chronicle*, Saturday, March 18, 2000.

"Hearst Sells Examiner to Owner of Local Papers," *New York Times*, Saturday, March 18, 2000.

"De Young Skyscraper to Get a Second Life as a Swanky Hotel," *San Francisco Chronicle*, Monday, August 15, 2005.

PERIODICALS AND MAGAZINE ARTICLES CONSULTED IN THE WRITING OF THIS BOOK:

Ayers, W. O., "Personal Recollections of the Vigilance Committee," *Overland Monthly*, August 1886.

Fracchia, Charles, "The Controversial Mayor Kalloch," *California Living Magazine*, October 12, 1980.

Kauer, Ralph, "The Workingmen's Party of California," *Pacific Historical Review*, Vol. 13, No. 3 (September 1944), pp. 278–291.

King, Charles J., "Reminiscences of Early Days in San Francisco," *Overland Monthly*, March 1888.

Malin, James C., "Dust Storms: Part One, 1850–1860," *Kansas Historical Quarterly*, Vol. 14, No. 2 (May 1946), pp. 129–145.

Mckee, Irving, "The Shooting of Charles de Young," *Pacific Historical Review*, Vol. 16, No. 3 (August 1947), pp. 271–284.

Rapaport, Richard, "The Chronicle Clan," *San Francisco Magazine*, November 1987.

Rosenwaike, Ira, "The Parentage and Early Years of M. H. De Young: Legend and Fact," *Western States Jewish Historical Quarterly*, April 1975, pgs. 210–217.

Scanland, F. M., "Early Journalism in San Francisco," *Overland Monthly*, September 1894.

Willard, J. T., "Bluemont Central College, the Forerunner of Kansas State College," *Kansas Historical Quarterly*, Vol. 13, No. 6, (May 1945) pp. 323–357.

MANUSCRIPTS, TRANSCRIPTS AND PAMPHLETS

Complete Report of the Trial of Rev. Isaac S. Kalloch, on Charge of Adultery. By the [Boston] *Times* reporter. 1857.

Faint Idea of a Terrible Life, A, Bancroft Library, U.C. Berkeley, XF869-S3.21-K141/K14, No. 3.

Full Report of R. H. Dana's Argument for Defence, in the Case of Rev. I. S. Kalloch, Pastor of the Tremont Temple Baptist Church. 1857.

History of the San Francisco Chronicle (dictation by M. H. de Young), Bancroft Library, U.C. Berkeley, BANC MSS C-D 370:1.

Though newspapers and periodicals provided the bulk of material for *War of Words*, a handful of books were relied upon in the telling of this story. Turned to most often was *The Golden Voice*, M. M. Marberry's 1947 biography of the Rev. Isaac S. Kalloch. The book was the primary source of information for Kalloch's younger years in Maine (see Chapter 3: "Son of a Preacher Man") and his time in the Midwest (Chapter 8: "The Coming Man"). Books consulted for the writing of *War of Words*:

Adams, Charles F., *Murder by the Bay: Historic Homicide in and about the City of San Francisco*, Quill Drive Books, San Francisco, 2005.

Bancroft, Hubert Howe, *History of California* (Vol. VIII, 1860-1890), The History Company, San Francisco, 1890.

Blackmar, Frank W., *Kansas: A Cyclopedia of State History, Embracing Events, Institutions, Industries, Counties, Cities, Towns, Prominent Persons, Etc.* (Vol. II), Standard Publishing Company, 1912.

Brands, H. W., *The Age of Gold: The California Gold Rush and the New American Dream*, Anchor Books, 2003.

Brechin, Gray, *Imperial San Francisco: Urban Power, Earthly Ruin* (California Studies in Critical Human Geography), University of California Press, 2d edition, 2006.

Bruce, John, *Gaudy Century: The Story of San Francisco's Hundred Years of Robust Journalism*, Random House, New York, 1948.

Coblentz, Stanton A., *Villains and Vigilantes: The Fabulous Story of James King of William and of Pioneer Justice in California*, Wilson-Erikson, Inc., 1936.

Ethington, Philip J., *The Public City: The Political Construction of Urban Life in San Francisco, 1850–1900*, University of California Press, 2001.

Lennon, Nigey, *The Sagebrush Bohemian: Mark Twain in California*, Marlowe & Co., 1993.

Marberry, M. M., *The Golden Voice*, Farrar, Straus and Company, New York, 1947.

Rhodes, James Ford, *History of the United States from Hayes to McKinley*, The Macmillan Company, New York, 1919.

Saxton, Alexander, *The Indispensable Enemy: Labor and the Anti-Chinese Movement in California*, University of California Press, 1975.

Secrest, Willaim B., *California Feuds: Vengeance, Vendettas, and Violence on the Old West Coast*, Word Dancer Press, 2004.

Sinclair, Mick, *San Francisco: A Cultural and Literary History*, Signal Books, 2004.

Young, John P., *Journalism in California* (Pacific Coast and Exposition Biographies, San Francisco), Chronicle Publishing, 1915.

ONLINE SOURCES

Online resources proved very helpful in the writing of this book. Specifically, the Virtual Museum of the City of San Francisco, which can be found at www.sfmuseum.com. The site is a treasure trove of firsthand accounts, old documents and colorful journalism that present a vibrant picture of San Francisco's unruly past.

Brewer, William H., *Up and Down California in 1860–1864: The Journal of William H. Brewer*, Book 4, Chapter 8, Crescent City and San Francisco:
http://www.yosemite.ca.us/library/up_and_down_california/4-8.html

Bryce, James, *The American Commonwealth*, MacMillan and Co., New York, 1889:
http://www.sfmuseum.net/hist9/bryce1.html

Hart, Jerome A., "The Sand Lot and Kearneyism," *In Our Second Century: From an Editor's Notebook*, Pioneer Press, San Francisco, 1931:
http://www.sfmuseum.org/hist2/kearneyism.html

"The Kearney-Kalloch Epoch," *In Our Second Century: From an Editor's Notebook*, Pioneer Press, San Francisco, 1931: http://www.sfmuseum.org/hist2/kalloch.html

Higgins, Pat, "How Maine Ran Afoul of Georgia Over a Fugitive Slave":
http:www.imaginemaine.com/mainestories/atticus.html

"The Panic of 1873":
http://www.thehistorybox.com/ny_city/panics/panics_article9a.htm

Tinkham, George H., "California Men and Events: Time 1769–1890," Panama-Pacific Exposition Edition, 1915: http://www.usgennet.org/usa/ca/state1/tinkhamtoc.html

Wilson, John L., M.D., *Stanford University School of Medicine and the Predecessor Schools:*
http://elane.stanford.edu/wilson/

"Execution of James P. Casey & Charles Cora," *Town Talk*, 1856: http://www.sfmuseum.org/hist6/hang.html

San Francisco Gold Rush Chronology 1846–1849:
http://www.sfmuseum.org/hist/chron1.html

"Chinatown Declared a Nuisance": http://www.sfmuseum.org/hist2/wpc1.html

SOURCE NOTES

Prologue: A Fallen King

1   "Subscriptions received . . . 11 to 12 only." Bruce, *Gaudy Century*, pg. 31; Scanland, pg. 265.

1   King details and physical description. Bruce, *Gaudy Century*, pg. 34.

2   Excels at language, literature. Wilson, *Stanford University School of Medicine and the Predecessor Schools*: Chapter 11 (online resource).

2   King's journey to San Francisco. King, pg. 277.

2   Montgomery Street bank. Wilson, *Stanford University School of Medicine and the Predecessor Schools*: Chapter 11 (online resource).

3   King publishes the *Bulletin*. King, pg. 281; Bruce, *Gaudy Century*, pg., 37.

3   "Whatever may be . . . the public good." *Daily Evening Bulletin*, 8 October 1855.

3   "The city . . . were thieves." Scanland, pg. 266.

3   "Necessity . . . by a few friends." *Daily Evening Bulletin*, 8 October 1855.

4   "A man . . . to uphold this iniquity." *Daily Evening Bulletin*, 13 October 1855.

4   King targets corruption. Scanland, pg. 267.

4   Editors duel. Scanland, pg. 266.

4   "One of . . . the leg." Scanland, pg. 266.

4   "Men warned . . . been assassinated." King, pg. 281.

5   "I have . . . be imperiled." King, pg. 281.

5   "James King . . . his hand." Ayers, pg. 164.

5   "the tool . . . a malignant misanthrope." Adams, *Murder by the Bay*, pg. 5.

5   *Bulletin* circulation. Coblentz, *Villains and Vigilantes*, pg. 139.

6   "Mr. Selover . . . not much farther." *Daily Evening Bulletin*, 6 December 1855.

6   "The fact . . . fraud of the people." *Daily Evening Bulletin*, 14 May 1856.

7   Casey background. *Daily Evening Bulletin*, 15 May 1856.

7   King and Casey exchange. *Daily Evening Bulletin*, 15 May 1856.

8   Casey following King. *Daily Evening Bulletin*, 15 May 1856.

8   "Draw and defend yourself." *Daily Evening Bulletin*, 15 May 1856.

8   "Hang him . . ." *Daily Alta California*, 15 May 1856.

9   "In less than three mintues . . . location of the prisoner." *Daily Alta California*, 15 May 1856.

9   King's condition. Bruce, *Gaudy Century*, pg. 47.

9   Gathering crowds. Bruce, *Gaudy Century*, pg. 47.

9   Medical treatment. *Daily Evening Bulletin*, 15 May 1856; Bruce, *Gaudy Century*, pg. 47.

10   "Hang . . . Take him out!" *Daily Alta California*, 15 May 1856.

10   Charles Cora background. Bruce, *Gaudy Century*, pg. 47; Coblentz, *Villains and Vigilantes*, pg. 109; *Daily Alta California*, 15 May 1856.

10   "Casey . . . the fate of us both!" Bruce, *Gaudy Century*, pg. 47.

10   Officers surrounding building. Coblentz, *Villains and Vigilantes*, pg. 109; *Daily Alta California*, 15 May 1856.

11   Crowd chases carriage. Ayers, pg. 165; Coblentz, *Villains and Vigilantes*, pg. 155.

11   "There they stood . . . intense excitement." Ayers, pg. 165.

11   Crowd demands Casey. Ayers, pg. 166; Coblentz, *Villains and Vigilantes*, pg. 156.

11   Mob jeering infantry. *Daily Alta California*, 15 May 1856.

11   "This did not . . . justice will be done." *Daily Alta California*, 15 May 1856.

12   "The various streets . . . almost to frenzy." *Daily Alta California*, 15 May 1856.

12   "The streets . . . we have ever seen." *Daily Alta California*, 15 May 1856.

13   "The Vigilance . . . has organized." Ayers, pg. 166.

13   "the peace . . . of San Francisco." Brands, *The Age of Gold*, pg. 265.

13   The Vigilance Committee. Brands, *The Age of Gold*, pp. 261–264.

13   Re-emergence of Vigilance Committee. *Daily Evening Bulletin*, 16 May 1856.

13   "A Committee . . . three thousand names." *Daily Evening Bulletin*, 16 May 1856.

13   Committee's military stylings. Bruce, *Gaudy Century*, pg. 48; Coblentz, *Villains and Vigilantes*, pg. 164.

14   "As a law-abiding man . . . shall be avenged." *Daily Evening Bulletin*, 15 May 1856.

14   "One lady enquired . . . 'the ladies will!'" *Daily Evening Bulletin*, 16 May 1856.

15   "Motives of delicacy . . . have a fair trial." *Daily Evening Bulletin*, 15 May 1856.

15   "It appears . . . not space to narrate." *Daily Evening Bulletin*, 16 May 1856.

15   "Just what . . . and then disband." Coblentz, *Villains and Vigilantes*, pg. 171.

15   The Law and Order Pary, Bruce, *Gaudy Century*, pg. 49.

16   "The entire . . . and order." Ayers, pg. 168; Bruce, *Gaudy Century*, pg. 48; Coblentz, *Villains and Vigilantes*, pg. 176.

16   "Mr. Scannell . . . and Cora." Ayers, pg. 168; Bruce, *Gaudy Century*, pg. 49.

17   "What? . . . I will go." Coblentz, *Villains and Vigilantes*, pp. 177–178.

17   "the door was opened." Ayers, pg. 168.

17   Casey leaving jail. *Daily Alta California*, 19 May 1856.

17   "The silence . . . of Egypt." Ayers, pg. 169 (description of the overall scene also comes from this same account).

18   "James King of Willian . . . not fully sensible." *Daily Evening Bulletin*, 20 May 1856.

18   "all bore . . . insignia of death." *Daily Evening Bulletin*, 21 May 1856.

18   Casey's trial. Coblentz, *Villains and Vigilantes*, pg. 187; *Town Talk*, San Francisco, 1856 (Virtual Museum of San Francisco).

19   "For some time . . . with tearful eyes." *Daily Evening Bulletin*, 21 May 1856.

19   "With a bold pen . . . and a corpse." *Daily Evening Bulletin*, 23 May 1856.

19   "Every trade . . . and unfortunate." *Daily Evening Bulletin*, 23 May 1856.

19   "nature . . . agony of grief." *Daily Evening Bulletin*, 23 May 1856.

20   Execution preparations. *Daily Evening Bulletin*, 23 May 1856.

20   Cora and Casey's composure. *Daily Evening Bulletin*, 23 May 1856.

20   "Both victim . . . the sleep of death." *Daily Evening Bulletin*, 23 May 1856.

20   "Behold! . . . of California Society." *Daily Evening Bulletin*, 21 May 1856.

21   "We are happy . . . has yet obtained." *Daily Evening Bulletin*, 23 May 1856.

Chapter 1: Young Blood

22   Approaching steamer. King, pg. 278.

22   De Young family rumors. Rapaport, pg. 40.

23   "Mrs. DY . . . looking husband." Rosenwaike, pg. 213 (details of family history also from this source, pp. 213–214).

23   Family leaves for California. Rosenwaike, pg. 214.

23   Family arrives in San Francisco. Rosenwaike, pg. 214; Bruce, *Gaudy Century*, pg. 128.

23   "His love . . . it certainly strengthened." *New York Times*, 25 April 1880.

24   "All the wickedness . . . of a mining State." *New York Times*, 25 April 1880.

24   Winnings paid in silver and gold. Wilson, *Stanford University School of Medicine and the Predecessor Schools*: Chapter 8 (online resource).

24   "It was among . . . character is principally formed." *New York Times*, 25 April 1880.

24   Young Charles' experiences. *New York Times*, 25 April 1880.

25   "Whatever may be the opinion . . . Californian 'honor.'" *New York Times*, 25 April 1880.

25   "quick and spasmodic . . . personal appearance." *New York Times*, 25 April 1880.

25   Union salaries. Scanland, pg. 260.

25   De Young's early newspaper experience. *San Francisco Chronicle*, 24 April 1880.

25   "The starting . . . the enterprise together." De Young dictation (Bancroft Library).

26   "This was the fund . . . to make it a newspaper." De Young dictation (Bancroft Library).

27   Robert Semple and the *Californian*. Scanland, pg. 262.

27   "But for . . . Mormon territory." Scanland, pg. 261.

27   "The whole . . . gold, gold." Scanland, pg. 263.

27   "The town . . . intellectual darkness." Scanland, pg. 264.

27   Competition increases. Scanland, pp. 264–265.

28 Price of papers, correspondents pay. Scanland, pg. 260.

28 "The newspapers . . . of civilization." Scanland, pg. 261.

29 "We make our politest bow . . . 'here below.'" *Daily Dramatic Chronicle*, 16 January 1865.

29 "with a Non-descript . . . GROTTO NYMPH." *Daily Dramatic Chronicle*, 16 January 1865.

29 "We do not think . . . and cabbage." *Daily Dramatic Chronicle*, 16 January 1865.

30 "During the performance . . . to-night as usual." *Daily Dramatic Chronicle*, 16 January 1865.

30 Approach to national coverage. *Daily Dramatic Chronicle*, 16 January 1865; Rapaport, pg. 41.

30 Charles de Young at work. Adams, *Murder by the Bay*, pg. 60.

30 "The *Chronicle* . . . on the Pacific Coast." *Daily Dramatic Chronicle*, 16 January 1865.

31 "We did . . . paper a success." De Young dictation (Bancroft Library).

31 Brothers recycling old papers. Rapaport, pg. 41.

31 "He was enterprising . . . a journalist was concerned." *San Francisco News Letter and California Advertister*, 26 March 1881.

31 "On Sunday morning last . . . kept it *hole-y*." *Daily Dramatic Chronicle*, 24 January 1865.

32 "So far . . . same number of deaths." *Daily Dramatic Chronicle*, 20 February 1865.

32 "Have you . . . been assassinated!" De Young dictation (Bancroft Library).

32 Michael de Young responds to news. De Young dictation (Bancroft Library).

32 "I ran . . . extras during the day." De Young dictation (Bancroft Library).

33 "The excitement got to be tremendous." De Young dictation (Bancroft Library).

33 Angry crowd gathers outside newspaper. Bruce, *Gaudy Century*, pp. 134–135.

33 Mob storms newsroom. Bruce, *Gaudy Century*, pp. 135.

33 "The extras issued . . . thrown into the street." *Daily Alta California*, 16 April 1865.

34 Rioters storm the *News Letter* offices. Bruce, *Gaudy Century*, pp. 135-136.

34 "I followed . . . taking items." De Young dictation (Bancroft Library).

34 Mob continues on its rampage. Bruce, *Gaudy Century*, pg. 136.

34 MacCrellish addresses the crowd. Bruce, *Gaudy Century*, pg. 136.

34 "We suggested . . . and hurriedly." Bruce, *Gaudy Century*, pp. 136–137.

35 "If opportunity . . . death of a good man." *Daily Evening Bulletin*, 17 April 1865.

35 Police call for Army intervention. Bruce, *Gaudy Century*, pg. 137.

35 "Gentlemen . . . The Army will now take over." Bruce, *Gaudy Century*, pg. 137.

35 "This is . . . seized and suppressed." Bruce, *Gaudy Century*, pg. 138.

35 "There are some things . . . law-abiding citizens." *Daily Dramatic Chronicle*, 17 April 1865.

36 Mid-1860s San Francisco. Lennon, *The Sagebrush Bohemian*, pg. 59; Rapaport, pg. 40; McKee, pg. 272.

36   "Every one . . . enjoy themselves." McKee, pg. 272.
37   "At the time . . . beer and German food." De Young dictation (Bancroft Library).
37   "Mark Twain . . . their brains to the *Chronicle.*" De Young dictation (Bancroft Library).
37   "We adopted . . . what our writers were saying." De Young dictation (Bancroft Library).
38   "The publication . . . the whole community." De Young dictation (Bancroft Library).
38   "Johns . . . consumptive Camille." De Young dictation (Bancroft Library).
38   Maguire's background. Ethington, *The Public City,* pg. 44; Sinclair, *San Francisco,* pg. 64; Bruce, *Gaudy Century,* pg. 129; De Young dictation (Bancroft Library).
39   "Though an ignorant . . . man controlling it." De Young dictation (Bancroft Library).
39   Gambling saloon entrance. McKee, pg. 274.
39   "The result . . . by these women of the town." de Young dictation (Bancroft Library).
39   Acresses "assaulted . . . outraged." De Young dictation (Bancroft Library).
39   Girls rendered limp. De Young dictation (Bancroft Library).
40   "We always . . . began to work." De Young dictation (Bancroft Library).
40   Maguire launches theatrical papers. McKee, pg. 274.
40   "The foundation . . . all the time." De Young dictation (Bancroft Library).
40   "In the prosecution . . . in San Francisco." De Young dictation (Bancroft Library).
40   "This statement . . . property of Hinckley's." De Young dictation (Bancroft Library).
40   "undoubtedly a brave Roman." Bruce, *Gaudy Century,* pg. 131.
41   "in which . . . with the thater." De Young dictation (Bancroft Library).
41   California Theater sinks Maguire. McKee, pg. 274.

CHAPTER 2: SON OF A PREACHER MAN

42   Kalloch the teen preacher. Marberry, *The Golden Voice,* pp. 26–27.
43   "Everyone knew . . . and the fame of it spread." Marberry, *The Golden Voice,* pg. 27.
43   Kalloch's early years and mother's death. Marberry, *The Golden Voice,* pg. 20.
44   Kalloch's imagination, family heroes. Marberry, *The Golden Voice,* pp. 21–22.
44   "was one . . . in the business." Marberry, *The Golden Voice,* pg. 24.
44   Amariah on stage. Marberry, *The Golden Voice,* pp. 24–25.
44   Amariah's famous acquaintances. Marberry, *The Golden Voice,* pg. 25.
44   Following in his father's footsteps. Marberry, *The Golden Voice,* pp. 27–28.
45   Kalloch's early education, meeting Laura. Marberry, *The Golden Voice,* pp. 27–28.
45   College and expulsion. Marberry, *The Golden Voice,* pp. 27–28.

45   "I know nothing . . . trial at Cambridge." *A Faint Idea of a Terrible Life* (Bancroft Library).

46   Classes canceled for the day. Marberry, *The Golden Voice*, pp. 29–30.

46   Father's influence at school, dropping out. Marberry, *The Golden Voice*, pg. 30.

47   Amariah's journey to California. *New York Times*, 25 April 1880; Marberry, *The Golden Voice*, pp. 31–32.

47   Amariah, wife succumbing to illness. Marberry, *The Golden Voice*, pg. 32.

47   Kalloch's marriage, birth of son. Marberry, *The Golden Voice*, pg. 33; *New York Times*, 12 December 1887; Seattle Post-Intelligencer, 16 March 1909.

47   Kalloch's physique, popularity. Marberry, *The Golden Voice*, pp. 33, 35, 43, 44; Adams, *Murder by the Bay*, pg. 58.

47   Journalism experience, drinking. Marberry, *The Golden Voice*, pp. 33, 35.

48   Job offer at Tremont Temple. Adams, *Murder by the Bay*, pg. 57; Marberry, *The Golden Voice*, pp. 43–44.

48   "He was . . . wondrously devout youth." *New York Times*, 25 August 1879.

48   Nature of Kalloch's sermons. Adams, *Murder by the Bay*, pg. 58; Marberry, *The Golden Voice*, pp. 43–44.

48   Tremont Temple description and layout. Marberry, *The Golden Voice*, pg. 47.

48   "Kalloch's fame . . . want of standing room." *Williamsburg (KS) Review*, 4 September 1879.

48   Lecture tours and political themes. Marberry, *The Golden Voice*, pg. 46.

49   Atticus stowing away on schooner. Higgins, *How the State of Maine . . .* (online resource).

49   Sagurs's pursuit, Atticus in Maine. Higgins, *How the State of Maine . . .* (online resource).

50   Atticus recaptured. Higgins, *How the State of Maine . . .* (online resource).

50   Critical complaints, Kalloch's salary. Marberry, *The Golden Voice*, pp. 44, 46.

CHAPTER 3: A TARNISHED HALO

51   Laura's visit. Marberry, *The Golden Voice*, pp. 51–52.

51   Laura's husband, purpose for visit. Marberry, *The Golden Voice*, pp. 51–52.

52   The Rev. David Thomas. Marberry, *The Golden Voice*, pg. 51.

52   Topic of speech, invite to lecture. Marberry, *The Golden Voice*, pg. 52.

52   Transportation to Cambridge. *Complete Report on the Trial of Rev. I. S. Kalloch . . .* (trial transcript).

52   Greeted by Ephraim P. Bailey. *Complete Report on the Trial of Rev. I. S. Kalloch . . .* (trial transcript).

53   "I am giving . . . a fire built upstairs." *Complete Report on the Trial of Rev. I. S. Kalloch . . .* (trial transcript).

53   "She had on . . . her eyes were dark blue." *Complete Report on the Trial of Rev. I. S. Kalloch . . .* (trial transcript).

53   "I guess . . . there's plenty." *Complete Report on the Trial of Rev. I. S. Kalloch . . .* (trial transcript).

54   Kalloch shown to his room. *Complete Report on the Trial of Rev. I. S. Kalloch . . .* (trial transcript).

54   "Can you furnish . . . know about it?" *Complete Report on the Trial of Rev. I. S. Kalloch . . .* (trial transcript).

54   Bailey brings Kalloch a drink. *Complete Report on the Trial of Rev. I. S. Kalloch . . .* (trial transcript).

54   Mrs. Griffin eavesdrop on Kalloch. *Complete Report on the Trial of Rev. I. S. Kalloch . . .* (trial transcript).

54   "I couldn't hear . . . in a low private manner." *Complete Report on the Trial of Rev. I. S. Kalloch . . .* (trial transcript).

54   "How can I help . . . to you—or nothing." *Complete Report on the Trial of Rev. I. S. Kalloch . . .* (trial transcript).

54   "What would they say . . . and so on." *Complete Report on the Trial of Rev. I. S. Kalloch . . .* (trial transcript).

55   Mrs. Griffin spying on guests. *Complete Report on the Trial of Rev. I. S. Kalloch . . .* (trial transcript).

55   Rev. F. W. Holland feeling stood-up. *Complete Report on the Trial of Rev. I. S. Kalloch . . .* (trial transcript).

55   Holland inviting Kalloch to tea. *Complete Report on the Trial of Rev. I. S. Kalloch . . .* (trial transcript); Marberry, *The Golden Voice*, pg. 51.

56   Kalloch excuses himself from tea. *Complete Report on the Trial of Rev. I. S. Kalloch . . .* (trial transcript).

56   "I really must get to my notes." *Complete Report on the Trial of Rev. I. S. Kalloch . . .* (trial transcript).

56   Guests leave, Mrs. Griffin shares secret. *Complete Report on the Trial of Rev. I. S. Kalloch . . .* (trial transcript).

56   Kalloch's speech, declines tea invite. *Complete Report on the Trial of Rev. I. S. Kalloch . . .* (trial transcript).

57   Bailey spies on Kalloch. *Complete Report on the Trial of Rev. I. S. Kalloch . . .* (trial transcript).

57   "There was . . . I should say." *Complete Report on the Trial of Rev. I. S. Kalloch . . .* (trial transcript).

57   "What do you suppose . . . knew you were here?" *Complete Report on the Trial of Rev. I. S. Kalloch . . .* (trial transcript).

58   Kalloch, Laura on the floor. *Complete Report on the Trial of Rev. I. S. Kalloch . . .* (trial transcript).

58   "How does . . . don't hurry." *Complete Report on the Trial of Rev. I. S. Kalloch . . .* (trial transcript).

58   Bailey and Giddings. *Complete Report on the Trial of Rev. I. S. Kalloch . . .* (trial transcript).

58 "I went upstairs . . . outside his pants." *Complete Report on the Trial of Rev. I. S. Kalloch* . . . (trial transcript).

58 Kalloch, Laura dressing. *Complete Report on the Trial of Rev. I. S. Kalloch* . . . (trial transcript).

59 Rumors circulating. Marberry, *The Golden Voice*, pg. 52.

59 Kalloch called to explain himself. Marberry, *The Golden Voice*, pg. 54.

59 Kalloch's explanation. Marberry, *The Golden Voice*, pg. 55.

60 "is a filthy sheet . . . renewed affection." Marberry, *The Golden Voice*, pg. 56.

60 "had caused . . . look askance." Marberry, *The Golden Voice*, pg. 57.

60 Villified by the press. Marberry, *The Golden Voice*, pp. 57, 59.

61 "Isaac S. Kalloch . . . to each other." *Complete Report on the Trial of Rev. I. S. Kalloch* . . . (trial transcript).

61 Kalloch responds to indictment. Marberry, *The Golden Voice*, pg. 59.

CHAPTER 4: IN JUDGMENT

62 "The number . . . worthy of praise." *Complete Report on the Trial of Rev. I. S. Kalloch* . . . (trial transcript).

62 "He appeared . . . clean his fingernails." *Complete Report on the Trial of Rev. I. S. Kalloch* . . . (trial transcript).

63 Richard H. Dana. Marberry, *The Golden Voice*, pg. 62.

63 Dana's background. Marberry, *The Golden Voice*, pg. 62.

63 Mr. Stein. Marberry, *The Golden Voice*, pg. 63.

63 Unless otherwise noted, trial testimony is taken from *Complete Report on the Trial of Rev. I. S. Kalloch* . . . (trial transcript).

66 "The trial . . . [Lechmere] House." *New York Times*, 3 April 1857

73 "Faith in . . . the last." *Full Report of R. H. Dana's Argument for Defense in the Case of Rev. I. S. Kalloch*

77 Kalloch's character. Marberry, *The Golden Voice*, pg. 121.

77 "He returned . . . to his vomit." *A Faint Idea of a Terrible Life* (Bancroft Library).

CHAPTER 5: VIOLENCE AND VILLAINY

78 "A new . . . *independent paper*." *Daily Morning Chronicle*, 1 September 1868.

79 "We shall . . . individual unnecessarily." *Daily Morning Chronicle*, 1 September 1868.

79 "We went . . . lie around on." De Young dictation (Bancroft Library).

79 "Nothing would . . . been since." De Young dictation (Bancroft Library).

80 "What would . . . Dramatic Chronicle." De Young dictation (Bancroft Library).

80 "Though not . . . reasonable ambition." *Daily Morning Chronicle*, 17 July 1865.

80 "by further . . . demand it." *Daily Morning Chronicle*, 16 March 1867.

81 "Human nature . . . 'forgive me!'" *Daily Morning Chronicle*, 17 April 1865.

81 "At that . . . a success." De Young dictation (Bancroft Library).

81 "The offers . . . daily paper." De Young dictation (Bancroft Library).

82 "make it a great paper." De Young dictation (Bancroft Library).

82 "As we . . . deal of attention." De Young dictation (Bancroft Library).

82 "You must . . . five dollars." Bruce, *Gaudy Century*, pg. 146.

83 "You sort . . . the five." Bruce, *Gaudy Century*, pg. 146.

83 George's homicidal impulse. Bruce, *Gaudy Century*, pg. 146.

83 Rounding out the *Chronicle*'s staff. De Young dictation (Bancroft Library).

83 "The 'Company' . . . business again." De Young dictation (Bancroft Library).

83 Bachelors and salary. Bruce, *Gaudy Century*, pg. 141.

83 New office, new sign. De Young dictation (Bancroft Library).

83 "The CHRONICLE . . . its existence" *Daily Morning Chronicle*, 1 September 1868.

84 "You have . . . with you." De Young dictation (Bancroft Library).

84 "If you . . . crush you." De Young dictation (Bancroft Library).

84 "The reason . . . crushing us." De Young dictation (Bancroft Library).

84 Seven-column paper. Bruce, *Gaudy Century*, pg. 141.

85 "Shortly after . . . *Bulletin* began." De Young dictation (Bancroft Library).

85 "Many acted . . . had come." *San Francisco Morning Call*, October 22, 1868

85 "As if the mountains . . . in pain." *Daily Morning Chronicle*, 22 October 1868.

85 "The scene . . . bring forth." *Daily Morning Chronicle*, 22 October 1868.

85 "In the . . . an extra." De Young dictation (Bancroft Library).

86 "Never . . . and fear." *Daily Morning Chronicle*, 21 October 1868.

86 "It was . . . with it." De Young dictation (Bancroft Library).

86 "The *Chronicle* . . . could display." De Young dictation (Bancroft Library).

86 "a dear, good-knowing twaddler." *Daily Dramatic Chronicle*, 7 February 1866.

87 "It is . . . right speedily." *Daily Dramatic Chronicle*, 25 January 1866.

87 "The dramatic . . . his head." *Daily Dramatic Chronicle*, 25 January 1866.

87 "Not having . . . to prevent." *Daily Dramatic Chronicle*, 27 January 1866.

87 "Do somebody . . . under awhile." *Daily Dramatic Chronicle*, 12 January 1866.

88 "The *Daily Humbugger*." McKee, pg. 274; Young, *Journalism in California*, pg. 74.

88 "The *Chronicle* . . . terrific one." De Young dictation (Bancroft Library).

88 "We branded . . . government here." De Young dictation (Bancroft Library).

88 "What do . . . every time." De Young dictation (Bancroft Library).

88 "equally as terrific." De Young dictation (Bancroft Library).

88 Accustomed foreman. Bruce, *Gaudy Century*, pg. 142.

89 "This paper . . . to appear." Bruce, *Gaudy Century*, pg. 142.

89 "Of course . . . the *Chronicle*." Bruce, *Gaudy Century*, pg. 142.

89 De Young's love of gossip. McKee, pg. 275.

89 "How any . . . cannot understand." *San Francisco Examiner*, 10 April 1871.

89 "Nearly one . . . 'high life.'" *San Francisco Chronicle*, 17 October 1869.

90 "San Francisco . . . the teeth." *San Francisco Chronicle*, 17 October 1869.

90 "yearned to . . . in Naples." *San Francisco Chronicle*, 17 October 1869.

90   "Alas! Alas! . . . to be." *San Francisco Chronicle*, 17 October 1869.

90   "He went . . . of April." *San Francisco Chronicle*, 17 October 1869.

91   Story appears ten months later. McKee, pg. 275.

91   "The most . . . every gentleman." McKee, pp. 275-276.

91   "The *Chronicle* . . . own savings." De Young dictation (Bancroft Library).

91   "We traded . . . financial failure." De Young dictation (Bancroft Library).

Chapter 6: Beatings and Litigation

92   De Young sued a dozen times. McKee, pg. 276.

92   Acquittals equaled indictments. Bruce, *Gaudy Century*, pg. 144.

93   Homicide "justifiable." Bruce, *Gaudy Century*, pg. 144.

93   "Higgins . . . an adversary." *San Francisco Chronicle*," 9 May 1871.

93   "a lamented son of James King of William." *San Francisco Chronicle*, 9 May 1871.

93   "Higgins plans at convention, " Secrest, *California Feuds*, pg. 97.

93   "I was . . . to strike." De Young dictation (Bancroft Library).

93   Michael's counterattack. De Young dictation (Bancroft Library); *San Francisco Chronicle*, 9 May 1871.

94   Higgins fights back. *San Francisco Chronicle*, 9 May 1871.

94   "At this . . . prostrate bravo." *San Francisco Chronicle*, 9 May 1871.

94   "You are . . . my pistol." *San Francisco Chronicle*, 9 May 1871.

94   "I did not . . . not prosecute." De Young dictation (Bancroft Library); *San Francisco Chronicle*, 9 May 1871.

95   "It is . . . and pistol." *San Francisco Chronicle*, 9 May 1871.

95   "On that . . . the 'draw.'" *San Francisco Chronicle*, 9 May 1871.

95   "The CHRONICLE . . . might conceive." *San Francisco Chronicle*, 9 May 1871.

95   "The afternoon . . . their way." *San Francisco Chronicle*, 2 July 1871; McKee, pg. 276.

96   "pretty girls and gallant officers." *San Francisco Chronicle*, 2 July 1871.

96   "'Sweet William' . . . in palm." *San Francisco Chronicle*, 2 July 1871.

96   Meeting on the street. *Daily Alta Californian*, 4 July 1871.

96   "The mean . . . right-thinking people." *Daily Alta California*, 4 July 1871.

97   McKinstry finds his range. *Daily Alta California*, 4 July 1871.

97   Fight ends. *Daily Alta California*, 4 July 1871.

97   "For several . . . future happiness." *San Francisco Examiner*, 5 July 1871.

97   "customary number . . . and gentleman." *San Francisco Examiner*, 5 July 1871.

98   "We are . . . *Chronicle* fellow." *San Francisco Examiner*, 5 July 1871.

98   "being humane . . . the lesson." *San Francisco Examiner*, 5 July 1871.

98   "I will . . . San Quentin yet!" De Young dictation (Bancroft Library).

98   "There was . . . the public." De Young dictation (Bancroft Library).

98   "It was . . . the bench." De Young dictation (Bancroft Library).

99   "It was . . . or not." De Young dictation (Bancroft Library).

99   "When the . . . nearly fainted." De Young dictation (Bancroft Library).

99   "They always . . . always did." De Young dictation (Bancroft Library).

99   "You are . . . the nomination!" De Young dictation (Bancroft Library).

100   "a passionate . . . to judge." De Young dictation (Bancroft Library).

100   "When (opponent) . . . my brother." De Young dictation (Bancroft Library).

100   "I had . . . his paper." *Daily Morning Call*, 2 December 1871.

101   "breathless with . . . violent efforts." *San Francisco Chronicle*, 2 December 1871.

101   Lake pulls gun. *San Francisco Chronicle*, 2 December 1871.

101   "a man . . . muscular strength." *San Francisco Chronicle*, 2 December 1871.

101   "And now . . . life began." *San Francisco Chronicle*, 2 December 1871.

101   "At length . . . being removed." *San Francisco Chronicle*, 2 December 1871.

101   Lake's bail, De Young's wounds. *Daily Morning Call*, 2 December 1871.

102   Mr. Wheeler's condition. *San Francisco Chronicle*, 2 December 1871.

102   "desperate struggle for life." *San Francisco Chronicle*, 2 December 1871.

102   "It may . . . four years." *San Francisco Chronicle*, 2 December 1871.

102   "a disgraceful attack." *Daily Morning Call*, 2 December 1871.

102   "It was . . . the world." *Daily Evening Bulletin*, 2 December 1871.

103   "There was . . . him $300." Bruce, *Gaudy Century*, pg. 156.

103   "one of . . . his death." De Young dictation (Bancroft Library).

103   "At that . . . generally Monday." De Young dictation (Bancroft Library).

104   "We started . . . been abducted." De Young dictation (Bancroft Library).

104   "We raised . . . man free." De Young dictation (Bancroft Library).

104   *Chronicle* circulation. De Young dication (Bancroft Library).

CHAPTER 7: UNDER FIRE

105   "offensive emanation." Bruce, *Gaudy Century*, pg. 156.

105   "a blackmail sheet." *San Francisco Chronicle*, 3 February 1874.

105   Corrupt Fitzgerald. *San Francisco Chronicle*, 3 February 1874.

106   "a thief . . . bigamy, etc." *San Francisco Chronicle*, 12 February 1874.

106   "the allegations . . . its circulation." *San Francisco Chronicle*, 12 February 1874.

106   Fitzgerald's marriages. *San Francisco Chronicle*, 13 February 1874.

106   Fitzgerald jumps bail. *San Francisco Chronicle*, 13 February 1874.

107   Fitzgerald arrives in San Francisco. *San Francisco Chronicle*, 13 February 1874.

107   "Napthaly . . . has none." *San Francisco Chronicle* (reprinting *Evening Post* article), 3 February 1874.

107   "leading an . . . dissolute life." *San Francisco Chronicle*, 14 February 1874.

107   Napthaly's misfortune. *San Francisco Chronicle*, 14 February 1874.

108   De Young hires Napthaly. *San Francisco Chronicle*, 14 February 1874.

108   "There goes a reporter!" *San Francisco Chronicle*, 14 February 1874.

108   "Sometimes . . . composing tables." *San Francisco Chronicle*, 14 February 1874.

108   Pressmen in saloons. *San Francisco Chronicle*, 14 February 1874.

108   Napthaly quits *Chronicle*. *San Francisco Chronicle*, 14 February 1874.

108   "I have . . . stay here." *San Francisco Chronicle*, 14 February 1874.

109   "You can . . . to come." *San Francisco Chronicle*, 14 February 1874.

109   "Very slight . . . with them." *San Francisco Chronicle*, 14 February 1874.

109   Fitzgerald hires Napthaly. *San Francisco Chronicle*, 14 February 1874.

109   "The thing . . . called a newspaper." *San Francisco Chronicle* (reprinting *Evening Post* article), 3 February 1874.

109   John Lander. *San Francisco Chronicle*, 12 February 1874.

110   "I told . . . read it." *San Francisco Chronicle*, 12 February 1874.

110   Blake talks with De Young. *San Francisco Chronicle*, 14 February 1874.

110   Quoted conversation. *San Francisco Chronicle*, 14 February 1874.

111   "Fitzgerald . . . of hoodlumism." *San Francisco Chronicle*, 31 January 1874.

111   "This first-class . . . and insignificant." *San Francisco Chronicle* (reprinting *Evening Post* article), 3 February 1874.

111   "It showed . . . prostituted." *San Francisco Chronicle*, 3 February 1874.

111   "Such an . . . respectable paper." *San Francisco Chronicle* (reprinting *Evening Post* article), 3 February 1874.

112   Gustavus visits Fitzgerald. *San Francisco Chronicle*, 3 February 1874.

112   Gustavus beats Fitzgerald. *San Francisco Chronicle*, 3 February 1874.

112   Gustavus leaves *Sun* offices. *San Francisco Chronicle*, 3 February 1874.

112   Charles and the "paddy wagon." *San Francisco Chronicle*, 3 February 1874.

113   "Such was . . . a piece." *San Francisco Chronicle* (reprinting *Evening Post* article), 3 February 1874.

113   News reaches Charles and Michael. *San Francisco Chronicle*, 3 February 1874.

113   "The police . . . a room." *San Francisco Chronicle* (reprinting *Evening Post* article), 3 February 1874.

114   "It is . . . remain hidden." *Daily Alta California*, 1 February 1874.

114   Gustavus opens fire. *Daily Alta California*, 3 February 1874.

114   Gustavus fires again. *Daily Alta California*, 3 February 1874.

115   Officer Ryan intervenes. *Daily Alta California*, 3 February 1874.

115   "You ought to have let me alone." *San Francisco Chronicle*, 10 February 1874.

115   "followed by an army of citizens." *Daily Alta California*, 3 February 1874.

115   Crowds and reporters gather. *San Francisco Chronicle* (reprinting *Evening Post* article), 3 February 1874.

115   Swarmed by reporters. *San Francisco Chronicle* (reprinting *Evening Post* article), 3 February 1874.

115   "Can you . . . was stunned." *San Francisco Chronicle* (reprinting *Evening Post* article), 3 February 1874.

116   "De Young . . . been shot." *San Francisco Chronicle* (reprinting *Evening Post* article), 3 February 1874; *San Francisco Chronicle*, 10 February 1874.

116   Napthaly's ordeal. *San Francisco Chronicle*, 10 February 1874.

116 "a scene . . . beggaring description." *San Francisco Chronicle* (reprinting *Evening Post* article), 3 February 1874; *Daily Alta California*, 3 February 1874.

117 "For God sake . . . man away!" *Daily Alta California*, 3 February 1874.

117 "Give me your pistol!" *Daily Alta California*, 3 February 1874.

117 Charles de Young surrenders weapon. *San Francisco Chronicle*, 10 February 1874.

117 "By this . . . of order." *San Francisco Chronicle* (reprinting *Evening Post* article), 3 February 1874.

117 Libel suit filed. *San Francisco Chronicle* (reprinting *Evening Post* article), 3 February 1874.

117 "For God's . . . even armed." *San Francisco Chronicle*, 10 February 1874.

117 "You dirty . . . on sight." *San Francisco Chronicle*, 10 February 1874; *Daily Alta California*, 8 February 1874.

117 Napthaly stays for the night. *San Francisco Chronicle* (reprinting *Evening Post* article), 3 February 1874.

118 "A fine . . . journalistic enterprises." *Daily Alta California* (reprinting *Daily Oakland News* article), 6 February 1874.

118 "He was . . . the rear." *Daily Alta California*, 5 February 1874.

118 "out of . . . of friendship." *Daily Alta California*, 8 February 1874.

118 "The Messrs. . . . summary vengeance." *San Francisco Chronicle*, 10 February 1874.

119 "as there . . . something extra" to report. *Daily Alta California*, 8 February 1874.

119 "The libeler . . . of police." *San Francisco Chronicle*, 6 February 1874.

119 "The De Young . . . Police Court." *Daily Alta California*, 5 February 1874.

120 "He paused . . . his tail." *San Francisco Chronicle*, 6 February 1874.

120 "While there . . . Bush Street." *San Francisco Chronicle*, 6 February 1874.

121 Charges "forgotten." Bruce, *Gaudy Century*, pg. 158.

121 "This does . . . by libel." Bruce, *Gaudy Century*, pg. 158.

121 Napthaly acquitted. *San Francisco Chronicle*, 17 June 1874.

122 "miserable dog's death." *San Francisco Chronicle*, 17 June 1874.

122 Charles de Young finds Napthaly. Bruce, *Gaudy Century*, pp. 158–159.

123 Napthaly enters police station. Bruce, *Gaudy Century*, pg. 159.

123 De Young sits in on game. Bruce, *Gaudy Century*, pg. 159.

123 Napthaly frequents post office. *New York Times* (reprinting *Daily Alta California*), 28 June 1874.

123 Charles de Young draws and fires. *New York Times* (reprinting *Daily Alta California*), 28 June 1874.

123 "There was . . . this kind." *New York Times* (reprinting *Daily Alta California*), 28 June 1874.

124 Young girl faints. Bruce, *Gaudy Century*, pg. 159.

124 Young boy shot. *New York Times* (reprinting *Daily Alta California*), 28 June 1874.

124 "Let's lynch . . . the streets!" *New York Times* (reprinting *Daily Alta California*), 28 June 1874.

124 "On leaving . . . the wound." *New York Times* (reprinting *Daily Alta California*), 28 June 1874.

124 Thomas Ryan's testimony. Bruce, *Gaudy Century*, pg. 160.

125 "You heard . . . stand down!" Bruce, *Gaudy Century*, pg. 160.

125 Napthaly's admiration. Bruce, *Gaudy Century*, pg. 160.

Chapter 8: The Coming Man

127 "believed . . . of justice." *A Faint Idea of a Terrible Life* (Bancroft Library).

127 "Here we . . . Baptist persuasion." Marberry, *The Golden Voice*, pg. 131.

127 Morse, a solitary figure. Marberry, *The Golden Voice*, pg. 124.

128 "men of . . . doubtful wisdom." *A Faint Idea of a Terrible Life* (Bancroft Library).

128 "The weak-kneed . . . be sure." *A Faint Idea of a Terrible Life* (Bancroft Library).

129 "Like Beecher . . . weak humanity." *A Faint Idea of a Terrible Life* (Bancroft Library).

129 A change of scenery. Marberry, *The Golden Voice*, pg. 146.

129 Heads to Kansas territory. Marberry, *The Golden Voice*, pg. 146.

129 Emigrant Aid Company. Marberry, *The Golden Voice*, pg. 145.

129 Kalloch's many pursuits. Marberry, *The Golden Voice*, pg. 147; *Kansas Historical Quarterly*, May 1945, pp. 332–333.

130 Fire and the Tremont Temple. Blackmar, *Kansas*, pg. 122; Marberry, *The Golden Voice*, pg. 149.

130 Smaller audience. Marberry, *The Golden Voice*, pg. 149.

130 "The man . . . their lives." *A Faint Idea of a Terrible Life* (Bancroft Library); Marberry, *The Golden Voice*, pp. 150–151.

131 Congregation restored, Marberry, *The Golden Voice*, pg. 150.

131 "The sanctity . . . his defilement." *A Faint Idea of a Terrible Life* (Bancroft Library).

131 Accusation against Kalloch. Marberry, *The Golden Voice*, pg. 152.

131 "The Committee . . . devotion!" Marberry, *The Golden Voice* (quoting the *New York Sunday Mercury*), pg. 153.

131 Kalloch considers Kansas again. Marberry, *The Golden Voice*, pg. 154.

132 Kalloch returns to Kansas. Marberry, *The Golden Voice*, pg. 156.

132 "The only . . . our remembrance." *New York Times*, 3 September 1860.

132 "The heat . . . as 108°." *Kansas Historical Quarterly*, May 1946, pg.139.

132 "gates of . . . thrown open." *Kansas Historical Quarterly*, May 1946, pg.139.

132 Kalloch at Laight Street. Marberry, *The Golden Voice*, pg. 158; *New York Times*, 25 August 1879.

133 "His height . . . his compliments." *New York Times*, 25 August 1879.

133 "While he . . . his reputation." *New York Times*, 25 August 1879.

133 "He soon . . . hear him." *New York Times*, 25 August 1879.

133 "contest . . . like water." *New York Times*, 1 May 1863.

134   Churchgoers and critics. *New York Times*, 25 August 1879.

134   "with scandalous flavors attached." *New York Times*, 25 August 1879.

134   New York accusations. *A Faint Idea of a Terrible Life* (Bancroft Library).

134   "I never . . . I say." *New York Times*, 25 August 1879.

135   Kalloch's Kansas mission. Marberry, *The Golden Voice*, pg. 164.

135   "in return . . . thirty years." *New York Times*, 24 May 1871.

135   Money borrowed. *New York Times*, 24 May 1871; Marberry, *The Golden Voice*, pg. 184.

135   Board accepts Kalloch's story. *New York Times*, 24 May 1871; Marberry, *The Golden Voice*, pp. 184–185.

136   "A wealthy . . . life itself." *New York Times*, 24 May 1871.

136   Kalloch launches paper, town company. Marberry, *The Golden Voice*, pp. 167–168, 176; City of Ottawa, KS, website.

136   Kalloch flees to Missouri. Marberry, *The Golden Voice*, pg. 188–189.

137   "The infamous . . . be known." Marberry, *The Golden Voice*, pg. 189.

137   Kalloch meets deadline. Marberry, *The Golden Voice*, pg. 187–189.

137   "I believe . . . lachrymal glands." *A Faint Idea of a Terrible Life* (Bancroft Library).

137   "The Coming Man . . . his belly." Marberry, *The Golden Voice*, pg. 196.

137   "Oh . . . around loose." *A Faint Idea of a Terrible Life* (Bancroft Library).

138   "If he . . . Isaac S. Kalloch." *A Faint Idea of a Terrible Life* (Bancroft Library).

138   Kalloch founds paper, purchases Eldridge House. Marberry, *The Golden Voice*, pp. 197, 201.

138   "never kept . . . for her." *A Faint Idea of a Terrible Life* (Bancroft Library).

138   "By way . . . same time." *A Faint Idea of a Terrible Life* (Bancroft Library).

139   Kalloch's political campaign. Marberry, *The Golden Voice*, pp. 206, 208–209.

139   Sameul C. Pomeroy. Marberry, *The Golden Voice*, pg. 209; "The Panic of 1873" (online resource).

139   Kalloch does not seek reelection. Marberry, *The Golden Voice*, pg. 213; "The Panic of 1873" (online resource)

139   Kalloch's bankruptcy, new pastoral position. Marberry, *The Golden Voice*, pp. 213, 214, 219.

140   Kalloch eyes San Francisco. Marberry, *The Golden Voice*, pp. 219, 224–225.

140   "go to . . . convert them." Marberry, *The Golden Voice*, pg. 226.

Chapter 9: Fire and Politics

141   "great anti-Coolie mass meeting." *San Francisco Examiner*, 26 July 1877.

142   One dollar and a sandwich. Bruce, *Gaudy Century*, pg. 162.

142   City's large Chinese population, resentment of white laborers. Bruce, *Gaudy Century*, pg. 161; Kauer, pg. 279.

142   "The majority . . . sight-seers." *San Francisco Examiner*, 26 July 1877.

142 "all railroad . . . public use." Hart, *The Sand Lot and Kearneyism* (Virtual Museum of San Francisco).

143 "As a windup . . . it down." *San Francisco Chronicle*, 26 July 1877.

143 "The centre . . . the platform. Hart, *The Sand Lot and Kearneyism* (Virtual Museum of San Francisco).

143 "Various agitators . . . the crowd." Hart, *The Sand Lot and Kearneyism* (Virtual Museum of San Francisco).

143 "appetite for mischief." *San Francisco Examiner*, 26 July 1877.

143 "boys ranging . . . them countenance." *San Francisco Examiner*, 26 July 1877.

143 "The two . . . be attacked." *San Francisco Chronicle*, 26 July 1877.

144 Shopkeepers take cover. *San Francisco Chronicle*, 26 July 1877.

144 "inspired by the gang." *San Francisco Chronicle*, 26 July 1877.

144 "This they . . . the house." *San Francisco Chronicle*, 26 July 1877.

144 Piercy threatens to shoot. *San Francisco Chronicle*, 26 July 1877.

145 Yee Wah's washhouse. *San Francisco Chronicle*, 26 July 1877.

145 "During the . . . about 250." *San Francisco Chronicle*, 26 July 1877.

145 Specators applaud. *San Francisco Chronicle*, 26 July 1877.

145 "hoodlum of tender years." *San Francisco Chronicle*, 26 July 1877.

146 A woman's pleas. *San Francisco Chronicle*, 26 July 1877.

146 "After a . . . the assault." *San Francisco Examiner*, 26 July 1877.

146 Teen arrested. *San Francisco Examiner*, 26 July 1877.

146 "This closed . . . the evening." *San Francisco Examiner*, 26 July 1877.

147 Stranger at the docks. *San Francisco Examiner*, 26 July 1877.

147 Fire at the docks. *San Francisco Examiner*, 26 July 1877; *San Francisco Chronicle*, 26 July 1877.

147 "In one . . . be had." *San Francisco Chronicle*, 26 July 1877.

147 Police go on the offensive. *San Francisco Examiner*, 26 July 1877.

148 Committee member shot. *San Francisco Examiner*, 26 July 1877.

148 "Many of . . . of stones." *San Francisco Examiner*, 26 July 1877.

148 "An engine . . . fatally injured." *San Francisco Examiner*, 26 July 1877.

148 "The thud . . . the officers." *San Francisco Examiner*, 26 July 1877.

149 "From one . . . the hoodlums." *San Francisco Examiner*, 26 July 1877.

149 The evening's casualties. *San Francisco Chronicle*, 26 July 1877.

149 $130,000 in damage. *San Francisco Chronicle*, 26 July 1877.

149 "The firemen . . . the engines." *San Francisco Examiner*, 26 July 1877.

149 Denis Kearney. Bruce, *Gaudy Century*, pg., 167.

150 Trade and Labor Union. Hart, *The Sand Lot and Kearneyism* (Virtual Museum of San Francisco).

150 "the beginning . . . the State." Hart, *The Sand Lot and Kearneyism* (Virtual Museum of San Francisco).

151 "The Central . . . the consequences." *Daily Evening Bulletin*, 5 November 1877.

151 Kearney holding a noose. Rhodes, *History of the United States* (1877–1896), pg. 186.

151 "Judge Lynch . . . we want!" Hart, *The Sand Lot and Kearneyism* (Virtual Museum of San Francisco).

151 "tax the . . . wealth impossible." Hart, *The Sand Lot and Kearneyism* (Virtual Museum of San Francisco); Kauer, pg. 280.

151 "We propose . . . their request." *San Francisco Chronicle*, 6 October 1877.

152 "California-street . . . of reformers." *San Francisco Chronicle*, 30 October 1877.

152 "thundered forth . . . the rich." Hart, *The Sand Lot and Kearneyism* (Virtual Museum of San Francisco).

152 "railroad magnets . . . scoundrelly officials." Hart, *The Sand Lot and Kearneyism* (Virtual Museum of San Francisco).

153 "destroy all . . . in California." Hart, *The Sand Lot and Kearneyism* (Virtual Museum of San Francisco).

153 "This is . . . be King." Kauer, pg. 281.

153 Speeches threatening destruction. Hart, *The Sand Lot and Kearneyism* (Virtual Museum of San Francisco).

153 "I'm tired . . . wants them." Kauer, pg. 281.

153 "bullets would replace ballots." Bruce, *Gaudy Century*, pg. 167.

153 Day surrenders presidency. Kauer, pg. 281.

153 Military organization. Kauer, pg. 281.

153 Kearney's repeated arrests. Kauer, pg. 281.

154 Workingmen's political victories, Marberry, *The Golden Voice*, pg. 236.

154 Election of delegates. Kauer, pg. 283.

154 Number of delegates. Hart, *The Sand Lot and Kearneyism* (Virtual Museum of San Francisco); Kauer, pg. 283.

154 "All those . . . San Francisco." Kauer, pg. 280.

154 "Many of . . . simply slaves." *San Francisco Chronicle*, 8 October 1877.

155 *Chronicle* supports the party. Marberry, *The Golden Voice*, pp. 236–237.

155 "mob-inspired monstrosity." Young, *Journalism in California*, pg. 91.

155 *Daily Record-Union* quote. Kauer, pg. 285.

155 "Never was . . . May 7th, 1879." Young, *Journalism in California*, pg. 94.

155 "One Hundred . . . Be Adopted." Young, *Journalism in California*, pg. 94.

155 "It must . . . put it." Young, *Journalism in California*, pg. 94.

156 "They adjourned . . . and stocks." Young, *Journalism in California*, pp. 94-95.

156 "There is . . . not good." Kauer, pg. 285.

156 ten-thousand-vote majority. Hart, *The Sand Lot and Kearneyism* (Virtual Museum of San Francisco).

156 New constitution. Bryce, *The Character of California* (Vitrual Museum of San Francisco).

156 "Charles de Young . . . political power." McKee, pg. 280.

157 "The last election . . . active operation?" *San Francisco Chronicle*, 13 May 1879.

157   "in which . . . existing party." *San Francisco Chronicle*, 13 May 1879.

157   "It is . . . common clodhopper." *San Francisco Chronicle*, 22 May 1879.

158   "The treacherous . . . impudent falsehood." *San Francisco Chronicle*, 25 May 1879.

158   "Kearney's Brutality." *San Francisco Chronicle*, 4 June 1879.

158   "Kearney's Vulgarity." *San Francisco Chronicle*, 7 June 1879.

158   "blackguard," "blatherskite," "a stupid bully." *San Francisco Chronicle*, 4 June 1879.

CHAPTER 10: A WAR OF WORDS

159   "It was . . . and handsome." Hart, *The Kearney-Kalloch Epoch* (Virtual Museum of San Francisco).

159   "always seemed . . . an organ." Marberry, *The Golden Voice*, pg. 229.

159   Kalloch's early days in San Francisco. Marberry, *The Golden Voice*, pg. 227.

160   Editors killed. Marberry, *The Golden Voice*, pg. 227.

160   Lankershim's contributions. Marberry, *The Golden Voice*, pg. 229.

161   Congregants pay ten cents admission. Bruce, *Gaudy Century*, pp. 171–172.

161   "The house . . . a theatre." Bancroft, *History of California*, pg. 412.

161   Admission supplements Kalloch's income. Bruce, *Gaudy Century*, pp. 171–172; Marberry, *The Golden Voice*, pp. 229–230.

161   "The Sunday . . . their tenseness." Hart, *The Kearney-Kalloch Epoch* (Virtual Museum of San Francisco).

161   Kalloch had plenty to say. Bancroft, *History of California*, pg. 412.

161   Kalloch's stance. Marberry, *The Golden Voice*, pg. 233.

162   "The Chinese . . . and huckstering." Bancroft, *History of California*, pg. 412.

162   "The Chinamen . . . from coming." Marberry, *The Golden Voice*, pg. 234.

162   "These howling . . . too effectually!" *San Francisco Chronicle*, 3 September 1879.

162   "They are . . . Gatling gun." *San Francisco Chronicle*, 3 September 1879.

163   "Napoleon's advice . . . of humanity." *San Francisco Chronicle*, 3 September 1879.

163   "anarchists . . . demagogues." Hart, *The Kearney-Kalloch Epoch* (Virtual Museum of San Francisco).

163   Democrats and Republicans form unified front. Marberry, *The Golden Voice*, pp. 236–237.

163   "We believe . . . be right." Saxton, *The Indispensable Enemy*, pp. 139–140.

164   Kalloch's about-face. Maberry, *The Golden Voice*, pp. 237–238.

164   "If the . . . sentiment left." Marberry, *The Golden Voice*, pg. 238.

164   "This sort . . . non-conservative classes." Bancroft, *History of California*, pg. 412.

164   "I have . . . its organization." *San Francisco Chronicle*, 3 September 1879.

165   "The Chinese Must Go." Maryberry, *The Golden Voice*, pp. 239, 241.

165   Workingmen songs. Marberry, *The Golden Voice*, pp. 239, 241.

165   Party's mistrust of Kalloch, acquiring influential statesman. Marberry, *The Golden Voice*, pg. 241.

165   "Kalloch saw . . . of Tarsus." Hart, *The Kearney-Kalloch Epoch* (Virtual Museum of San Francisco).

165   "At the head . . . at heart!" Adams, *Murder by the Bay*, pg. 63.

166   "I do . . . been acquitted." *San Francisco Chronicle*, 21 June 1879.

166   "Instead of . . . about him." *San Francisco Chronicle*, 21 June 1879.

166   "There was . . . Terry had." *San Francisco Chronicle*, 21 June 1879.

167   "New York . . . fancy farmer." *San Francisco Chronicle*, 21 June 1879.

167   "Why have . . . the Workingmen." Marberry, *The Golden Voice*, pg. 247.

167   "We have . . . our support." *San Francisco Chronicle*, 21 June 1879.

167   "We expect . . . with success." *San Francisco Chronicle*, 21 June 1879.

167   "rally around . . . all quarters." *San Francisco Chronicle*, 21 June 1879.

167   "had the ammunition . . . a preacher." Tinkham, *California Men and Events: Time 1769-1890*: Chapter XVII (online resource).

167   "Give Mr. De Young . . . to hell." *Daily Evening Bulletin*, 23 August 1879.

168   "If Kalloch . . . do it, too." Marberry, *The Golden Voice*, pg. 248.

168   "How would . . . that Sun." Marberry, *The Golden Voice*, pg. 250.

168   "Kalloch . . . a satyr." *San Francisco Chronicle*, 20 August 1879.

169   "a disgrace . . . of office," *San Francisco Chronicle*, 20 August 1879.

170   Revealing Kalloch's past. *San Francisco Chronicle*, 20 August 1879.

170   "A letter . . . to women." *San Francisco Chronicle*, 20 August 1879.

170   "The Leavenworth . . . his vicinity." *San Francisco Chronicle*, 20 August 1879.

170   "A lady . . . the city!" *San Francisco Chronicle*, 20 August 1879.

171   "He has . . . do so." *San Francisco Chronicle*, 20 August 1879.

171   "Mr. Kalloch . . . their support." *San Francisco Chronicle*, 20 August 1879.

171   "Corrupt Kalloch . . . its occupant." *San Francisco Chronicle*, 21 August 1879.

172   "A most . . . twenty-four hours." *San Francisco Chronicle*, 21 August 1879.

172   "It is . . . and corrupt." *San Francisco Chronicle*, 21 August 1879.

172   "became a . . . the Union." *San Francisco Chronicle*, 21 August 1879.

172   "Kalloch . . . a hypocrite." *San Francisco Chronicle*, 21 August 1879.

173   "The attention . . . 8 o'clock." *Daily Alta California*, 21 August 1879.

173   "While he . . . years ago." *San Francisco Chronicle*, 22 August 1879.

174   "scum . . . and brutes." *San Francisco Chronicle*, 22 August 1879.

174   "A decent . . . family circles." *Daily Alta California*, 22 August 1879.

174   "an accumulation . . . and bitterness." *Daily Evening Bulletin*, 23 August 1879.

174   "All else . . . unadulterated lie." *Daily Evening Bulletin*, 23 August 1879.

174   "I stood . . . in Boston." *Daily Evening Bulletin*, 23 August 1879.

175   "It is . . . is frustrated." *Daily Evening Bulletin*, 23 August 1879.

176   "unbecoming . . . the church." *Daily Alta California*, 24 August 1879.

176   "The De Youngs . . . of prostitution." *San Francisco Morning Call*, 24 August 1879.

176   "fighting language . . . be revived." *Daily Alta California*, 24 August 1879.

CHAPTER 11: THE SPARK OF MANHOOD

177   Smith picks up customer. *San Francisco Morning Call*, 24 August 1879.

178   "Smith returned . . . a moment." *San Francisco Morning Call*, 24 August 1879.

178   Ride to the Metropolitan Temple. *San Francisco Morning Call*, 24 August 1879.

178   "I don't . . . last night." *Daily Alta California*, 24 August 1879.

178   "Do you . . . see him." *San Francisco Morning Call*, 24 August 1879.

178   Kalloch approaches. *Daily Evening Bulletin*, 23 August 1879.

179   Kalloch is shot. *San Francisco Morning Call*, 24 August 1879.

179   "I asked . . . his heart." *Daily Alta California*, 24 August 1879.

179   "When asked . . . his suffering." *Daily Alta California*, 24 August 1879.

179   De Young threatens crowd. *San Francisco Morning Call*, 24 August 1879.

179   "I'll kill . . . on me." *Daily Alta California*, 24 August 1879.

180   "There was . . . be demented." *Daily Evening Bulletin*, 23 August 1879.

180   Officer Fredericks responds. *San Francisco Morning Call*, 24 August 1879.

180   "I saw . . . with him." *San Francisco Morning Call*, 24 August 1879.

180   Gould, De Young wrestle." *San Francisco Morning Call*, 24 August 1879.

180   "The coupe . . . 'Lynch him!'" *San Francisco Morning Call*, 24 August 1879.

181   "A number . . . the head." *San Francisco Morning Call*, 24 August 1879.

181   Calls for De Young's hanging. *San Francisco Morning Call*, 24 August 1879.

181   "The crowd . . . De Young's death." *San Francisco Morning Call*, 24 August 1879.

181   "I know . . . night's work." *San Francisco Morning Call*, 24 August 1879.

181   De Young brought to City Hall. *San Francisco Morning Call*, 24 August 1879.

182   "When De Young . . . his person." *San Francisco Morning Call*, 24 August 1879.

182   De Young's injuries. *San Francisco Morning Call*, 24 August 1879.

182   "was responded . . . their coats." *Daily Alta California*, 24 August 1879.

182   "that within . . . the sidewalks." *Daily Alta California*, 24 August 1879.

183   "where crowds . . . hostile expressions." *Daily Alta California*, 24 August 1879.

183   "that the . . . impending riot." *San Francisco Morning Call*, 24 August 1879.

183   "Kearney who . . . cowardly act." *San Francisco Morning Call*, 24 August 1879.

183   "They wished . . . in custody." *Daily Alta California*, 24 August 1879.

183   "Mr. de Young . . . to come." *San Francisco Morning Call*, 24 August 1879.

184   "Many men . . . the tragedy." *San Francisco Morning Call*, 24 August 1879.

184   O'Brien and Wellock. *San Francisco Morning Call*, 24 August 1879.

184   "If we . . . *Chronicle* office." *San Francisco Morning Call*, 24 August 1879.

185   "This great . . . for life." *San Francisco Morning Call*, 24 August 1879.

185   "They say . . . 'must go!'" *San Francisco Morning Call*, 24 August 1879.

185   "Whereas . . . be suppressed." *San Francisco Morning Call*, 24 August 1879.

186   March of the Third Ward Club. *San Francisco Morning Call*, 24 August 1879.

186   Secretary of War's support. Marberry, *The Golden Voice*, pg. 260.

186   De Young in jail. *Daily Alta California*, 24 August 1879.

186   "Every possible . . . him comfortable." *Daily Evening Bulletin*, 23 August 1879.

186   "As the . . . the situation." *Daily Alta California*, 24 August 1879.

187   "succession of lusty cheers." *Daily Alta California*, 24 August 1879.

187   "almost indescribable." *Daily Alta California*, 24 August 1879.

187   "The street . . . exciting crowd." *Daily Alta California*, 24 August 1879.

188   "Friends . . . ten minutes." *Daily Alta California*, 24 August 1879.

188   "You will . . . be hung." *Daily Alta California*, 24 August 1879.

188   "Hang him . . . peaceful manner." *Daily Alta California*, 24 August 1879.

189   Bryant orders militia. *San Francisco Morning Call*, 24 August 1879.

189   "believed . . . *Chronicle* office." *San Francisco Morning Call*, 24 August 1879.

189   "still confined . . . change there." *Daily Alta California*, 24 August 1879.

189   "Well now . . . my wounds." *Daily Alta California*, 24 August 1879.

189   "coolly puffing . . . start up." *Daily Alta California*, 24 August 1879.

189   "It seems . . . of affairs." *Daily Alta California*, 24 August 1879.

190   "Mr. Kalloch . . . he did." *Daily Alta California*, 24 August 1879.

190   "That was . . . without retraction." *Daily Alta California*, 24 August 1879.

190   "No matter . . . in him." *Daily Alta California*, 24 August 1879.

190   "I have . . . the inevitable." *San Francisco Morning Call*, 24 August 1879.

190   "because of . . . will do." *San Francisco Morning Call*, 24 August 1879.

190   Kearney maintains a vigil. *San Francisco Morning Call*, 24 August 1879.

CHAPTER 12: A VOTE OF SYMPATHY

191   "belched forth . . . of danger." *Daily Alta California*, 24 August 1879.

192   "destined to . . . Apache Indian." *San Francisco Morning Call*, 27 August 1879.

192   "For years . . . attends cruelty." *San Francisco Morning Call*, 27 August 1879.

192   Quotes from national papers. *San Francisco Chronicle*, 26 August 1879.

193   "We do . . . in character." *San Francisco Chronicle*, 24 August 1879.

194   "There was . . . his father." *New York Times*, 25 April 1880.

194   "from a . . . San Francisco." *New York Times*, 25 April 1880.

194   Milton travels to San Francisco. *New York Times*, 25 April 1880.

194   "The bullet . . . intense pain." *Daily Alta California*, 25 August 1879.

194   "Thus, it . . . will recover." *Daily Alta California*, 25 August 1879.

194   "From private . . . infuriated populace." *Daily Alta California*, 25 August 1879.

194   "Some were . . . and order." *Daily Alta California*, 25 August 1879.

195   "Throw the . . . the stage." *Daily Alta California*, 25 August 1879.

195   "Workingmen! . . . to us." *Daily Alta California*, 25 August 1879.

195   "By God . . . against reporters." *Daily Alta California*, 25 August 1879.

195   "seething, stinking . . . of corruption." *Daily Alta California*, 25 August 1879.

195   "I want . . . this morning." *Daily Alta California*, 25 August 1879.

196   "Mr. Kalloch . . . the Workingman." *Daily Alta California*, 25 August 1879.

196   "I expect . . . kill him!" *Daily Alta California*, 25 August 1879.

196   "murderer . . . assassin." *San Francisco Chronicle*, 26 August 1879.

196   De Young in his cell. *San Francisco Chronicle*, 26 August 1879.

197   "A Purely . . . a newspaper." *San Francisco Chronicle*, 25 August 1879.

197   "filthy speech . . . and confusion." *San Francisco Chronicle*, 25 August 1879.

197   "The same . . . or antagonism." *San Francisco Chronicle*, 25 August 1879.

198   "We put . . . a dog." *San Francisco Chronicle*, 25 August 1879.

198   "recognized . . . is remarkable." *Daily Alta California*, 26 August 1879.

198   "Mr. Pickering . . . his head." *San Francisco Chronicle*, 26 August 1879.

199   "slunk . . . away." *San Francisco Chronicle*, 26 August 1879.

199   "Blair's forbearance . . . the penitentiary." *San Francisco Chronicle*, 26 August 1879.

199   "A man . . . recent occurrences." *San Francisco Chronicle*, 26 August 1879.

199   "It was . . . a duty." *San Francisco Chronicle*, 25 August 1879.

200   "Charles de Young . . . indignant populace." *San Francisco Morning Call*, 27 August 1879.

200   "They ran . . . a [cannon]." *San Francisco Morning Call*, 27 August 1879.

200   "His vermillion . . . the day." *San Francisco Morning Call*, 27 August 1879.

201   "The appearance . . . kill Kalloch." *Daily Alta California* (reprinting a *Bulletin* article), 26 August 1879.

201   Lees's testimony. *Daily Alta California* (reprinting a *Bulletin* article), 26 August 1879.

201   "It was . . . locked up." *Daily Alta California* (reprinting a *Bulletin* article), 26 August 1879.

202   Cold, hard facts. *Daily Alta California* (reprinting a *Bulletin* article), 26 August 1879.

202   "The board . . . coming in." *Daily Alta California*, 26 August 1879.

202   "There were . . . the trouble." *San Francisco Chronicle*, 27 August 1879.

202   Personal grudge. *San Francisco Chronicle*, 28 August 1879.

202   "I was . . . and resentment." *San Francisco Chronicle*, 28 August 1879.

203   Napthaly visits the De Youngs. *San Francisco Chronicle*, 27 August 1879.

203   "excultingly announced . . . had one." *San Francisco Chronicle*, 27 August 1879.

204   Reverend was determined. *San Francisco Chronicle*, 27 August 1879.

204   "Kalloch did . . . he expect?" *San Francisco Chronicle*, 27 August 1879.

204   "If there . . . bore him." *San Francisco Chronicle*, 27 August 1879.

205   "After careful . . . was wounded." *Daily Alta California*, 27 August 1879.

205   "Good morning . . . kill me." *Daily Alta California* (reprinting a *Bulletin* article), 31 August 1879.

205   "Before the . . . not object." *Daily Alta California* (reprinting a *Bulletin* article), 31 August 1879.

206   "grizzly bear." Adams, *Murder by the Bay*, pg. 69.

206   "You have . . . being elected." *San Francisco Chronicle* (reprinted article), 26 August 1879.

206   "If Kalloch . . . suitable now." *San Francisco Chronicle*, 26 August 1879.

206   "If a . . . Wednesday's lottery." *Daily Alta California*, 29 August 1879.

207   Early returns. Marberry, *The Golden Voice*, pg. 275.

207   "We hear . . . 'the ground.'" *Daily Alta California*, 3 September 1879.

207   "The crack . . . the Mayoralty." Marberry, *The Golden Voice*, pg. 276.

207   "When the . . . speedily recovered." Hart, *The Kearney-Kalloch Epoch* (San Francisco Virtual Museum).

207   Workingmen political victories. Marberry, *The Golden Voice*, pg. 276.

207   "Not . . . been elected." *San Francisco Chronicle* (reprting a *Call* article), 8 September 1879.

CHAPTER 13: FINAL EDITION

208   Kalloch's swearing-in. Marberry, *The Golden Voice*, pg. 278.

208   "There must . . . an assassin." Marberry, *The Golden Voice*, pg. 278.

209   "pretentious building . . . Bush streets." McKee, pg. 282.

209   First building of its kind. McKee, pg. 282.

209   Monument to success. Young, *Journalism in California*, pp. 108–109.

209   "the most . . . the coast." *San Francisco Chronicle*, 29 September 1879.

209   *Chronicle* presses. Young, *Journalism in California*, pp. 108–109.

209   Proponent of electricity. Young, *Journalism in California*, pp. 109–110.

210   "It was . . . does things." Young, *Journalism in California*, pg. 110.

211   Bullets removed. Marberry, *The Golden Voice*, pp. 278–279.

212   Accusations against Kalloch. Marberry, *The Golden Voice*, pg. 280.

212   "animosity on both sides." Marberry, *The Golden Voice*, pg. 280.

212   Chinatown investigation. Marberry, *The Golden Voice*, pg. 281.

212   sixteen-page pamphlet. *Chinatown Declared a Nuisance* (Virtual Museum of San Francisco).

212   "The first . . . the city." *Chinatown Declared a Nuisance* (Virtual Museum of San Francisco).

212   "smoke and . . . American race." *Chinatown Declared a Nuisance* (Virtual Museum of San Francisco).

213   "These vile . . . infamous race." *Chinatown Declared a Nuisance* (Virtual Museum of San Francisco).

213   "If it . . . insurance policies." *Chinatown Declared a Nuisance* (Virtual Museum of San Francisco).

213   "slaughter and fire." *Chinatown Declared a Nuisance* (Virtual Museum of San Francisco).

213   "How stands . . . kept it." *Chinatown Declared a Nuisance* (Virtual Museum of San Francisco).

214 "a retribution . . . to anticipate." *Chinatown Declared a Nuisance* (Virtual Museum of San Francisco).

214 "Mr. De Young . . . human sacrifice." *Chinatown Declared a Nuisance* (Virtual Museum of San Francisco).

215 Pamphlet appears. McKee, pg. 282; *Daily Alta California*, 24 April 1880.

215 Pamphlet's title. *San Francisco Morning Call*, 24 April 1880.

215 "It is . . . insidious enemy." *San Francisco Morning Call*, 24 April 1880.

216 Milton Kalloch. *New York Times*, 25 April 1880.

217 Milton's City Hall job. Marberry, *The Golden Voice*, pg. 298.

217 "to offer . . . his trial." *Daily Alta California*, 24 April 1880.

217 Rumors. *Daily Alta California*, 24 April 1880.

217 Milton's stakeout. *San Francisco Chronicle*, 25 April 1880.

218 Milton arms himself. *San Francisco Morning Call*, 13 March 1881; Marberry, *The Golden Voice*, pg. 298.

218 "His associations . . . marked degree." *New York Times*, 25 April 1880.

218 Milton frequents saloons. Marberry, *The Golden Voice*, pg. 298.

218 "His hat . . . his nose." *San Francisco Chronicle*, 25 April 1880.

218 "thinking it . . . particularly sullen." *San Francisco Chronicle*, 25 April 1880.

219 De Young enters his home. *San Francisco Chronicle*, 25 April 1880.

220 Thralls spy on neighboring residence. *San Francisco Chronicle*, 25 April 1880.

220 Young man in tan overcoat. *San Francisco Chronicle*, 25 April 1880.

220 "We were . . . his hand." *San Francisco Chronicle*, 24 April 1880.

220 Milton opens fire. *San Francisco Examiner*, 24 April 1880.

221 De Young is shot. *San Francisco Chronicle*, 24 April 1880.

221 "Charles de Young . . . him sinking." *San Francisco Chronicle*, 24 April 1880.

221 Elias and Dreypolcher. *San Francisco Chronicle*, 24 April 1880.

222 Officers Peckinpah and Ward respond. *San Francisco Chronicle*, 24 April 1880.

222 Milton hauled off to jail. *San Francisco Chronicle*, 24 April 1880.

222 "a tremendous . . . Kearny streets." *San Francisco Chronicle*, 24 April 1880.

222 "I was . . . the office." *Daily Evening Bulletin*, 28 April 1880.

222 Initial examination. *Daily Evening Bulletin*, 28 April 1880.

222 "was a corpse." *San Francisco Chronicle*, 24 April 1880.

223 "M. H. de Young . . . complete prostration." *San Francisco Morning Call*, 24 April 1880.

223 "The workings . . . intense emotion." *San Francisco Morning Call*, 24 April 1880.

223 "They heard . . . the basement." *San Francisco Morning Call*, 24 April 1880.

223 "A few . . . all present." *San Francisco Morning Call*, 24 April 1880.

223 "In short . . . the wagon." *San Francisco Morning Call*, 24 April 1880.

224 "an expression . . . utmost coolness." *San Francisco Chronicle*, 24 April 1880.

224 "You shot . . . with that." *San Francisco Chronicle*, 24 April 1880.

224 Sheriff Desmond. *San Francisco Chronicle*, 24 April 1880.

224 "Well, Milton . . . the house." *San Francisco Chronicle*, 24 April 1880.

225 Reporter interview, Milton smokes. *San Francisco Chronicle*, 24 April 1880.
225 "A boisterous . . . reverend leader." *Daily Alta California*, 24 April 1880.
225 Workingmen beaten. *San Francisco Chronicle*, 24 April 1880.
225 Police form human cordon. *Daily Alta California*, 24 April 1880.
225 Entrance on Bagley Place. *San Francisco Morning Call*, 24 April 1880.
226 "The few . . . clotted blood." *San Francisco Morning Call*, 24 April 1880.
226 "There was . . . the deceased." *San Francisco Morning Call*, 24 April 1880.
226 Mustache hid wound. *Daily Alta California*, 24 April 1880.
226 "A bowie . . . his side." *San Francisco Morning Call*, 24 April 1880.
226 "Until a . . . very cowardice." *Daily Alta California*, 24 April 1880.

Chapter 14: Bad Business

227 "The external . . . the features." *San Francisco Chronicle*, 25 April 1880.
227 "He was . . . the dock." *San Francisco Chronicle*, 25 April 1880.
228 Home guarded by Workingmen. *San Francisco Chronicle*, 25 April 1880.
228 "This community . . . of society." *San Francisco Morning Call*, 24 April 1880.
228 "The killing . . . sufficiently notorious." *Daily Alta California*, 24 April 1880.
229 "cast a . . . the city." *Daily Evening Bulletin*, 24 April 1880.
229 "There is . . . leading motive." *Daily Evening Bulletin*, 24 April 1880.
229 *Chronicle* praises De Young. *San Francisco Chronicle*, 24 April 1880.
229 "And when . . . and farewell!" *San Francisco Chronicle*, 24 April 1880.
230 "The man who demanded a retraction." Marberry, *The Golden Voice*, pg. 301.
230 "The *Chronicle* . . . Charles de Young." *Daily Alta California*, 25 April 1880.
230 "strong evidence . . . deep-laid plot." *San Francisco Chronicle*, 25 April 1880.
230 "to be excited over something." *San Francisco Chronicle*, 25 April 1880.
230 City auditor and former sheriff. *San Francisco Chronicle*, 25 April 1880; Marberry, *The Golden Voice*, pg. 304.
230 "It was . . . Pine Street." *San Francisco Chronicle*, 25 April 1880.
230 "I took . . . City Prison. *San Francisco Chronicle*, 25 April 1880.
231 "The *Chronicle* . . . his son." *New York Times*, 26 April 1880.
231 "I want . . . or not." *San Francisco Chronicle*, 25 April 1880.
231 Ransome's rheumatism. *San Francisco Chronicle*, 25 April 1880.
231 The casket. *San Francisco Chronicle*, 26 April 1880.
232 "Among the . . . 'HIS MOTHER.'" *San Francisco Chronicle*, 26 April 1880.
232 "To Charles, from Mother, 1880." *Daily Alta California*, 26 April 1880.
232 "It was . . . the tragedy." *Daily Alta California*, 26 April 1880.
232 "The top . . . was delivered." *San Francisco Chronicle*, 26 April 1880.
232 Elderly woman. *San Francisco Chronicle*, 26 April 1880.
233 "I want . . . so sorry." *San Francisco Chronicle*, 26 April 1880.
233 "Many were . . . who desired." *San Francisco Chronicle*, 26 April 1880.
233 "Many assembled . . . murdered man." *Daily Alta California*, 26 April 1880.

233   Picture of Charles de Young. *Daily Alta California*, 26 April 1880.

233   "What more . . . of life." *San Francisco Chronicle*, 26 April 1880.

234   Funeral procession. *San Francisco Chronicle*, 26 April 1880.

234   "When it . . . get aboard." *Daily Alta California*, 26 April 1880.

235   "Earth to . . . to dust." *San Francisco Chronicle*, 26 April 1880.

235   Family says good-byes. *San Francisco Chronicle*, 26 April 1880.

235   "It was . . . bad business." *Daily Alta California* (reprinting *New York Sun* article), 26 April 1880.

236   "You don't . . . the people." Marberry, *The Golden Voice*, pg. 306.

236   "In that . . . my revenge." Maberry, *The Golden Voice*, pg. 306.

236   "I stayed . . . the Kallochs." *Daily Evening Bulletin*, 28 April 1880.

237   Milton returns fire. *Daily Evening Bulletin*, 28 April 1880.

237   "When Kalloch . . . man's face." *Daily Evening Bulletin*, 28 April 1880.

237   "I saw . . . his chin." *Daily Evening Bulletin*, 28 April 1880.

237   "Kalloch . . . and scared." *Daily Evening Bulletin*, 28 April 1880.

238   Name hard to pronounce. *Daily Evening Bulletin*, 28 April 1880.

238   "Mr. De Young's . . . uniform cartridges." *Daily Alta California*, 28 April 1880.

238   "We find . . . of murder." *Daily Evening Bulletin*, 28 April 1880.

238   "His reputation . . . character generally." *San Francisco Chronicle*, 30 April 1880.

239   "less serious . . . swindles outright." *San Francisco Chronicle*, 30 April 1880.

239   Reappears in De Young case. *San Francisco Chronicle*, 30 April 1880.

239   "Can this . . . are one." *San Francisco Chronicle* (reprinting *Salt Lake City Herald* article), 30 April 1880.

239   "The announcement . . . 'All right.'" *San Francisco Chronicle*, 29 April 1880.

239   "illegal lying." Bruce, *Gaudy Century*, pg. 177.

240   "The police . . . the spectators." *San Francisco Morning Call*, 30 April 1880.

240   Milton enters courtroom. *San Francisco Morning Call*, 30 April 1880.

240   Mayor, Michael de Young are absent. *San Francisco Morning Call*, 30 April 1880.

240   Testimony given. *San Francisco Morning Call*, 30 April 1880.

240   "I have . . . prevent it." *San Francisco Morning Call*, 30 April 1880.

240   "I do . . . my exculpation." *San Francisco Morning Call*, 30 April 1880.

241   "The people . . . his son." San Francisco Chronicle (reprinting New York World article), 29 April 1880.

CHAPTER 15: IMPEACHMENT AND TRIAL

242   Charges against Kalloch. Kauer, pg. 288.

242   "counseling the . . . evil-disposed." *Daily Alta California*, 4 May 1880.

243   "The report . . . San Francisco." *Daily Alta California*, 4 May 1880.

243   "If he . . . as Mayor." *San Francisco Chronicle*, 28 May 1880.

243   "The precincts . . . and companions." *San Francisco Chronicle*, 27 May 1880.

243   "State what . . . was bad." *San Francisco Chronicle*, 27 May 1880.

243 Judge postpones proceedings. *San Francisco Chronicle*, 27 May 1880.

244 "The truth . . . poured forth." *San Francisco Chronicle*, 1 April 1880.

244 "For sale . . . not Bulldosed." *A Faint Idea of a Terrible Life* (Bancroft Library).

244 "The Rev. . . . them known." *A Faint Idea of a Terrible Life* (Bancroft Library).

245 "When under . . . heard of." *A Faint Idea of a Terrible Life* (Bancroft Library).

245 Kalloch pays for every girl. *A Faint Idea of a Terrible Life* (Bancroft Library).

246 "In a nude . . . any knowledge." *A Faint Idea of a Terrible Life* (Bancroft Library).

246 "He is . . . chief-magistrate." *A Faint Idea of a Terrible Life* (Bancroft Library).

246 William McCann Neilson. *San Francisco Chronicle*, 3 June 1880.

246 "I did . . . for it." *San Francisco Chronicle*, 4 June 1880.

246 "It was . . . the people." *San Francisco Chronicle*, 4 June 1880.

247 Alexander Kydd. *San Francisco Chronicle*, 4 June 1880.

247 "a gentleman . . . we live." *San Francisco Chronicle*, 4 June 1880.

247 "I expect . . . do now." *San Francisco Chronicle*, 4 June 1880.

247 Police search for Kalloch. *San Francisco Chronicle*, 4 June 1880.

247 "It was . . . his business." *San Francisco Chronicle*, 5 June 1880.

247 "This proceeding . . . infamous publication. *San Francisco Chronicle*, 5 June 1880.

247 Intricate publicity stunt. *San Francisco Chronicle*, 5 June 1880.

248 "there must . . . police department." *San Francisco Chronicle*, 5 June 1880.

248 "A pretty . . . a church." Marberry, *The Golden Voice*, pg. 329.

248 "The three . . . Friday night." *San Francisco Chronicle*, 6 June 1880.

248 "I am . . . recent experience." *San Francisco Chronicle*, 6 June 1880.

248 Publicize Nelison's efforts. *San Francisco Chronicle*, 6 June 1880.

248 "On the . . . and investigation." Marberry, *The Golden Voice*, pg. 330.

249 "It was . . . be collusive." *San Francisco Chronicle*, 6 June 1880.

249 Neilson reprimanded. Marberry, *The Golden Voice*, pg. 330.

249 "At two . . . obtain admission." *San Francisco Morning Call*, 20 February 1881.

249 "If these . . . also there." *San Francisco Morning Call*, 20 February 1881.

250 "I expected . . . shooting then." *San Francisco Morning Call*, 22 February 1881.

250 "the line of decent journalism." *San Francisco Morning Call*, 12 March 1881.

250 "Charles de Young . . . physical destruction." *San Francisco Morning Call*, 2 March 1881.

251 Caroline Kalloch takes the stand. *San Francisco Morning Call*, 12 March 1881.

251 "After his . . . than before." *San Francisco Morning Call*, 12 March 1881.

251 Caroline never imagined. *San Francisco Morning Call*, 12 March 1881.

251 "Did you . . . his paper." *San Francisco Morning Call*, 12 March 1881.

252 "Your Honor . . . for you." *San Francisco Morning Call*, 12 March 1881.

253 Judge dimisses Murphy's concerns. *San Francisco Morning Call*, 12 March 1881.

253 "I stood . . . the jury." *San Francisco Morning Call*, 12 March 1881.

253 "Do you . . . your presence?" *San Francisco Morning Call*, 13 March 1881.

253 "As well . . . I haven't." *San Francisco Morning Call*, 13 March 1881.

254 "I had . . . protect myself." *San Francisco Morning Call*, 13 March 1881.

254 "When I . . . his death." *San Francisco Morning Call*, 13 March 1881.

254 "While it . . . seeing him." *San Francisco Morning Call*, 13 March 1881.

255 "When I . . . about it." *San Francisco Morning Call*, 13 March 1881.

255 "I wish . . . the trouble." *San Francisco Morning Call*, 13 March 1881.

255 "When you . . . shooting him." *San Francisco Morning Call*, 13 March 1881.

256 "Did you . . . his paper?" *San Francisco Morning Call*, 15 March 1881.

256 "No, sir . . . do not." *San Francisco Morning Call*, 15 March 1881.

256 "After the . . . paper read." *San Francisco Morning Call*, 25 March 1881.

257 "The street . . . impatient humanity." *San Francisco Morning Call*, 25 March 1881.

257 "Gentlemen of . . . not guilty." *San Francisco Morning Call*, 25 March 1881.

258 Public, bailiff react. *San Francisco Morning Call*, 25 March 1881.

258 Crowd clamors for glimpse. *San Francisco Morning Call*, 25 March 1881.

258 "At the . . . the *Chronicle*." *San Francisco Morning Call*, 25 March 1881.

259 "The excitement . . . beggars description." *San Francisco Morning Call*, 25 March 1881.

259 "Here he is, mother!" *San Francisco Morning Call*, 25 March 1881.

259 "I have . . . San Francisco are." *San Francisco Morning Call*, 25 March 1881.

259 Groaning and chanting. *San Francisco Morning Call*, 25 March 1881.

259 Longest case. *San Francisco Chronicle*, 25 March 1881; *San Francisco Morning Call*, 25 March 1881.

260 "In a . . . dead man." *Daily Alta California*, 25 March 1881.

260 "Let us . . . the future." *Daily Alta California*, 25 March 1881.

260 "It would . . . was acquitted." *San Francisco Morning Call*, 25 March 1881.

261 "The verdict . . . of California." *San Francisco Chronicle*, 25 March 1881.

261 "Charles de Young's . . . the heart." *Daily Alta California* (reprinting *The Stock Exchange* article), 25 April 1880.

EPILOGUE

261 "Had De Young . . . had achieved." *Daily Alta California* (reprinting *The Stock Exchange* article), 25 April 1880.

262 Kalloch's end. Marberry, *The Golden Voice*, pg. 350; McKee, pg. 283; *New York Times*, 12 December 1887.

263 Milton Kalloch. McKee, pg. 283.

263 Spreckels shoots Michael de Young. McKee, pg. 283.

264 West's first skyscraper, current location. *San Francisco Chronicle*, 15 August 2005.

264 Michael de Young dies. McKee, pg. 284.

264 *Chronicle* sale. *San Francisco Chronicle*, 7 August 1999; *San Francisco Chronicle*, 18 March 2000; *New York Times*, 18 March 2000.

INDEX

ABOUT THE AUTHOR

SIMON READ, a former Bay Area newspaper reporter, now lives in the Sierra foothills of Northern California. He is the author of three previous works of nonfiction, *On the House: The Bizarre Killing of Michael Malloy, In the Dark: The True Story of the Blackout Ripper,* and *The Killing Skies: RAF Bomber Command at War,* and is currently researching his next book. He can be reached through his website at www.simon-read.com.